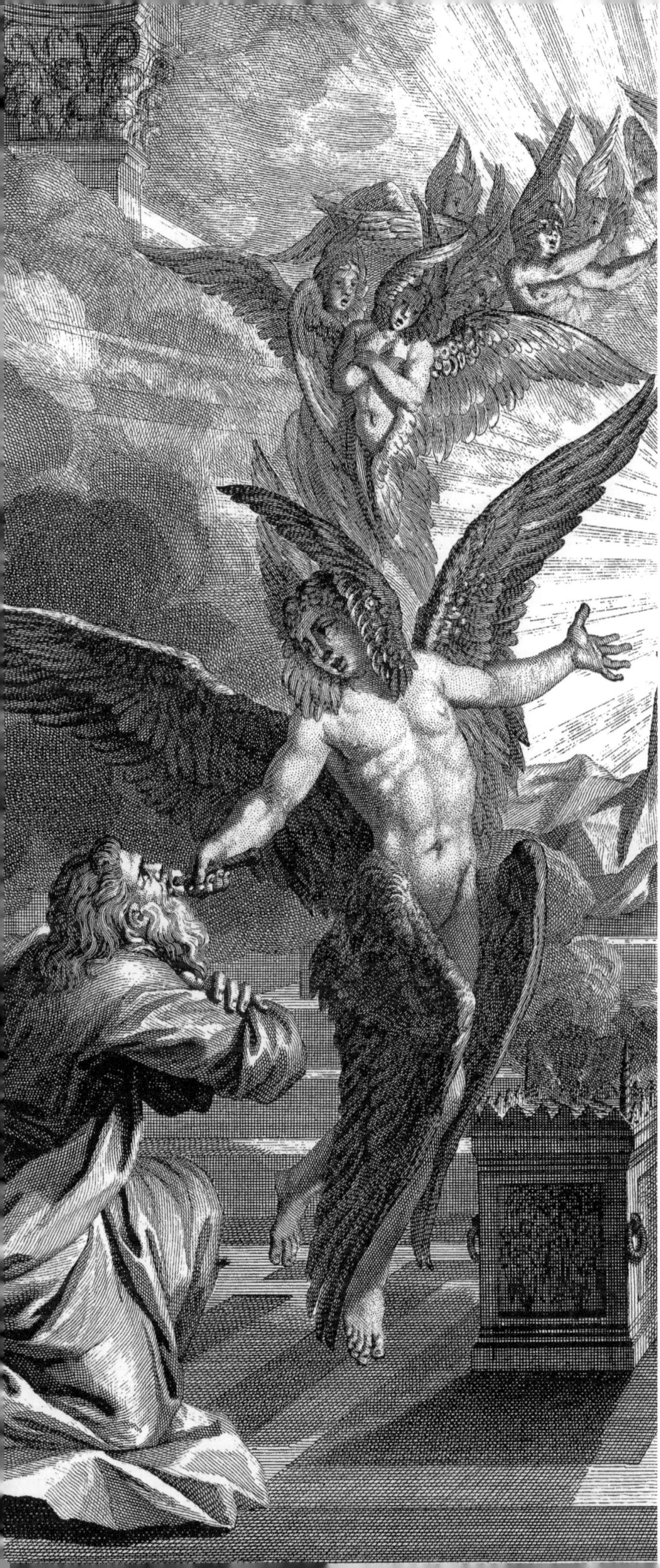

ANGELS & CHERUBS

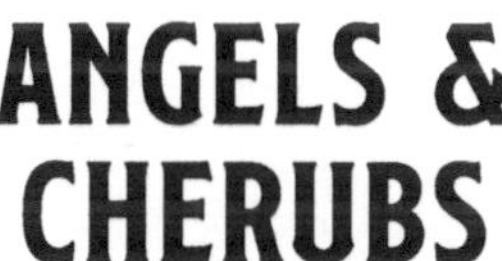

AN IMAGE ARCHIVE FOR
ARTISTS *And* **DESIGNERS**

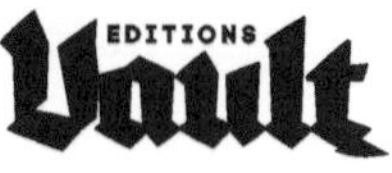

INTRODUCTION

Angels have inspired artists for centuries as a
sign of hope, peace and divinity; in contemporary
culture, angels often symbolise protection or a guide
through challenging times. Artists have used angels
in various religious and secular scenarios to inspire
awe and convey beauty and grace. In a historical
religious context, they were divine beings that
helped bridge the gap between the spiritual realm
and everyday life. Over time these representations
became less literal and more symbolic, and today,
angels are a popular metaphor for the afterlife, moral
courage, and protection against harm. Cherubs are
depicted as playful angelic children, traditionally
associated with romantic love. Majestic angels
and lively cherubs continue to inspire artists and
designers today, which is why we have created this
comprehensive reference book.

Our high-resolution images are perfect for drawing
references, tattoo flash designs or printed and
framed to make stunning decorative artworks.
Angels and Cherubs: An Image Archive contains
159 fascinating images to inspire you to take your
creative skills to the next level. A downloadable
version of all images featured is included.

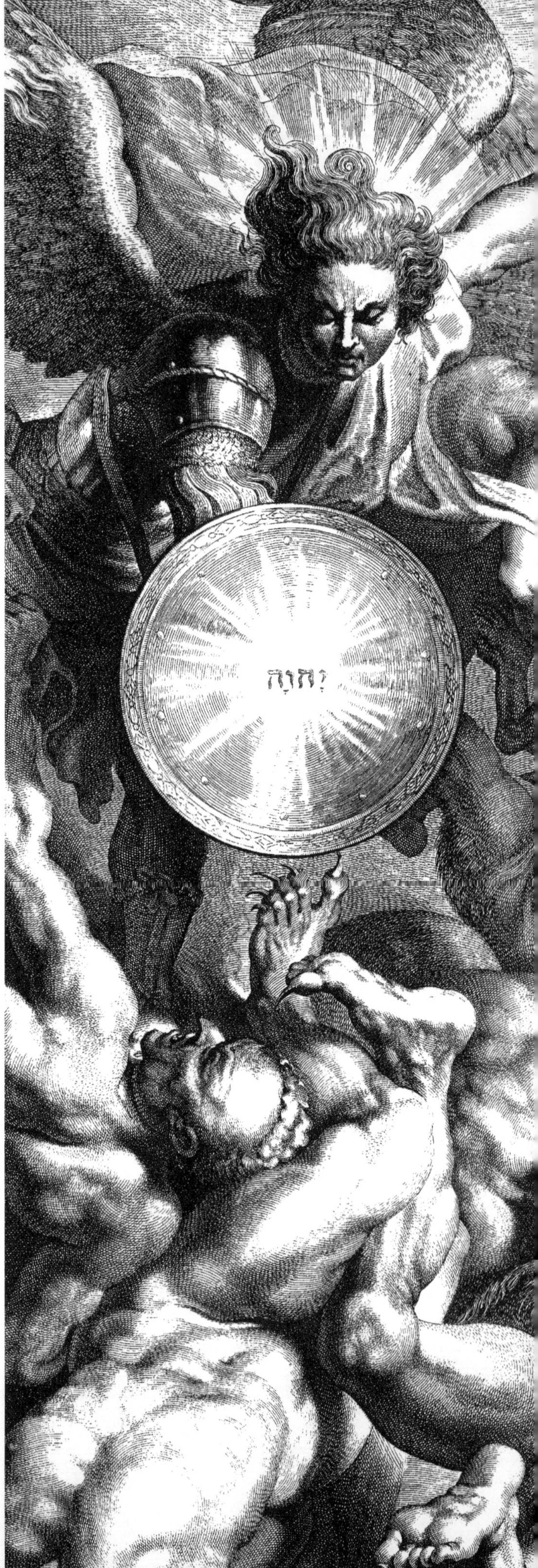

TABLE OF CONTENTS

DOWNLOAD YOUR FILES

Downloading your files is simple. To access your digital files, please go to the last page of this book and follow the instructions.

For technical assistance, please email:
info@vaulteditions.com

Bibliographical Note

This book is a new work created by Vault Editions Ltd.

ISBN: 978-1-922966-03-2

ANGELS & CHERUBS

VAULT EDITIONS

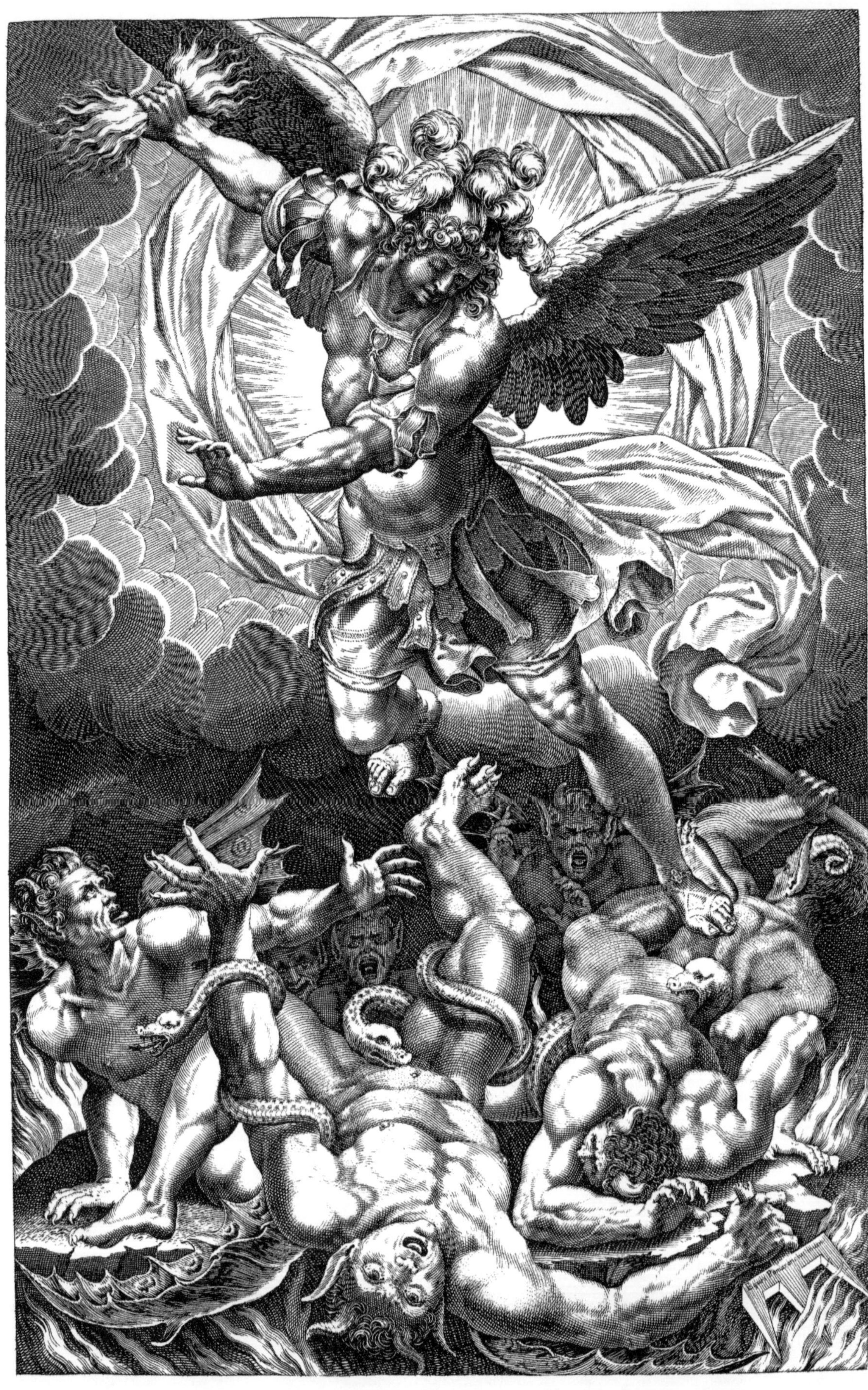

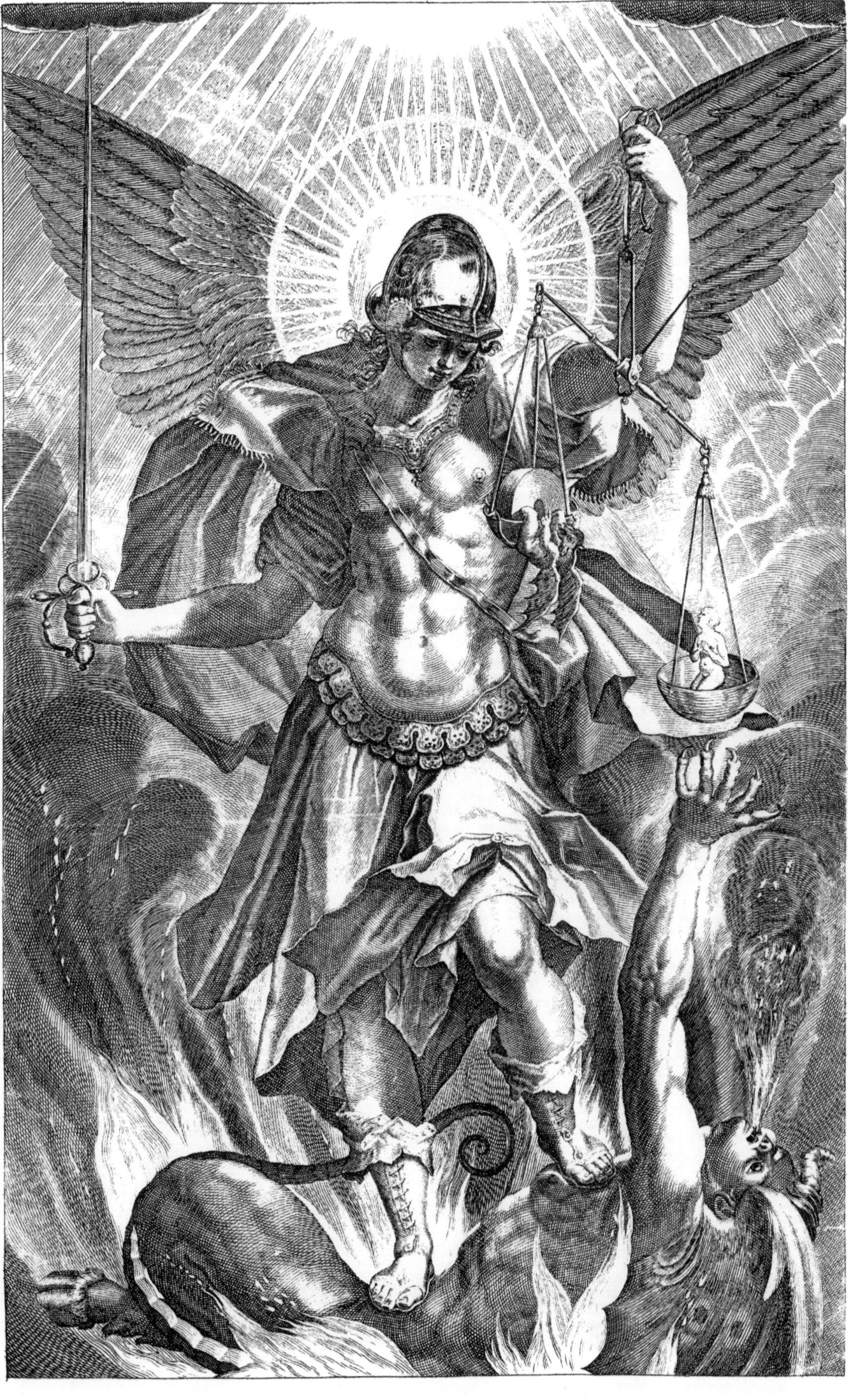

03

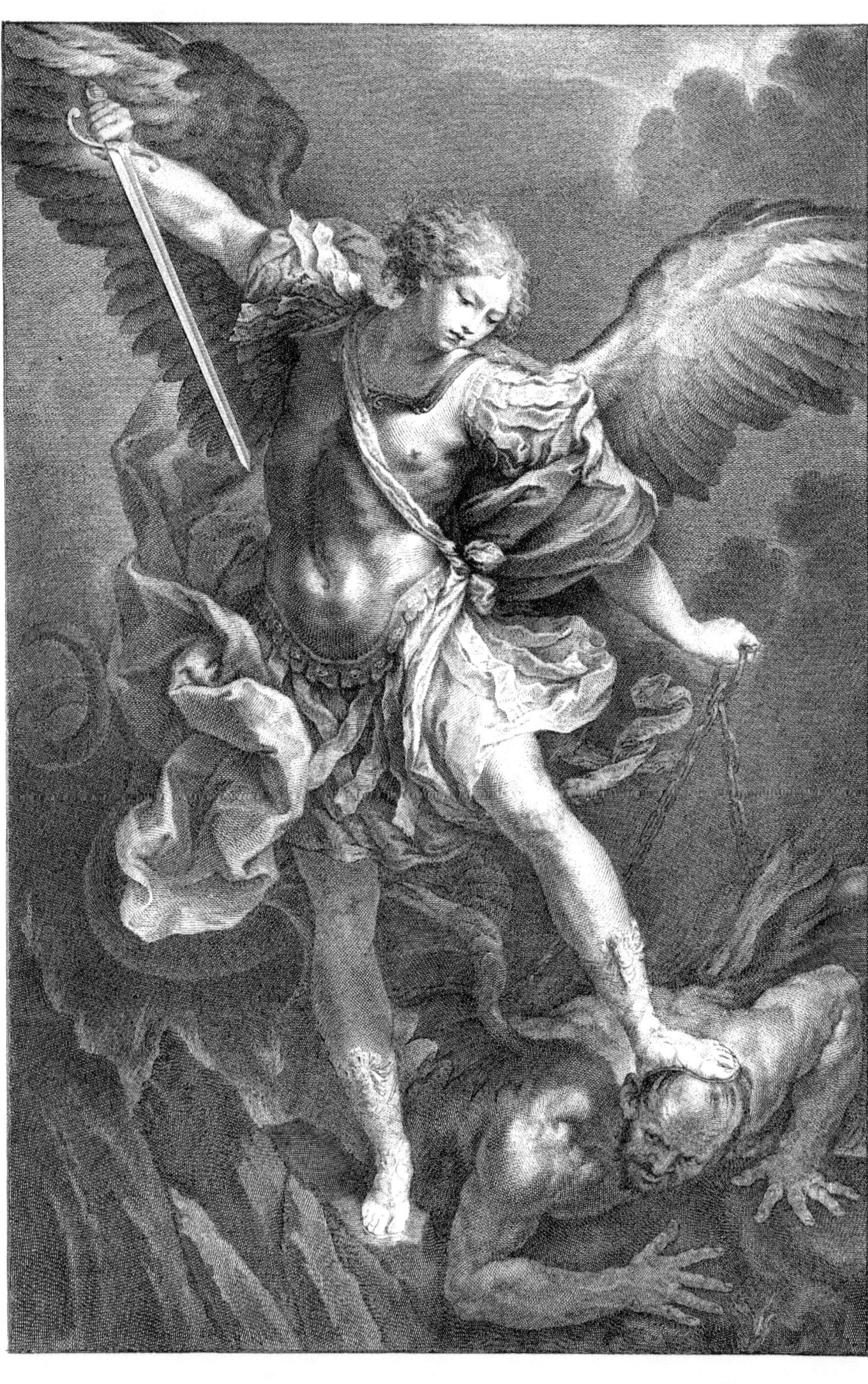

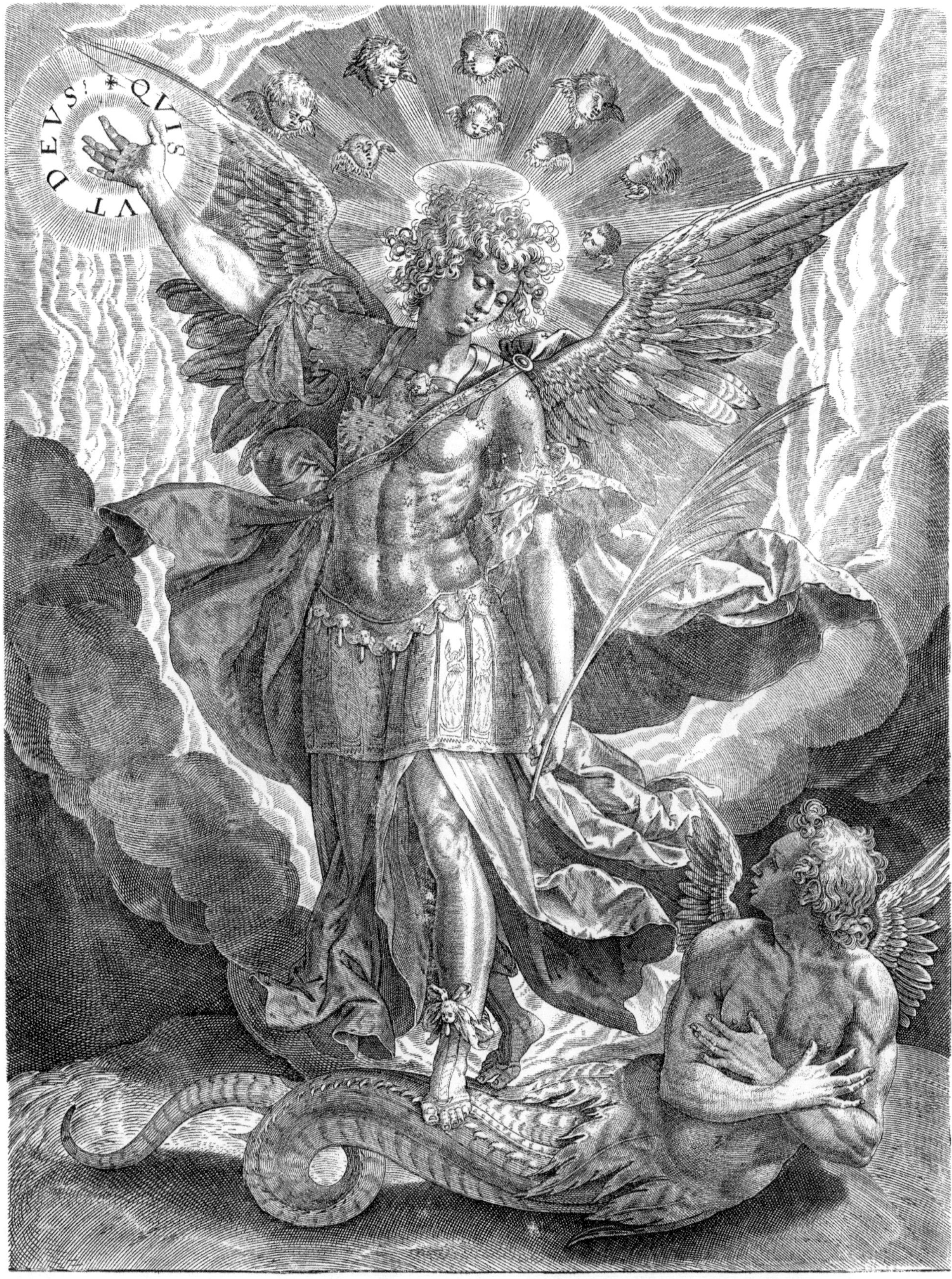
QVIS + DEVS!
VT

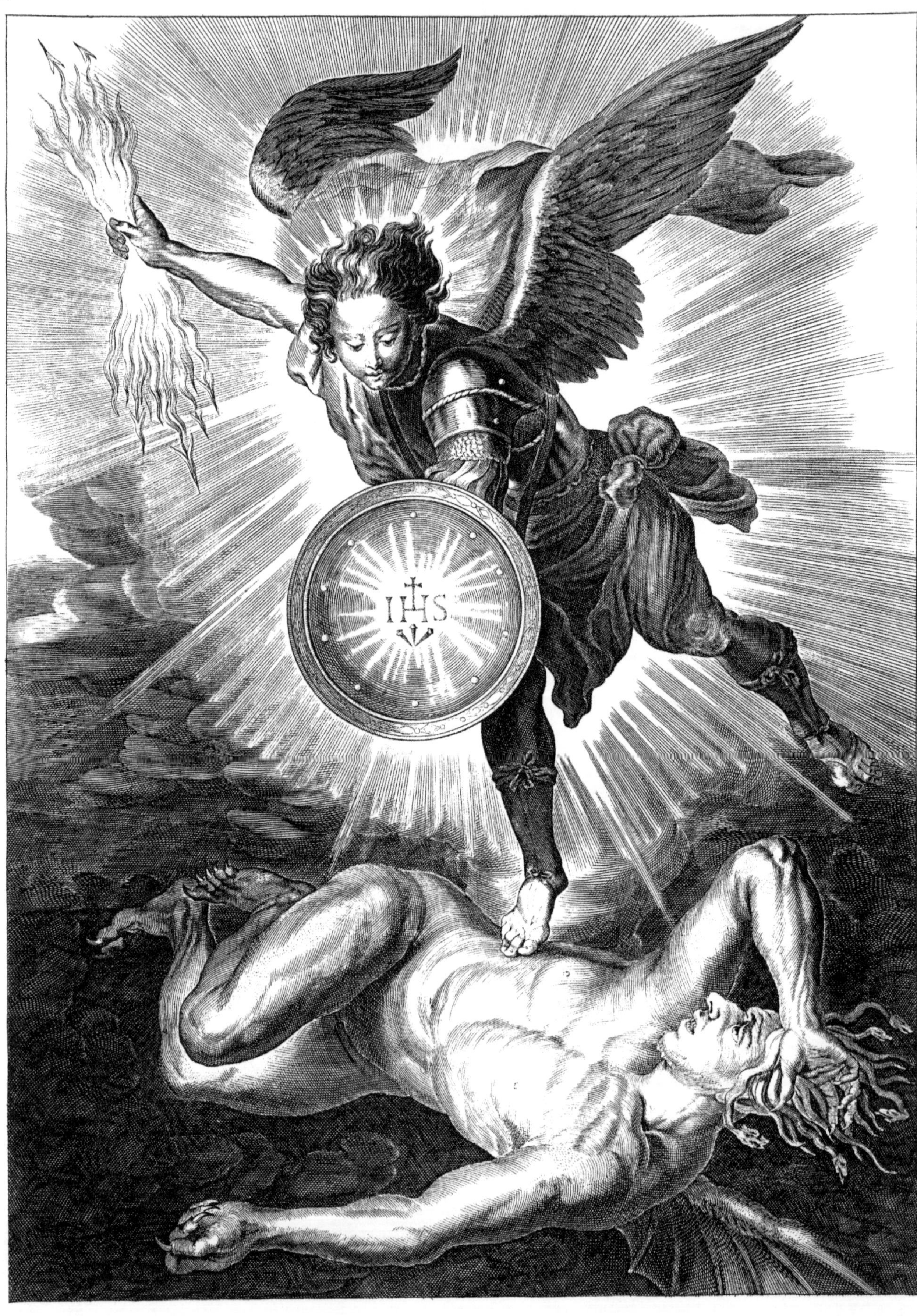

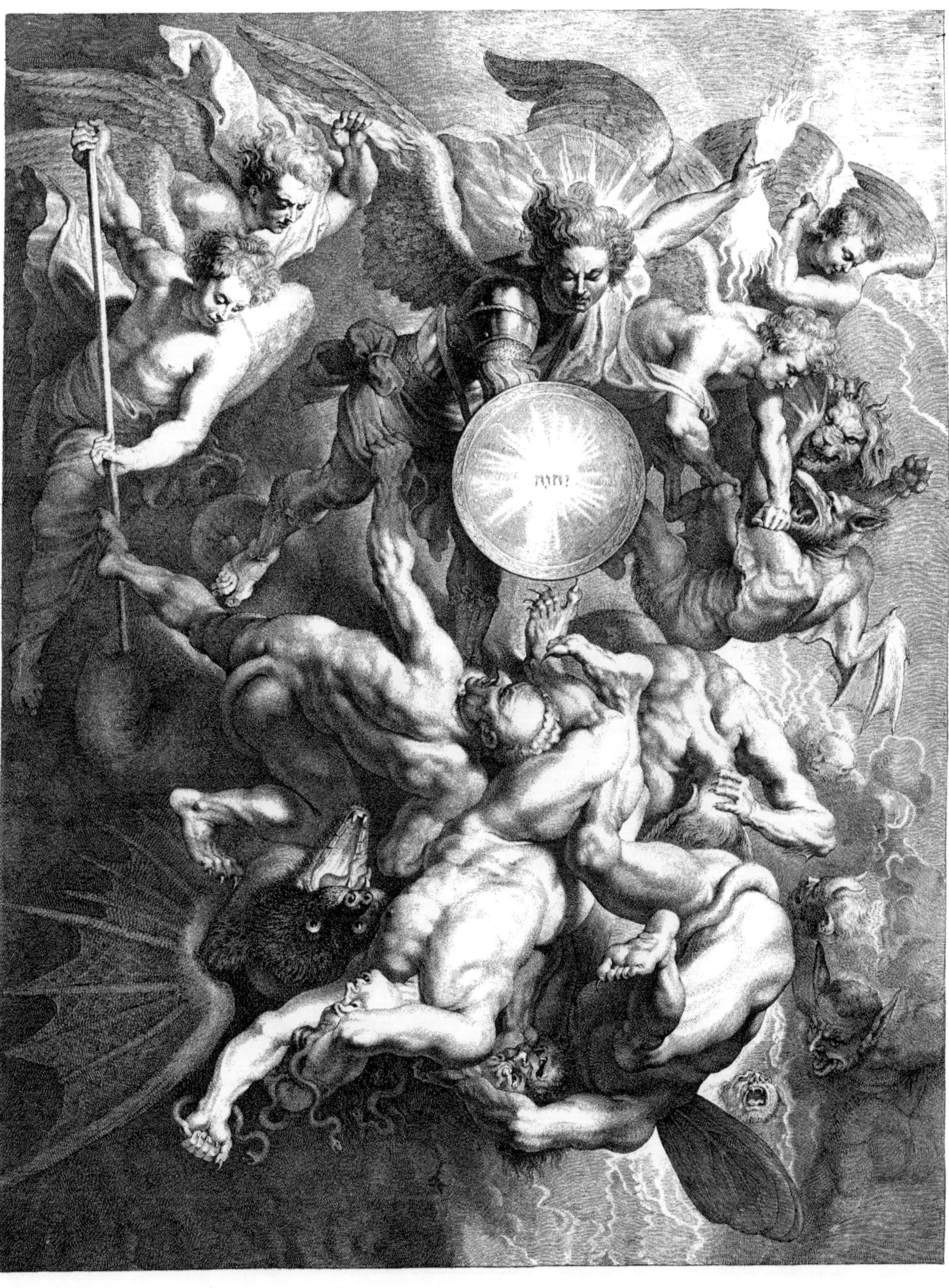

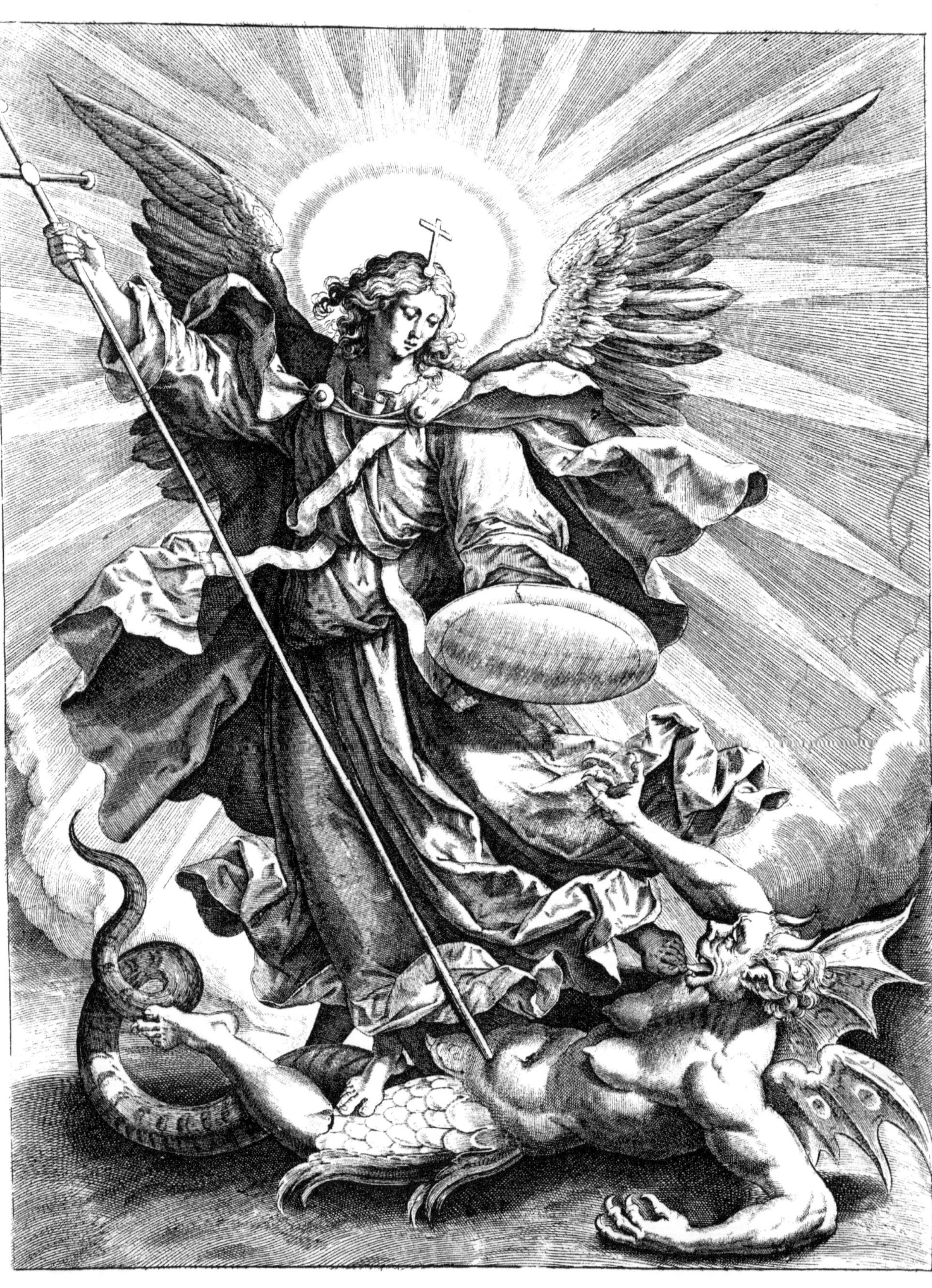

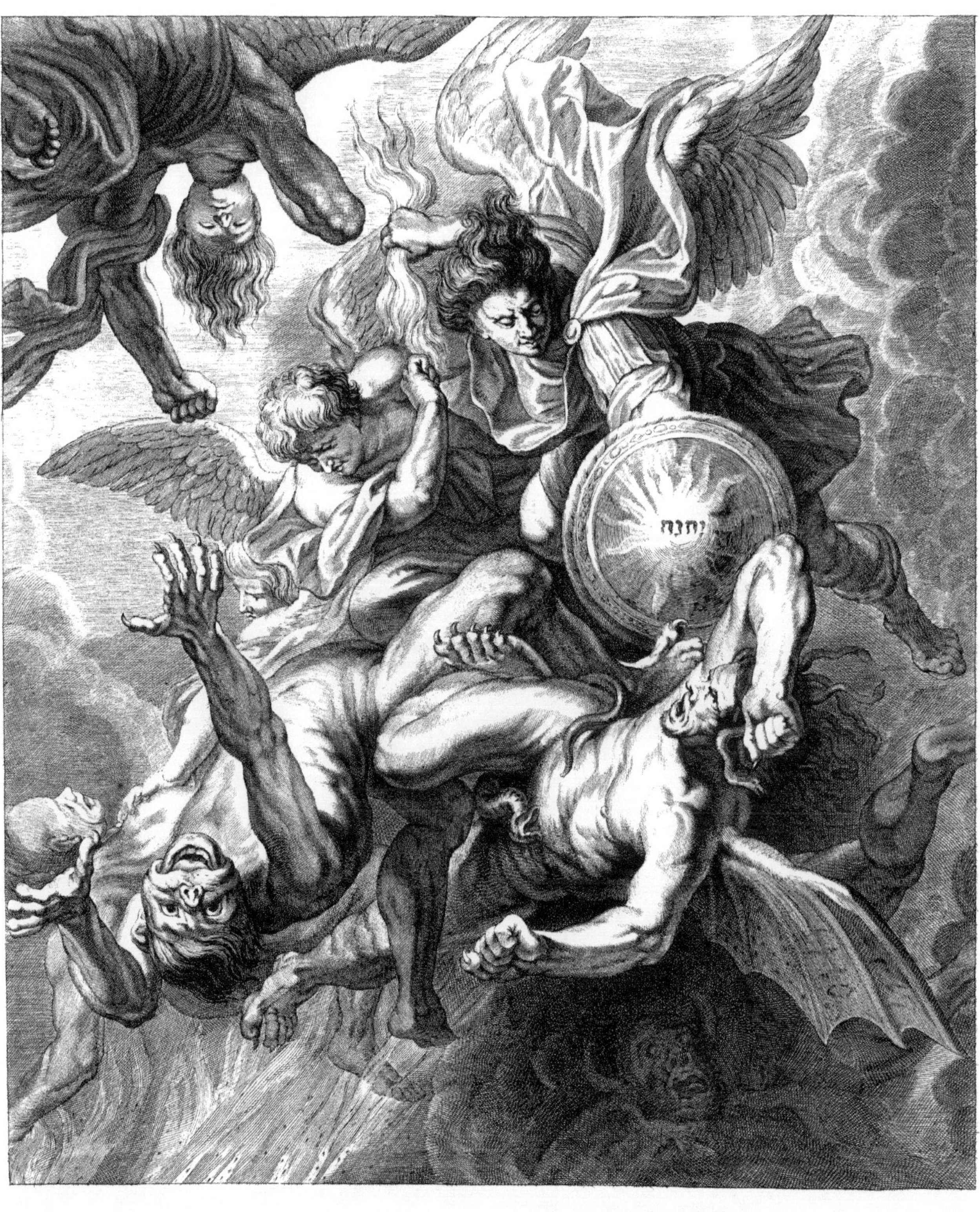

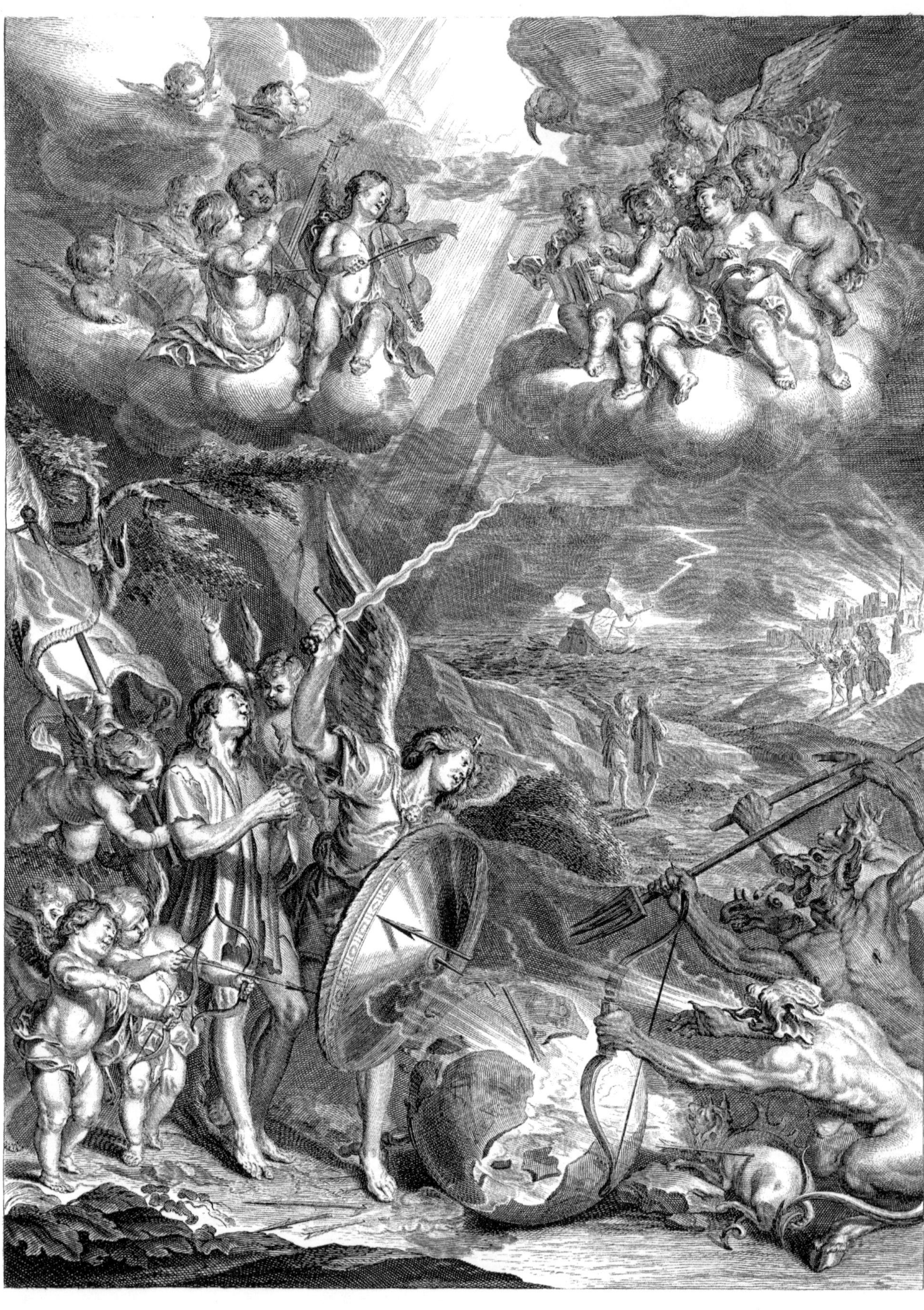

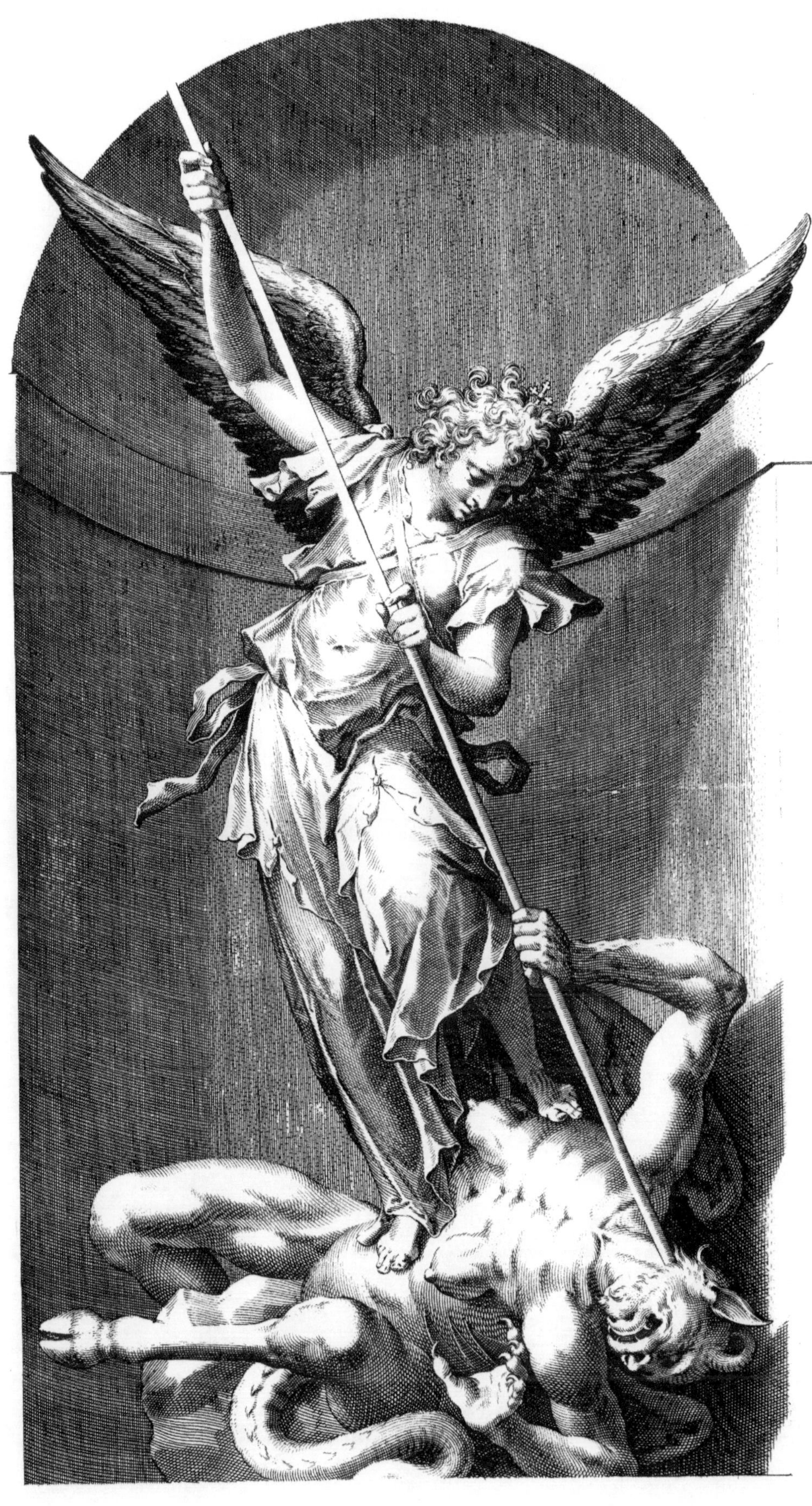

ANGELS & CHERUBS

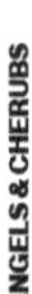

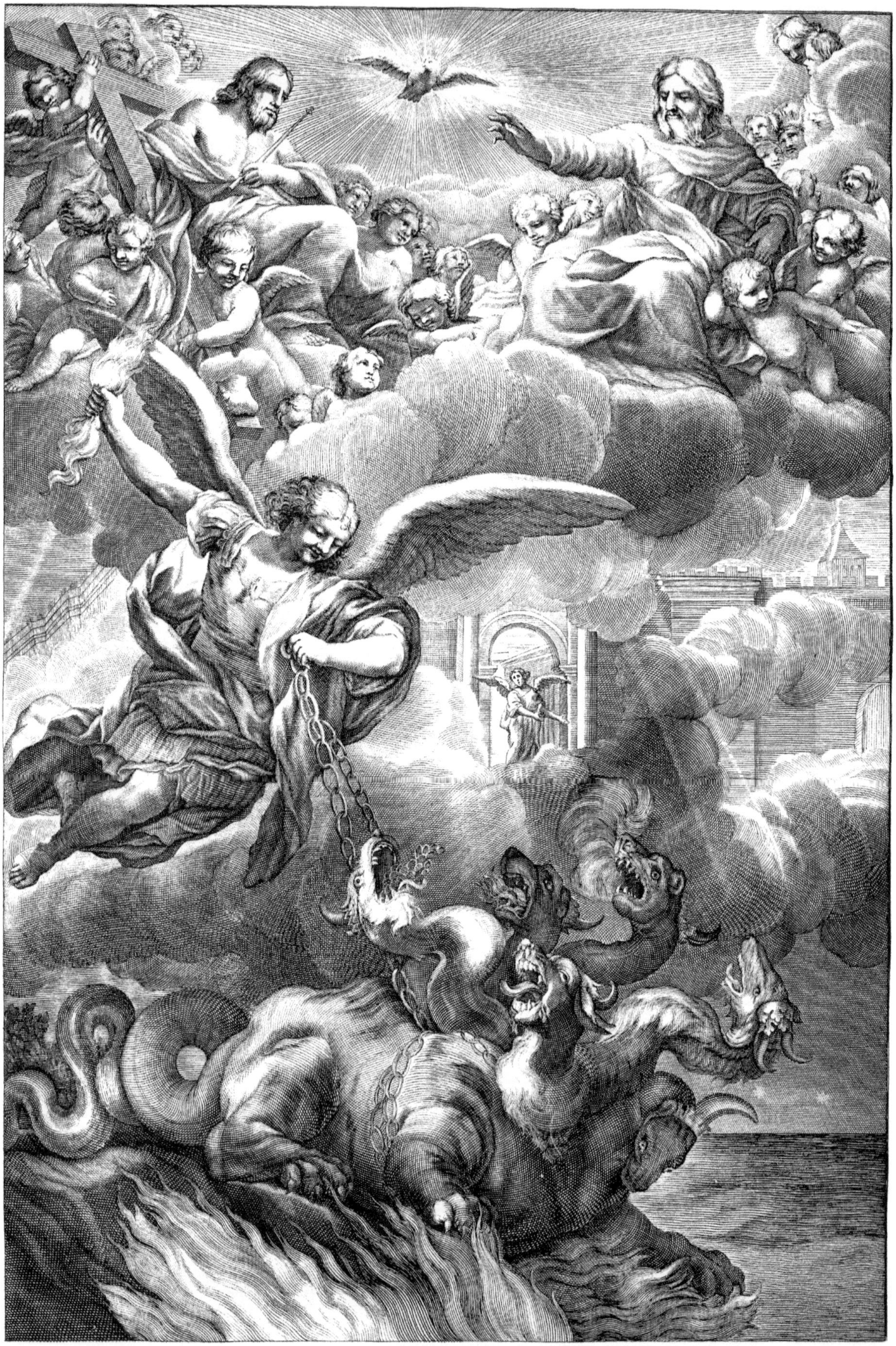

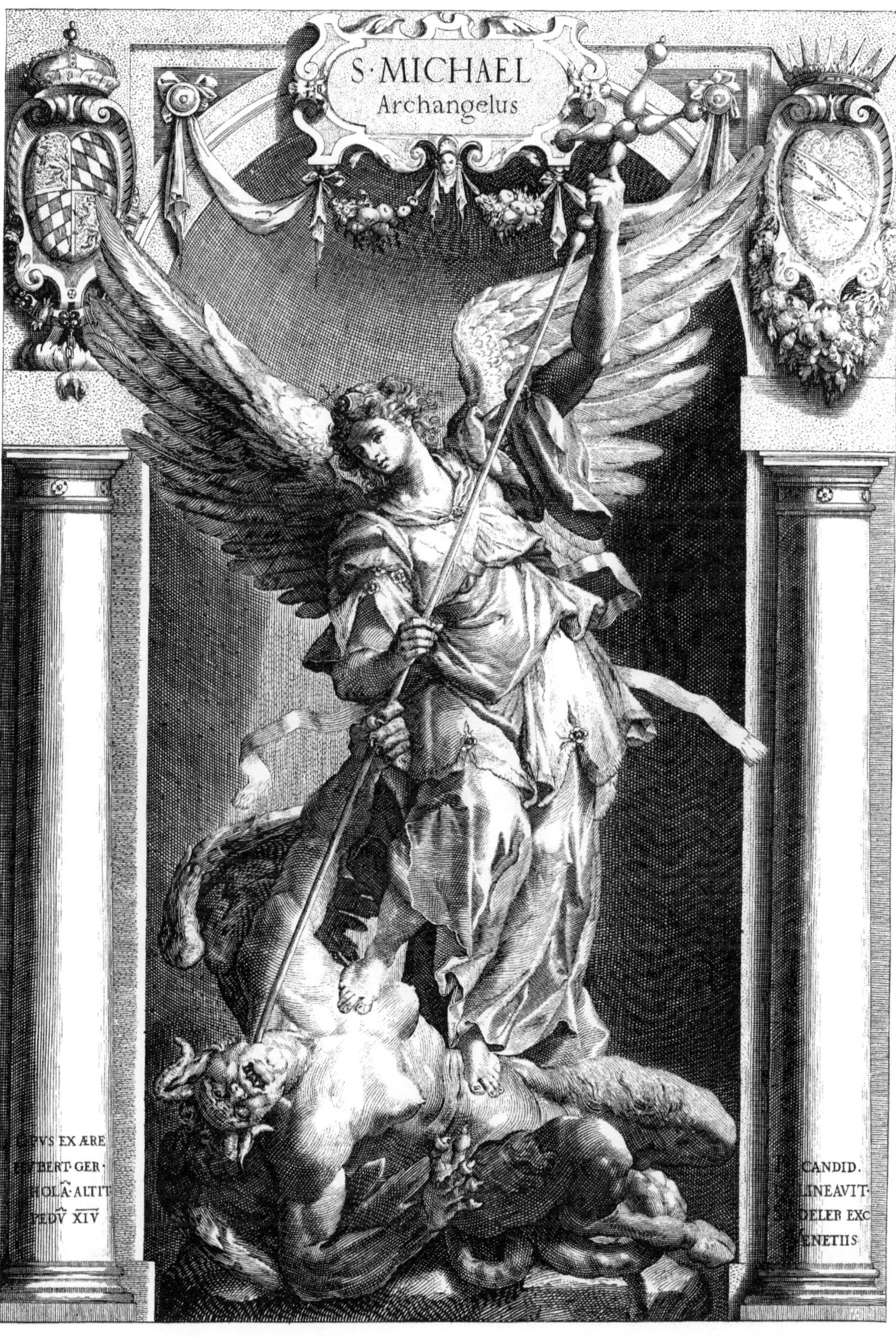
S·MICHAEL
Archangelus
...VS EX ÆRE
...BERT·GER·
...OLÂ·ALTIT
PEDŪ XIV
CANDID.
LINEAVIT·
...DELER EXC
...ENETIIS

13

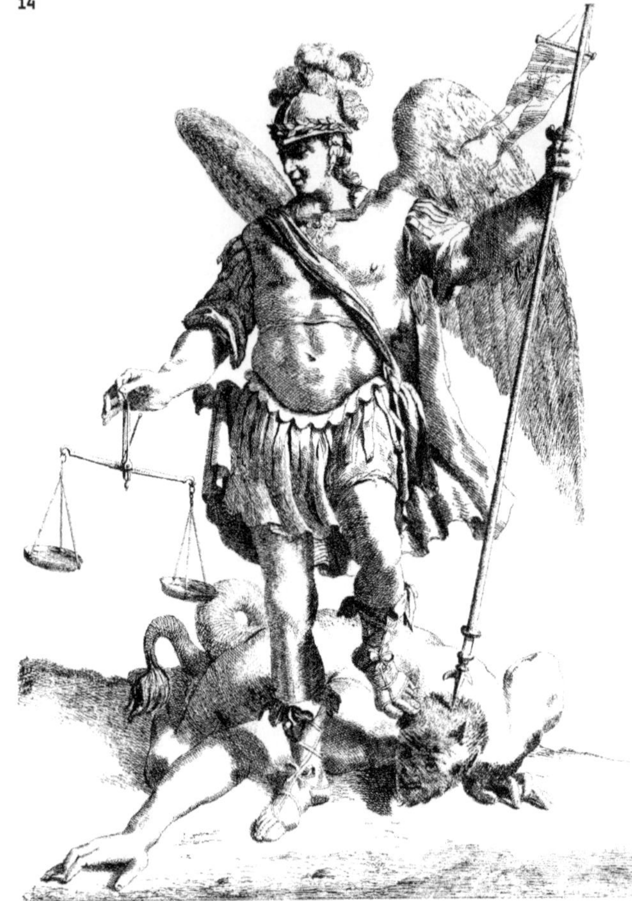

14

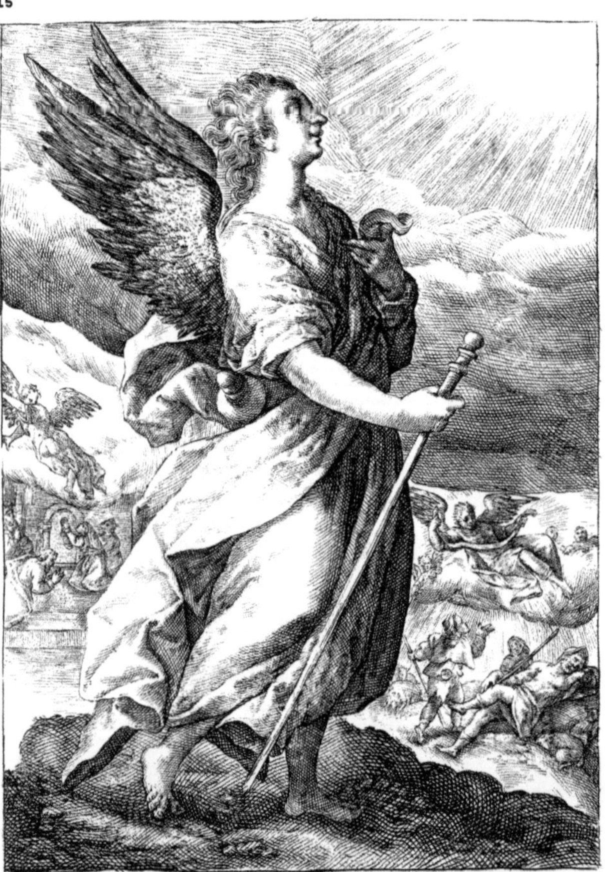

15

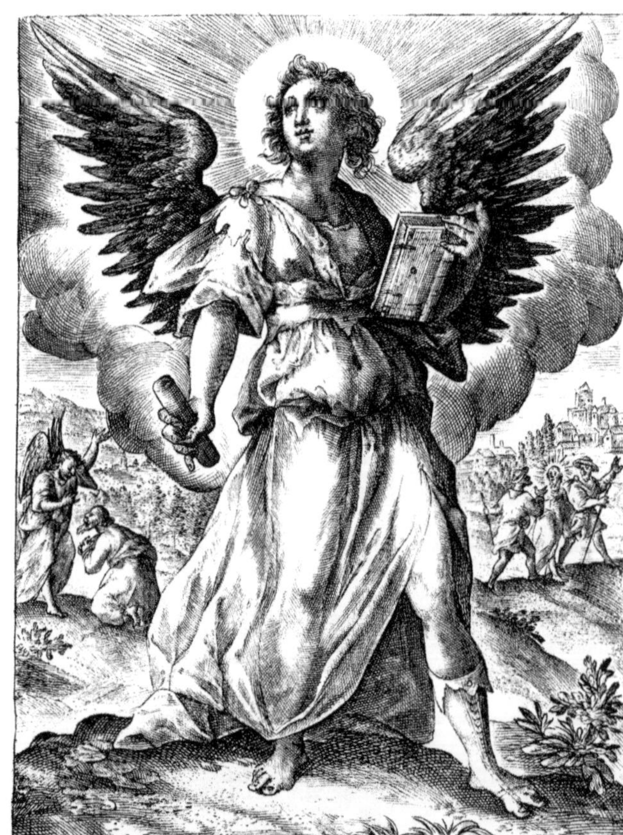

16

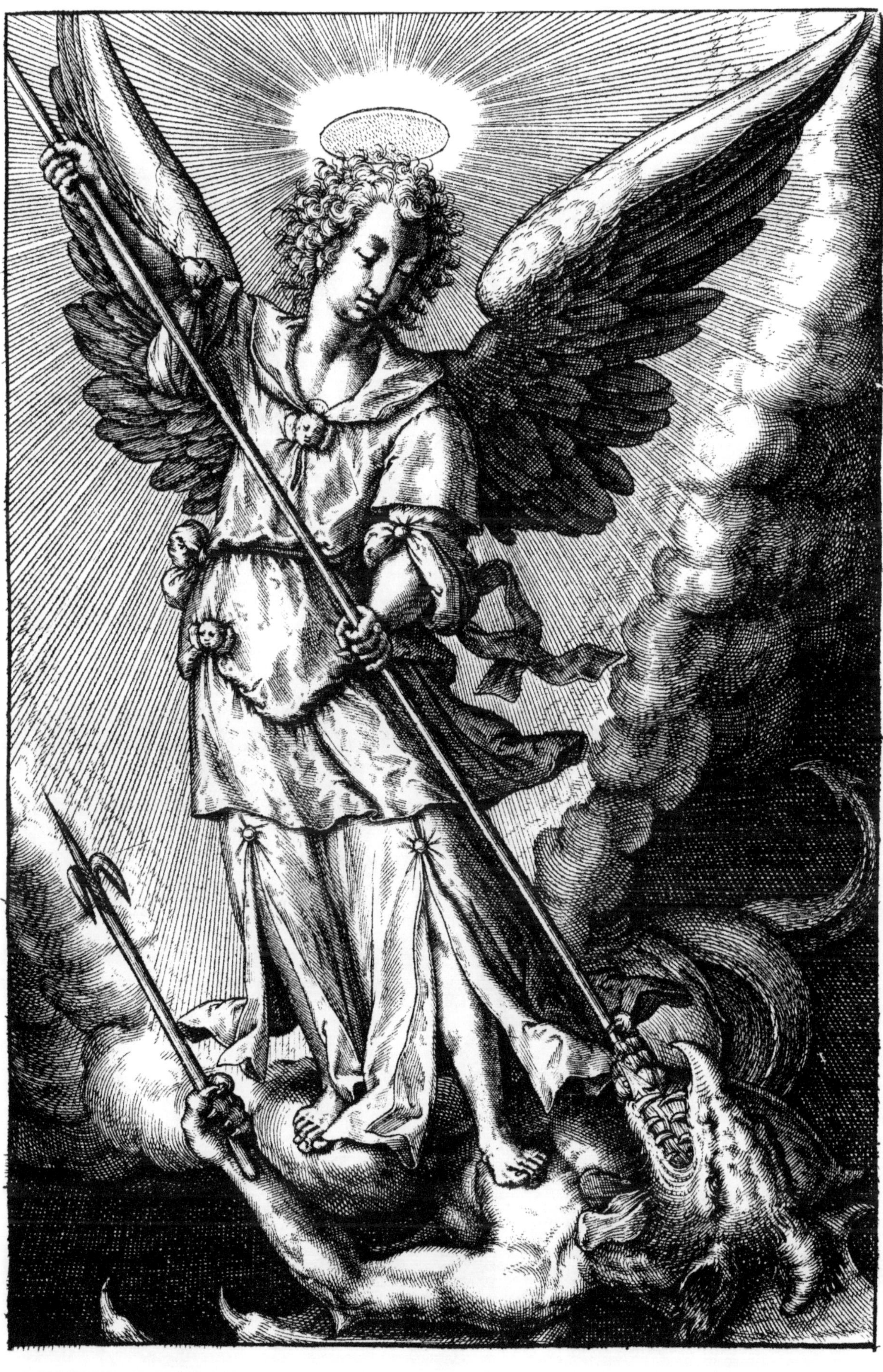

18

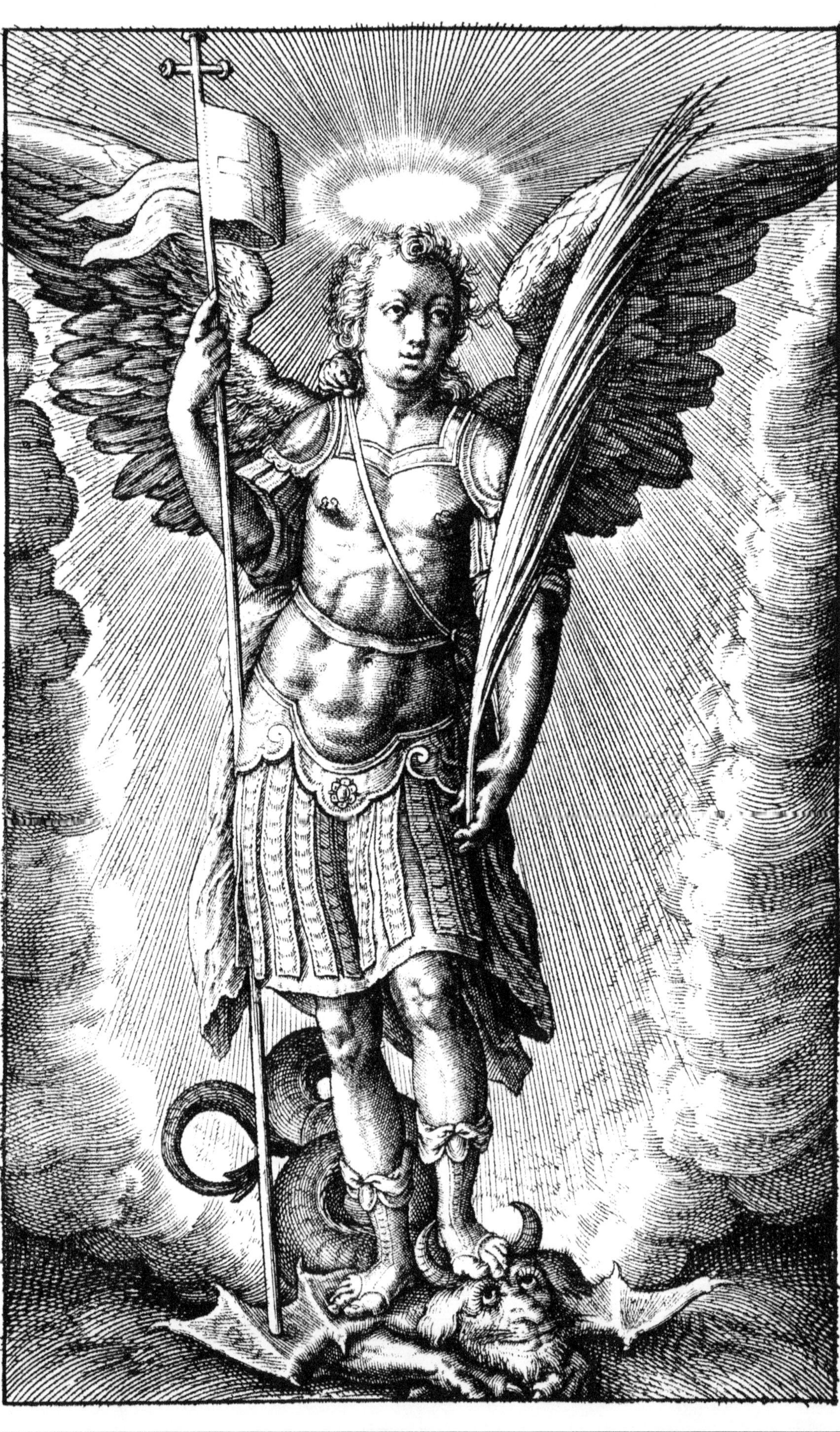

19

20

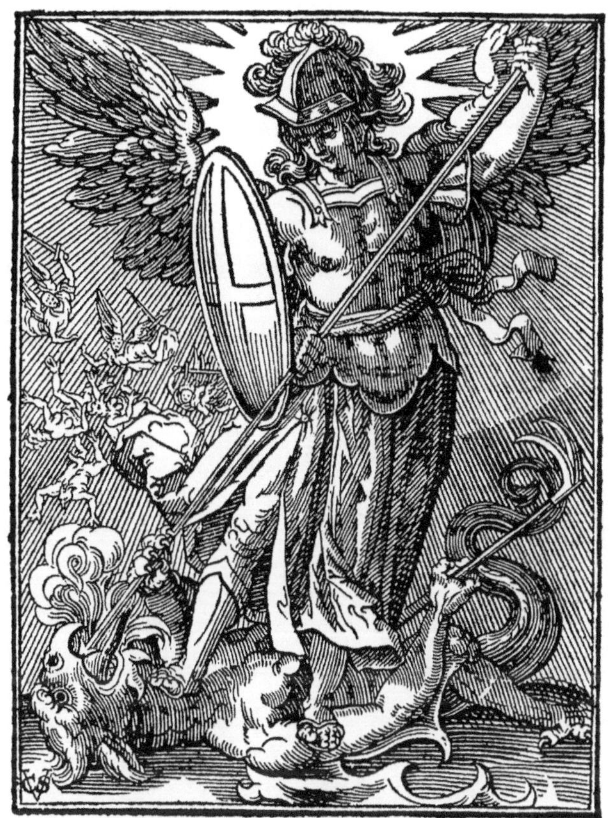

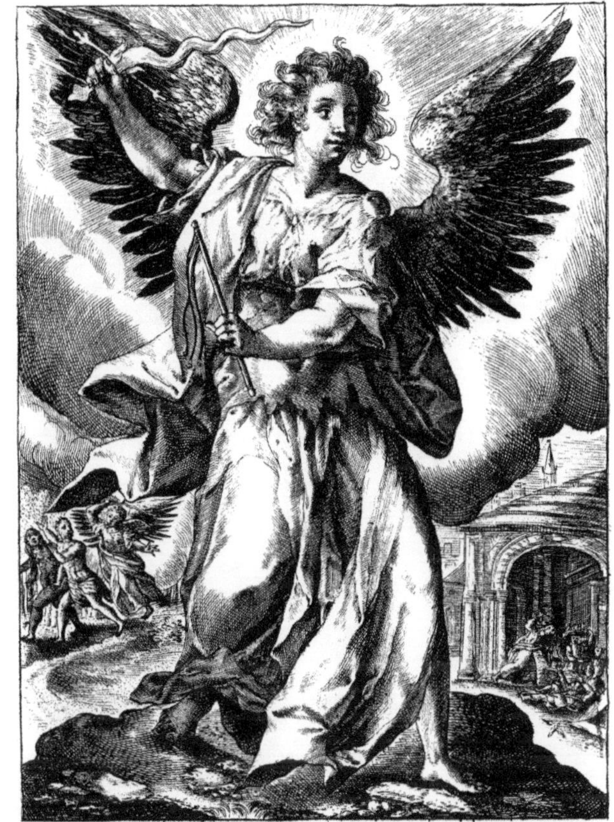

21

22

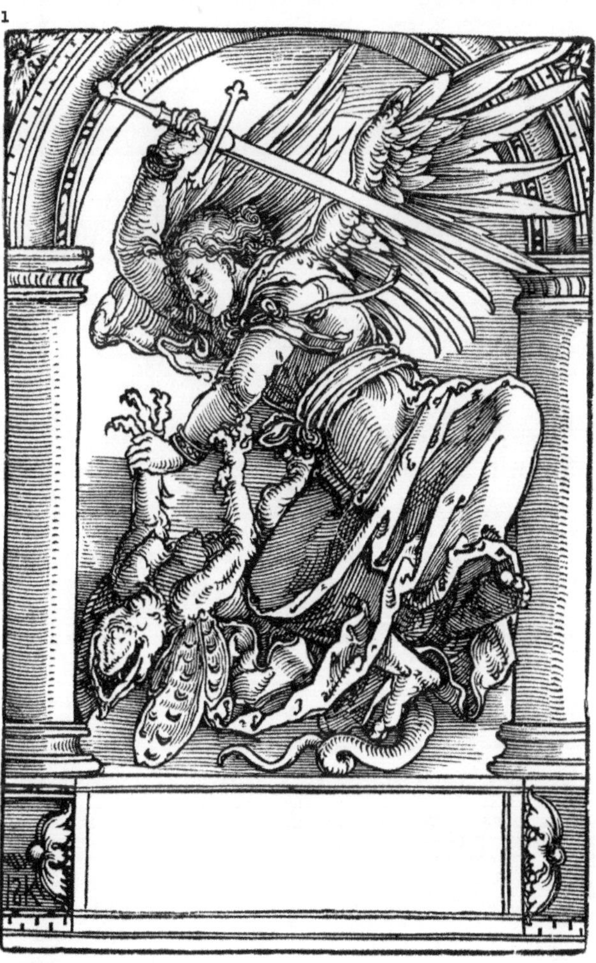

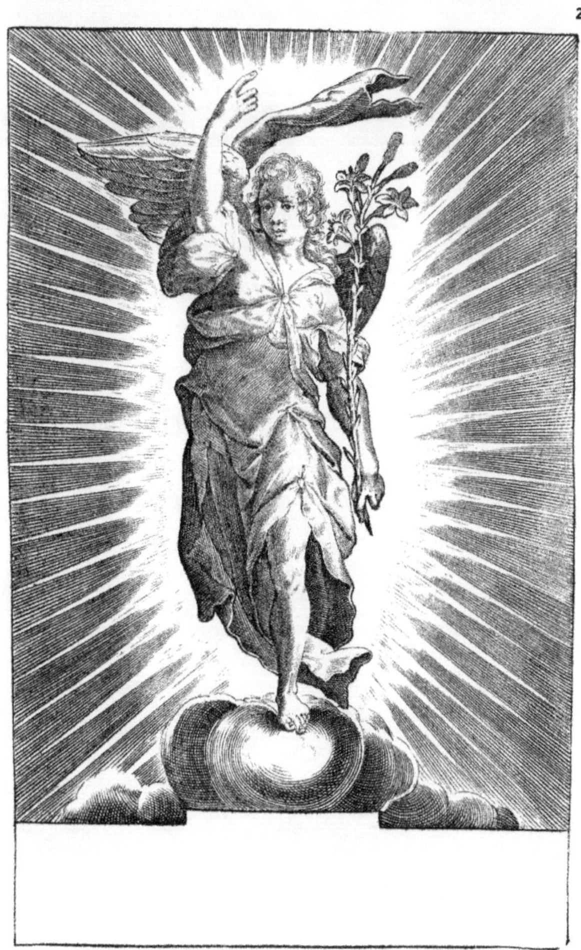

23

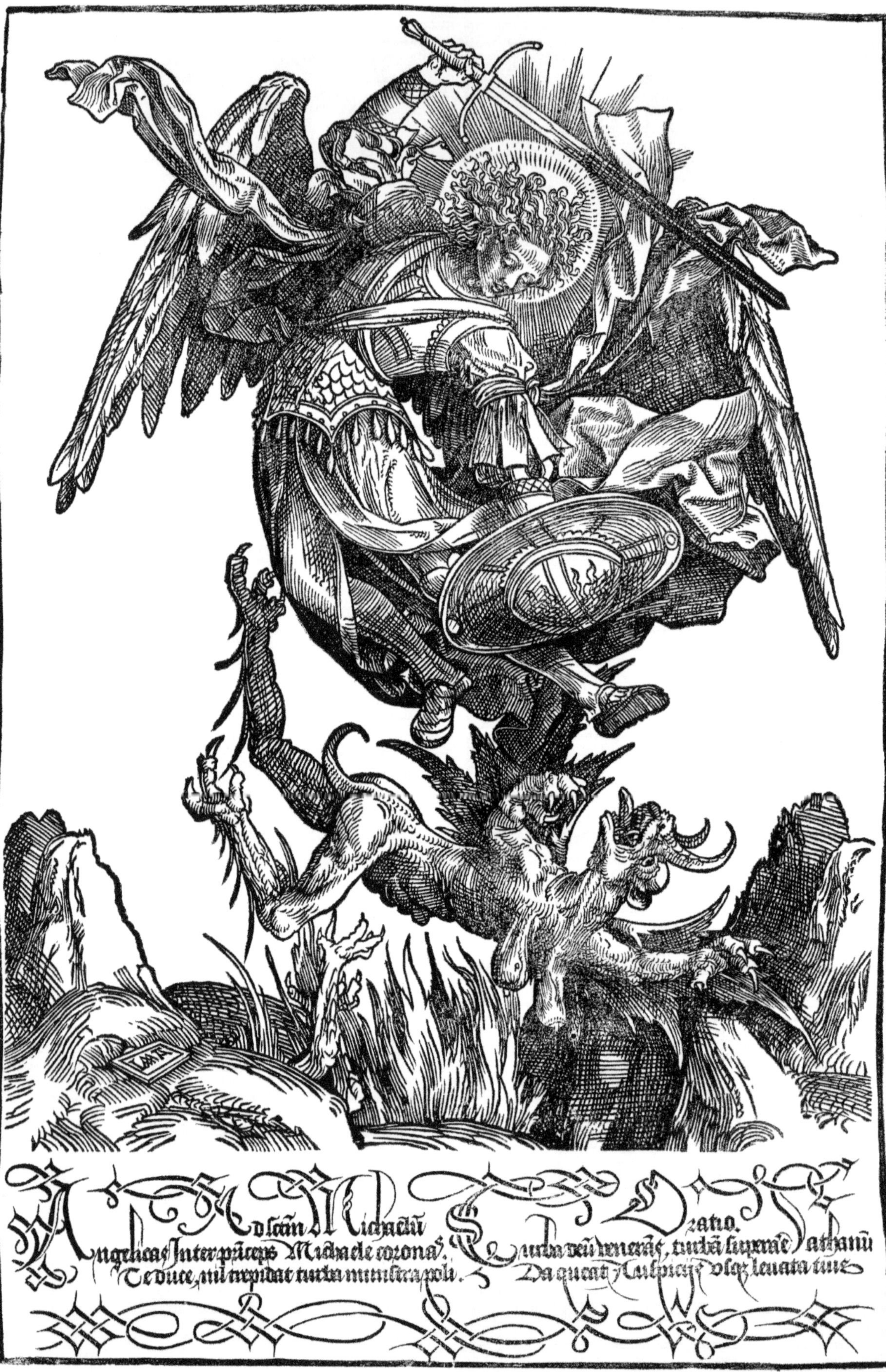

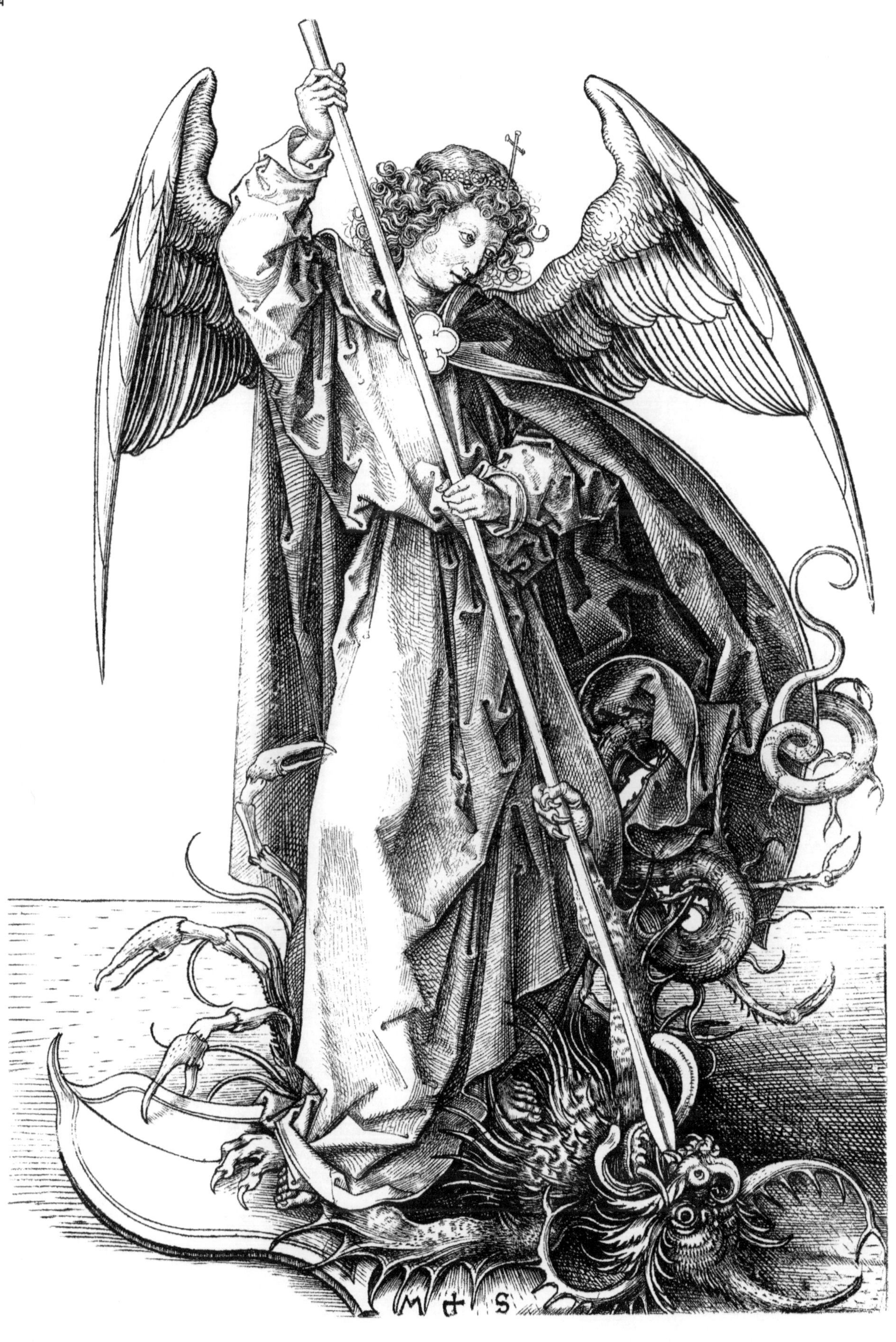

25

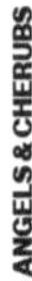

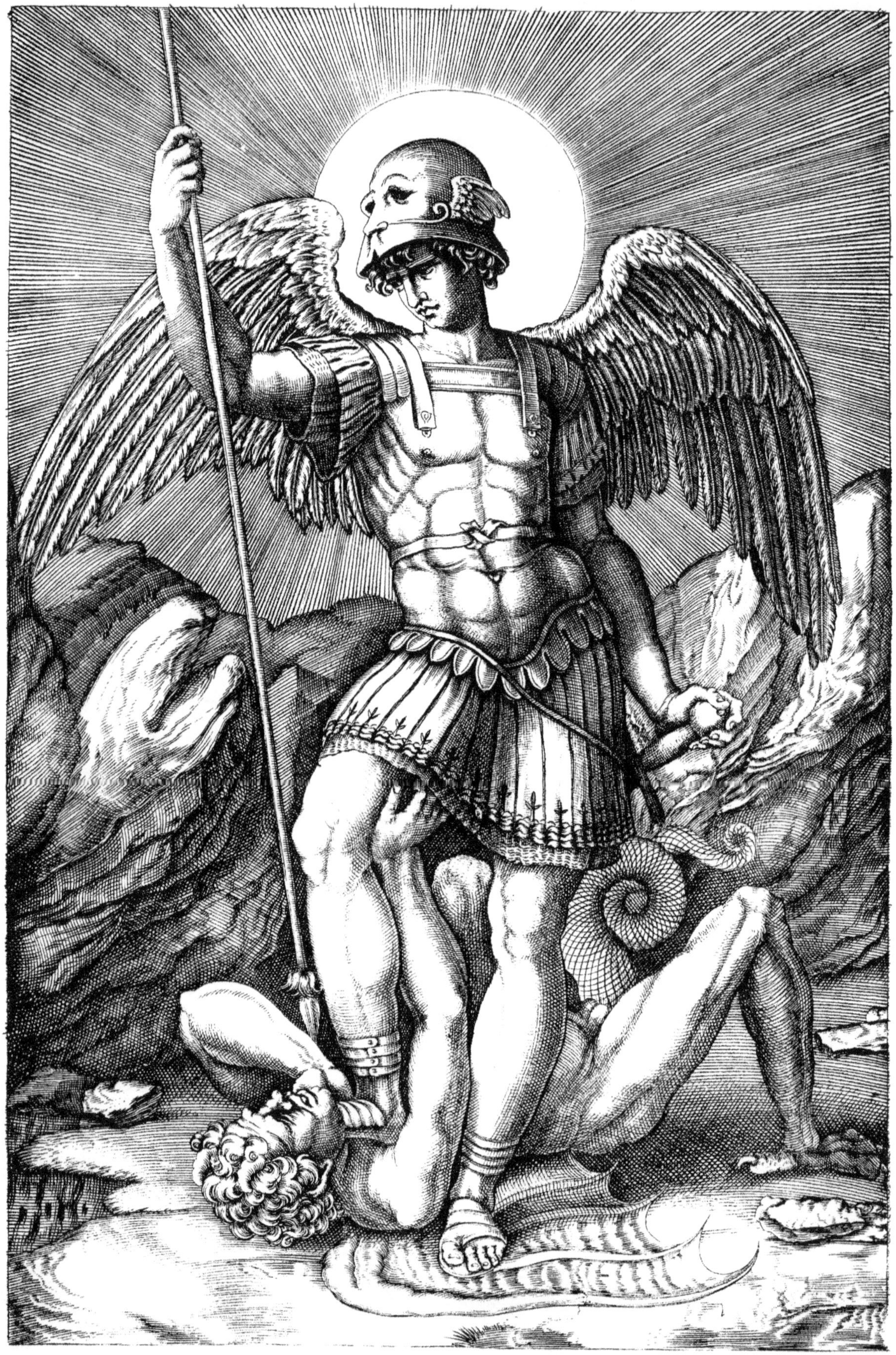

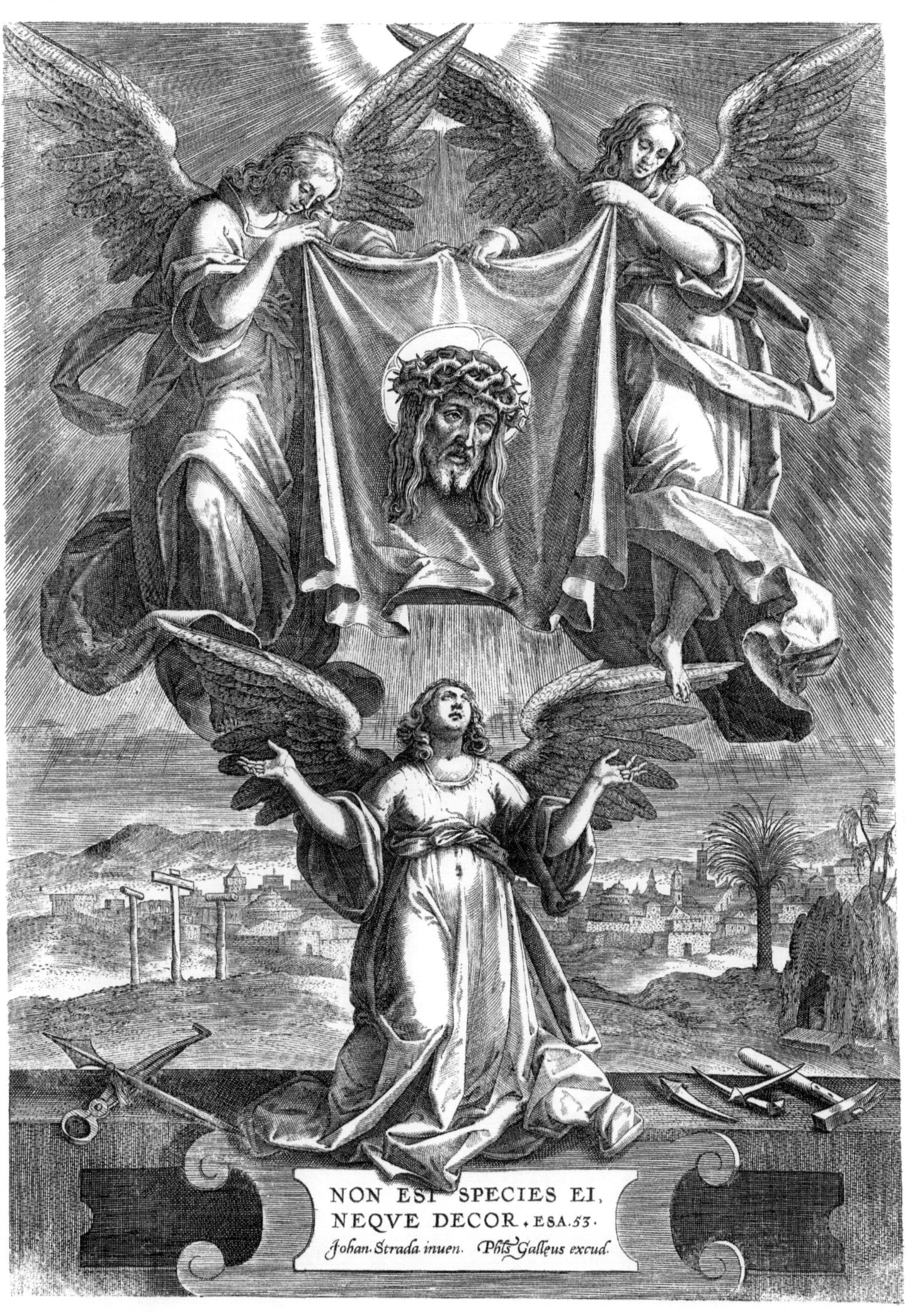

NON EST SPECIES EI,
NEQVE DECOR. ESA.53.
Johan. Strada inuen. Phls Galleus excud.

27

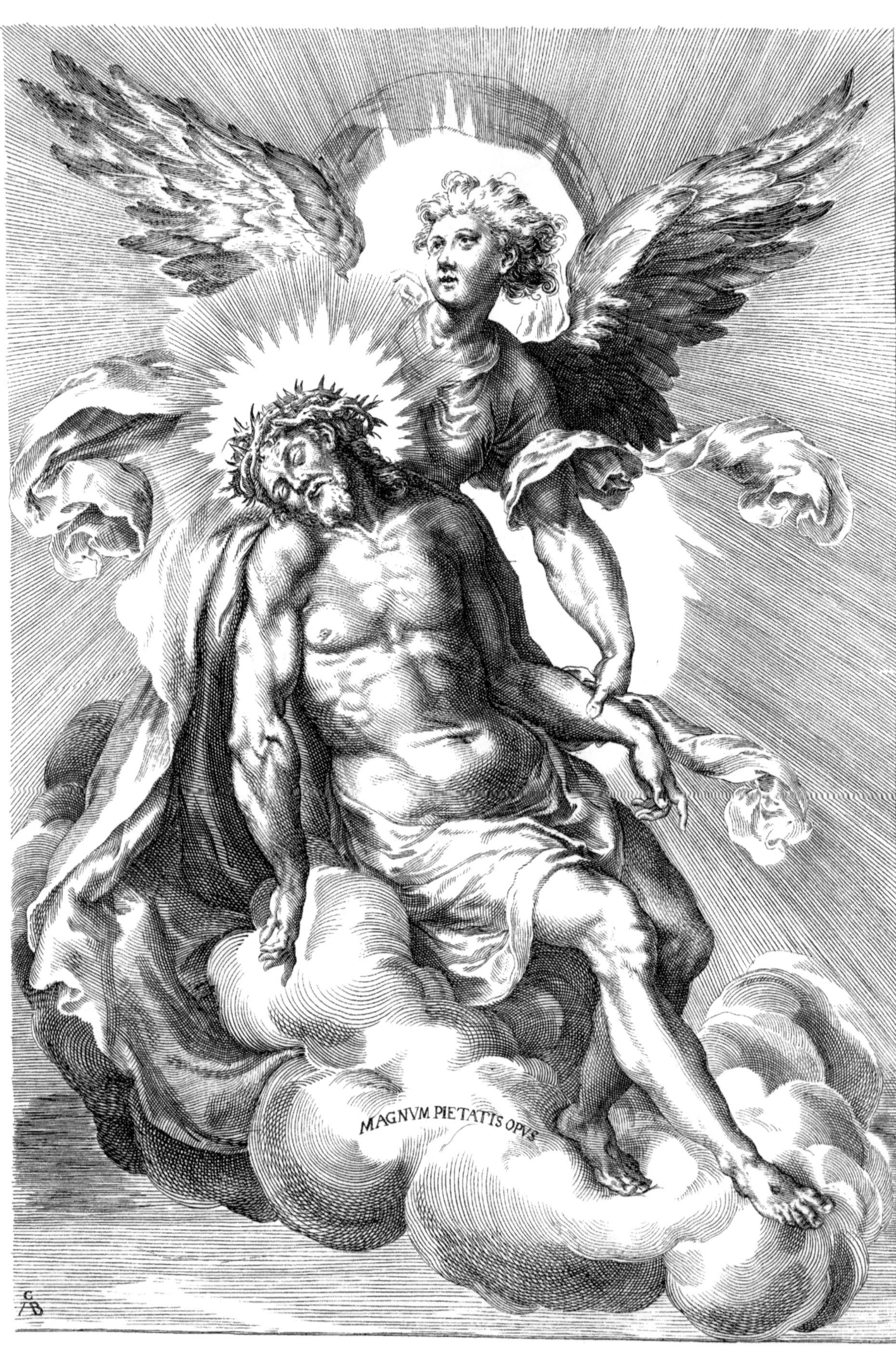

28

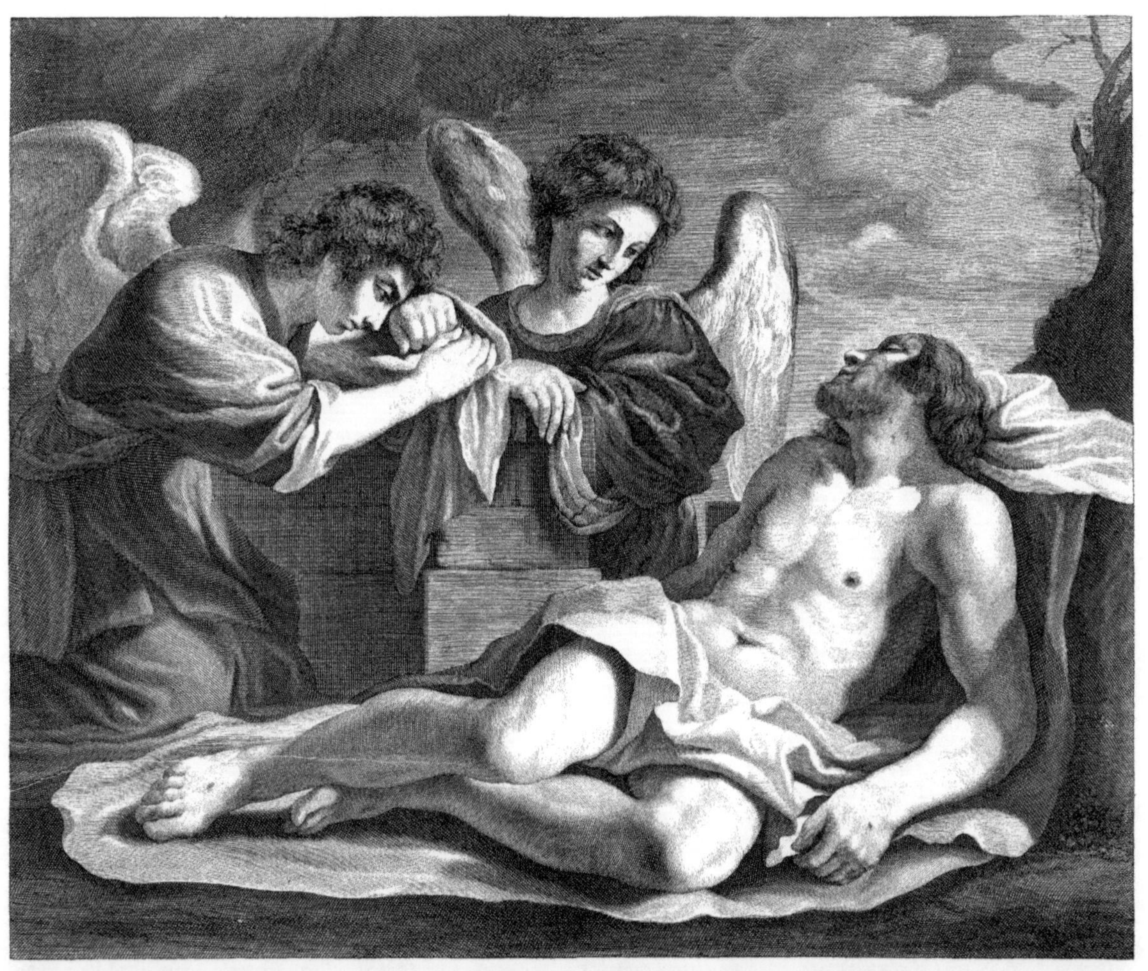

29

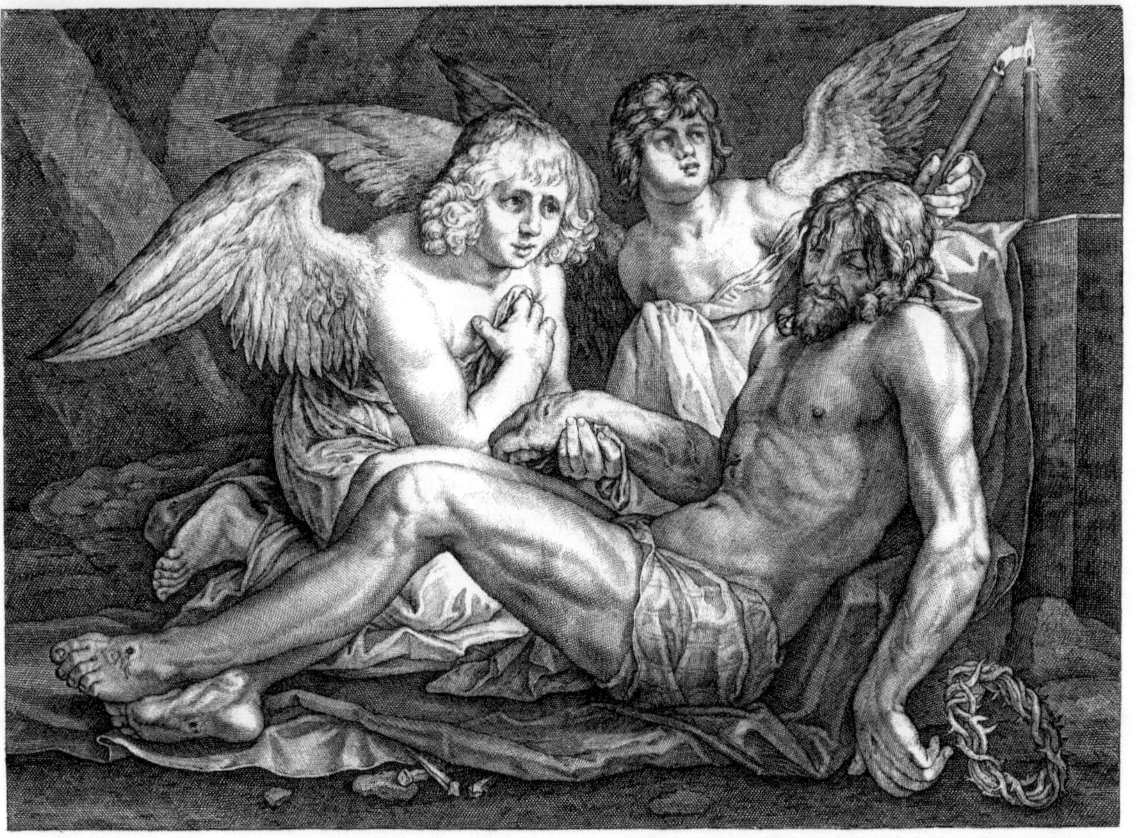

30

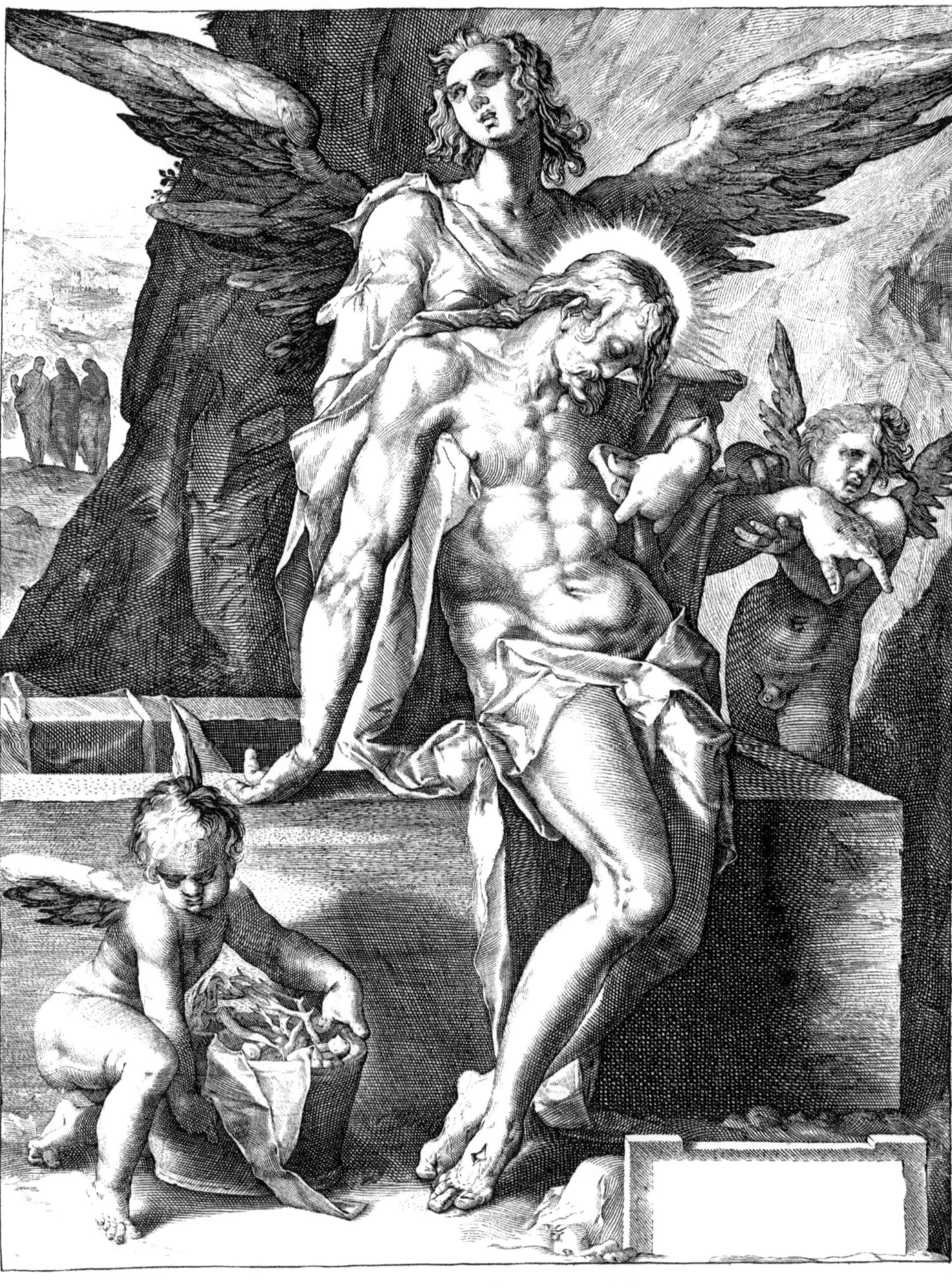

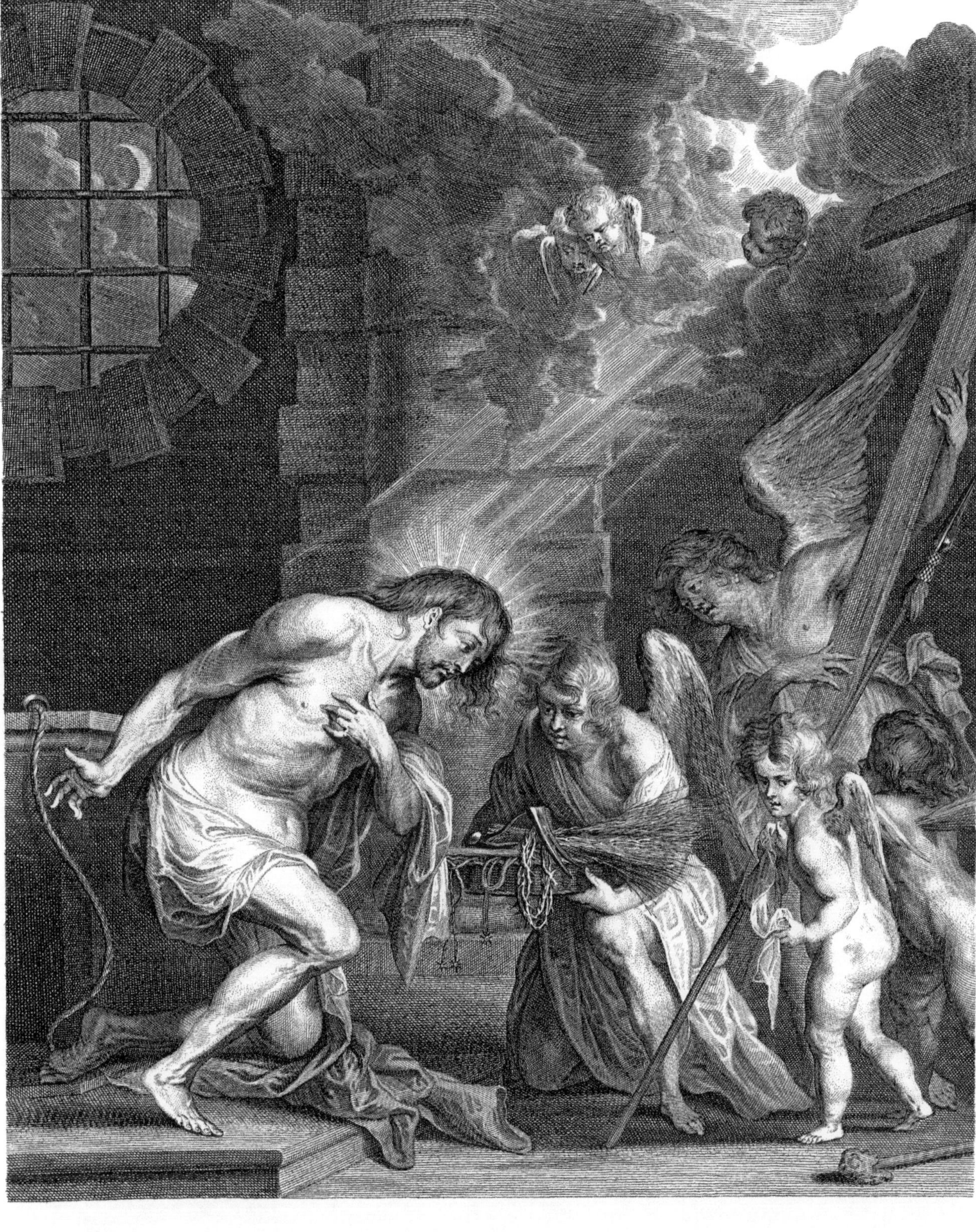

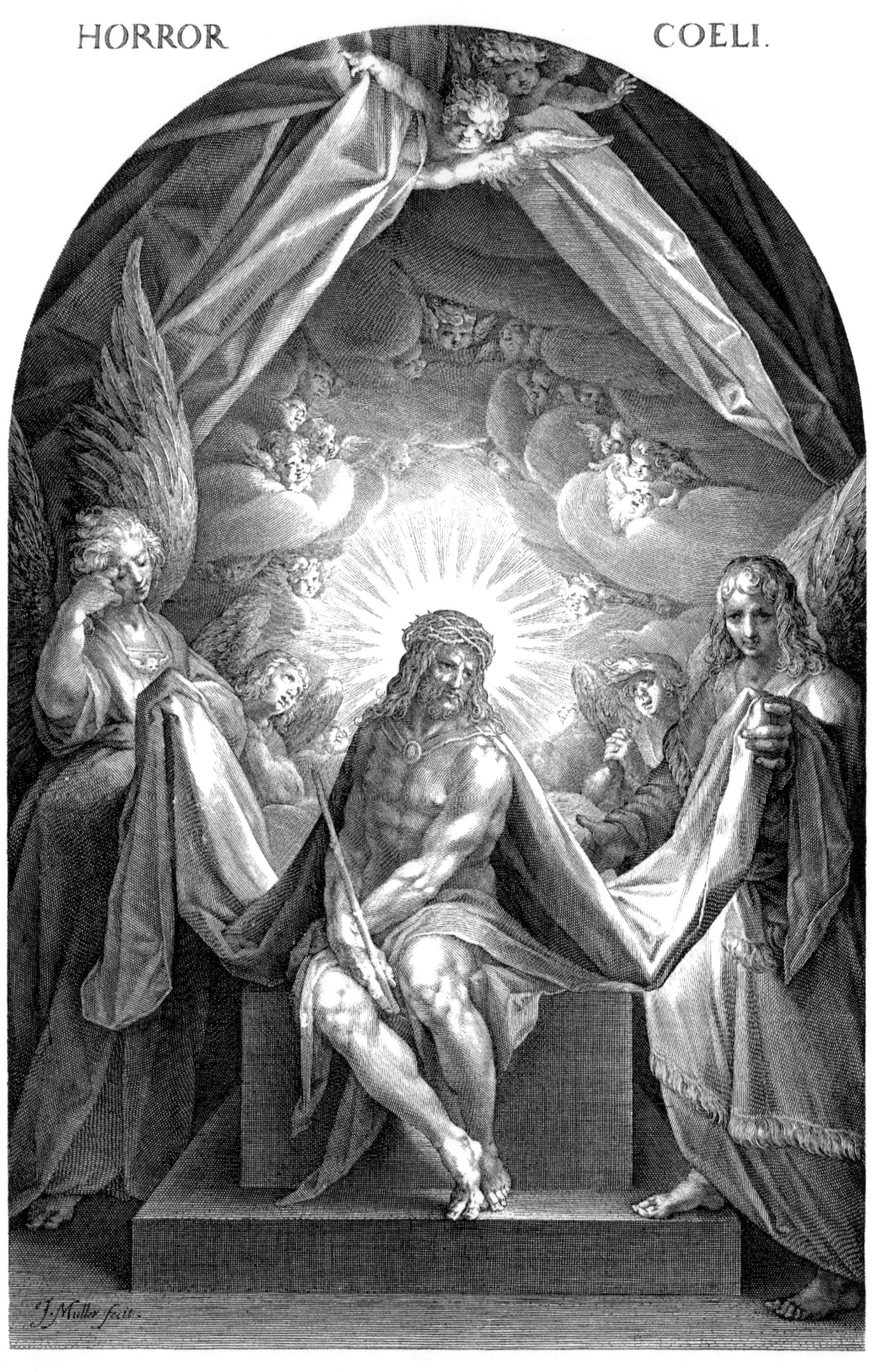

HORROR
COELI.
J. Muller fecit.

33

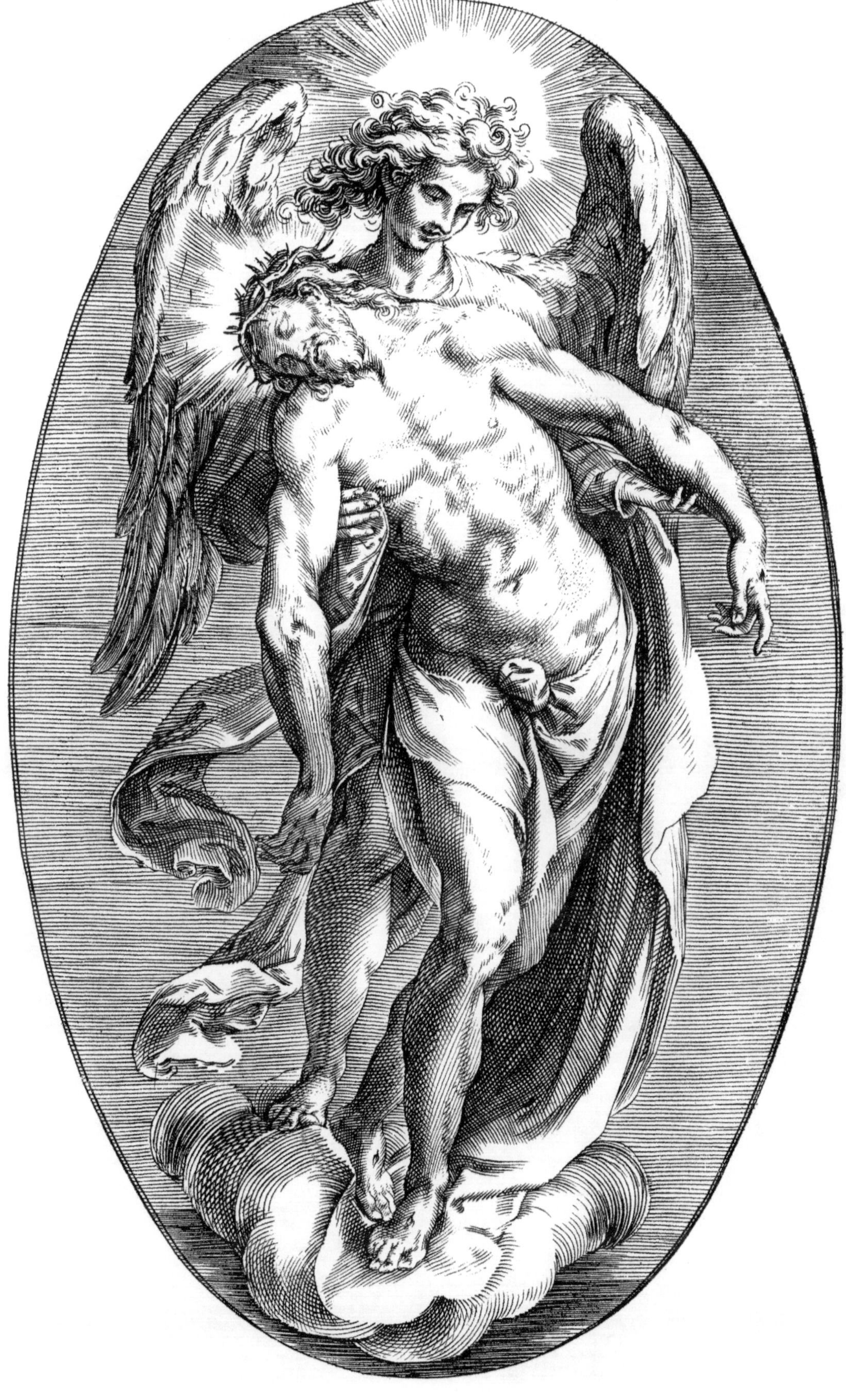

34

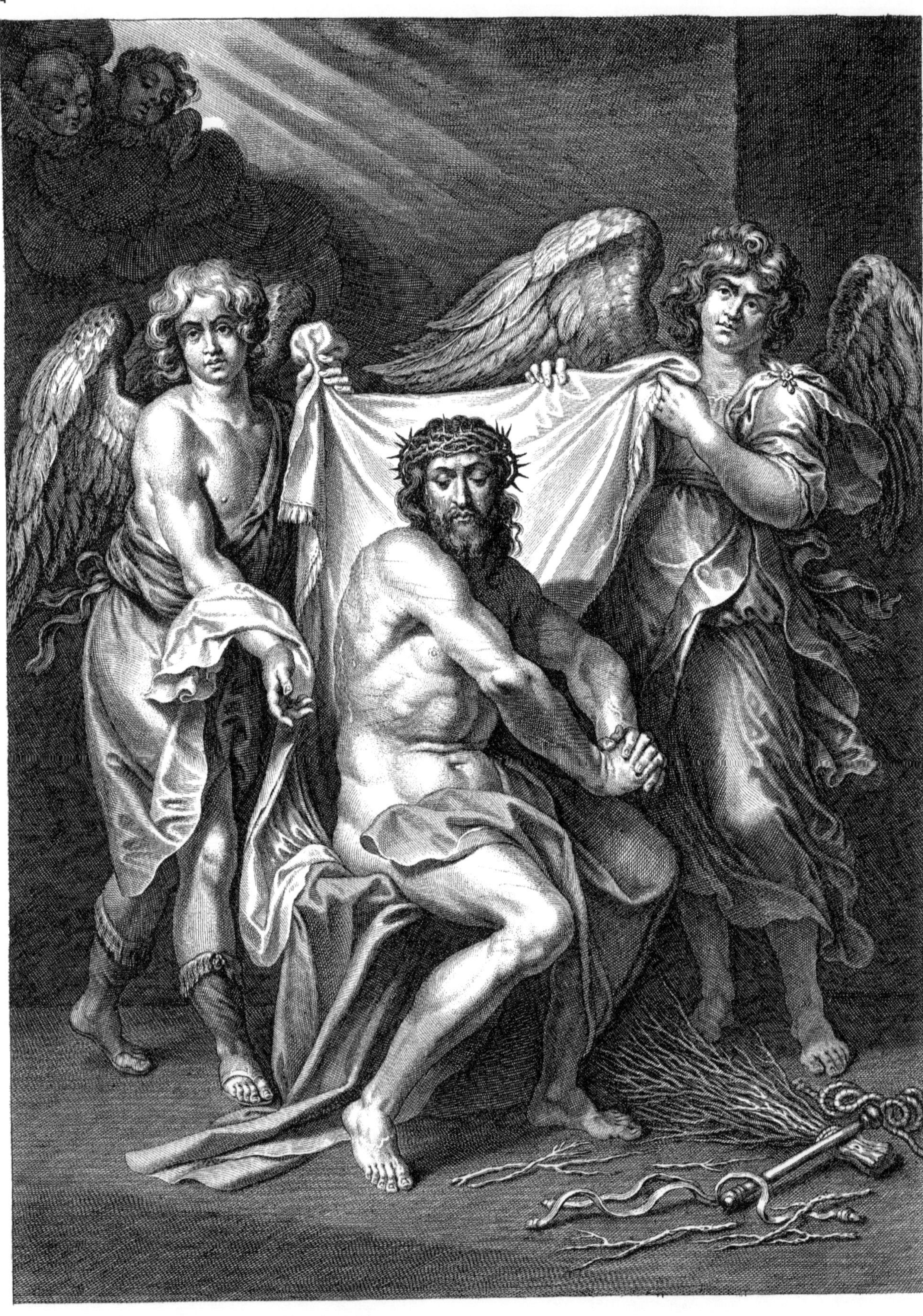

35

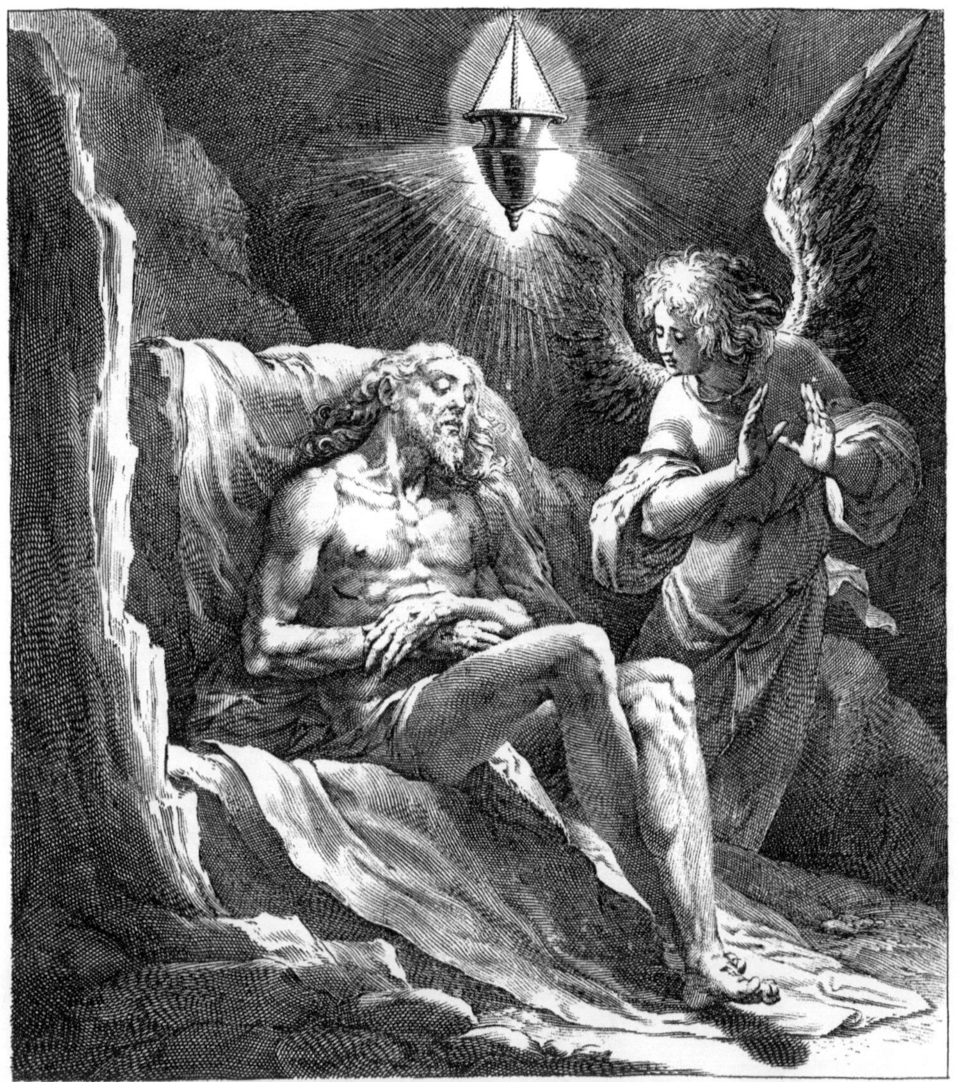

36

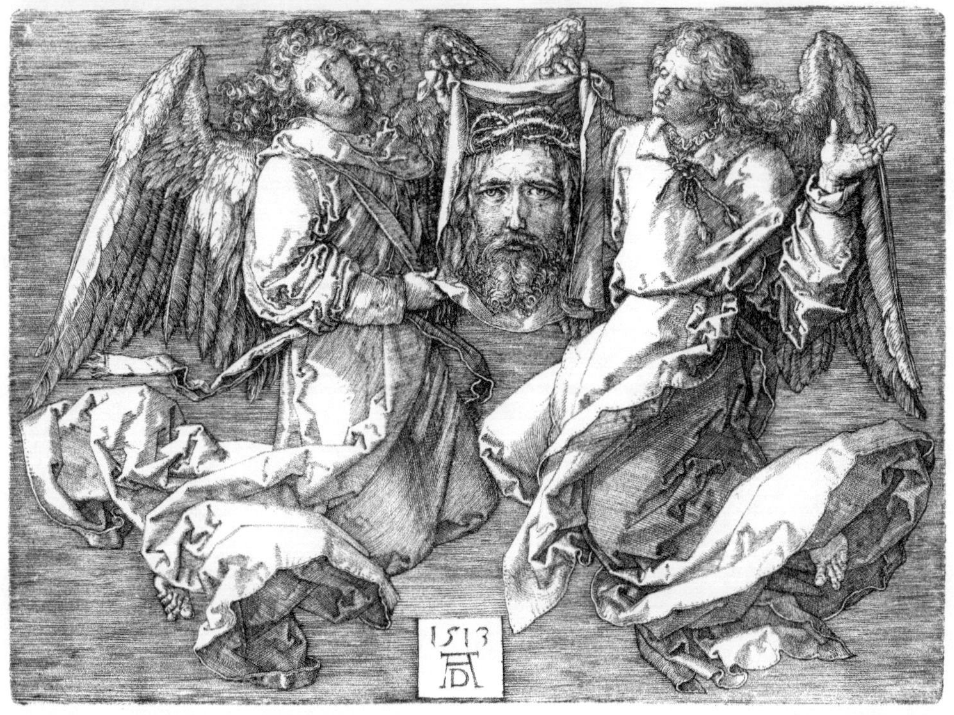

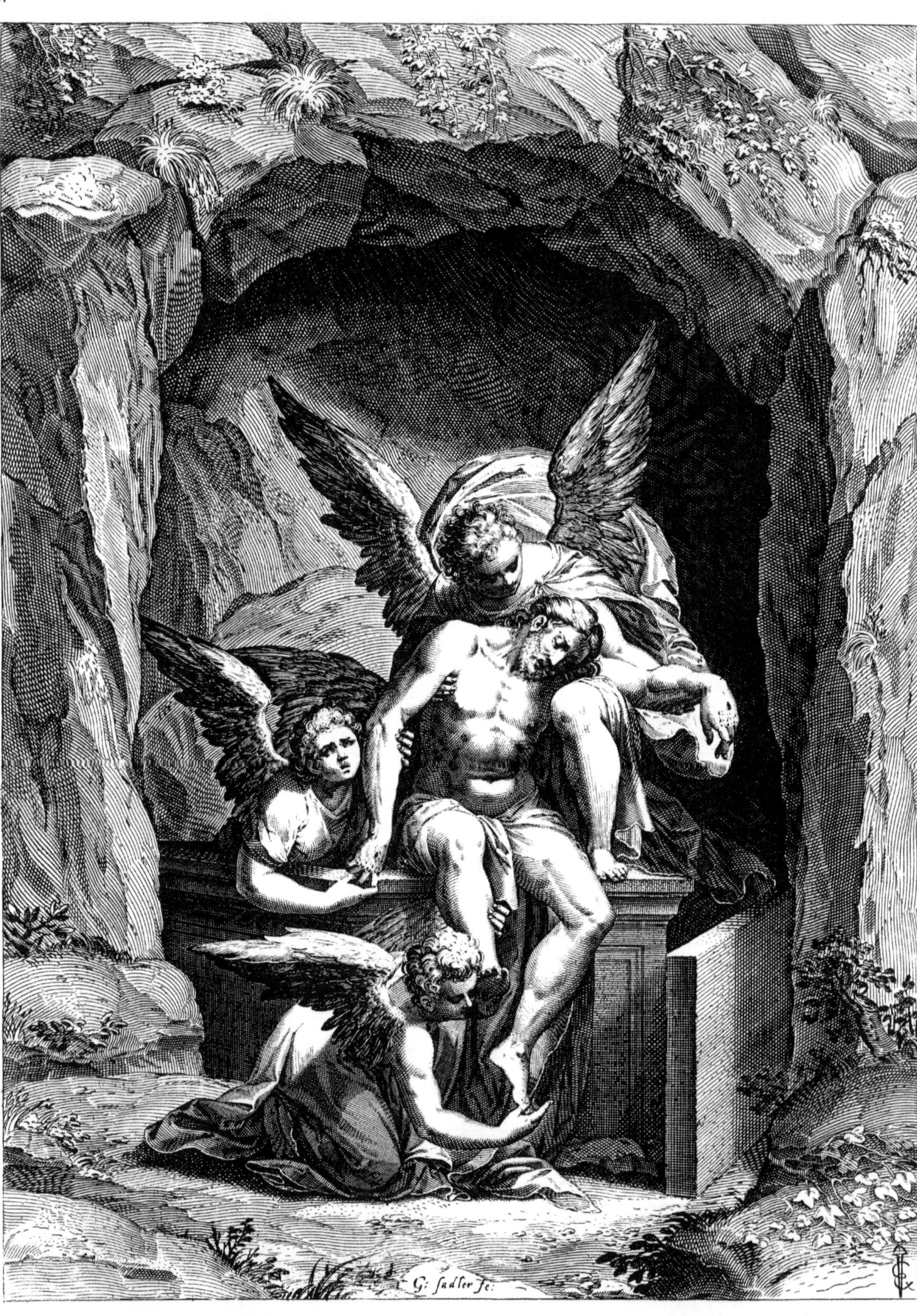
G: Sadler fe:

38

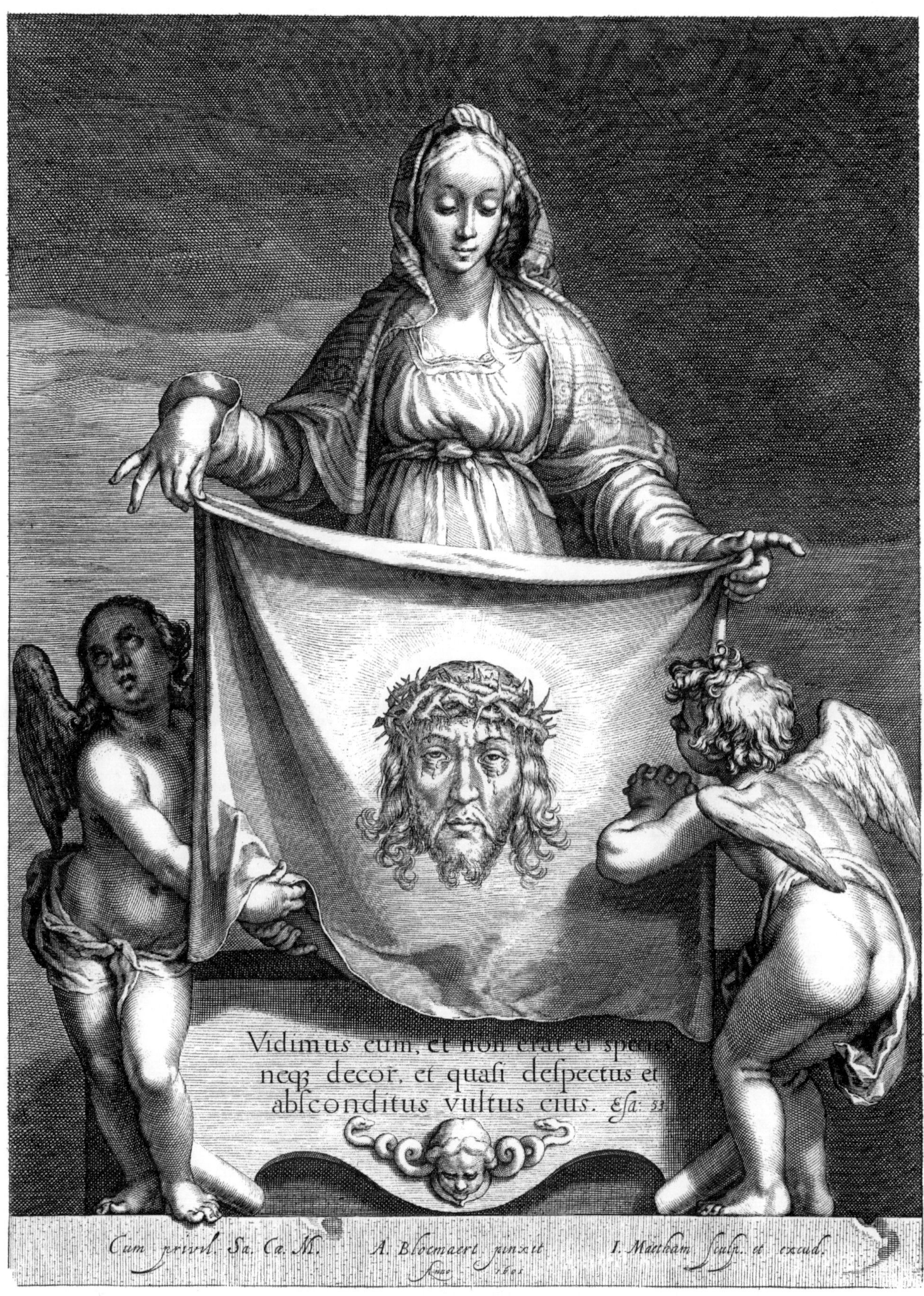

Vidimus eum, et non erat ei species
neq; decor, et quasi despectus et
absconditus vultus eius. Esa: 53

Cum privil. Sa. Ca. M.   A. Bloemaert pinxit   I. Matham sculp. et excud.
Anno 1605

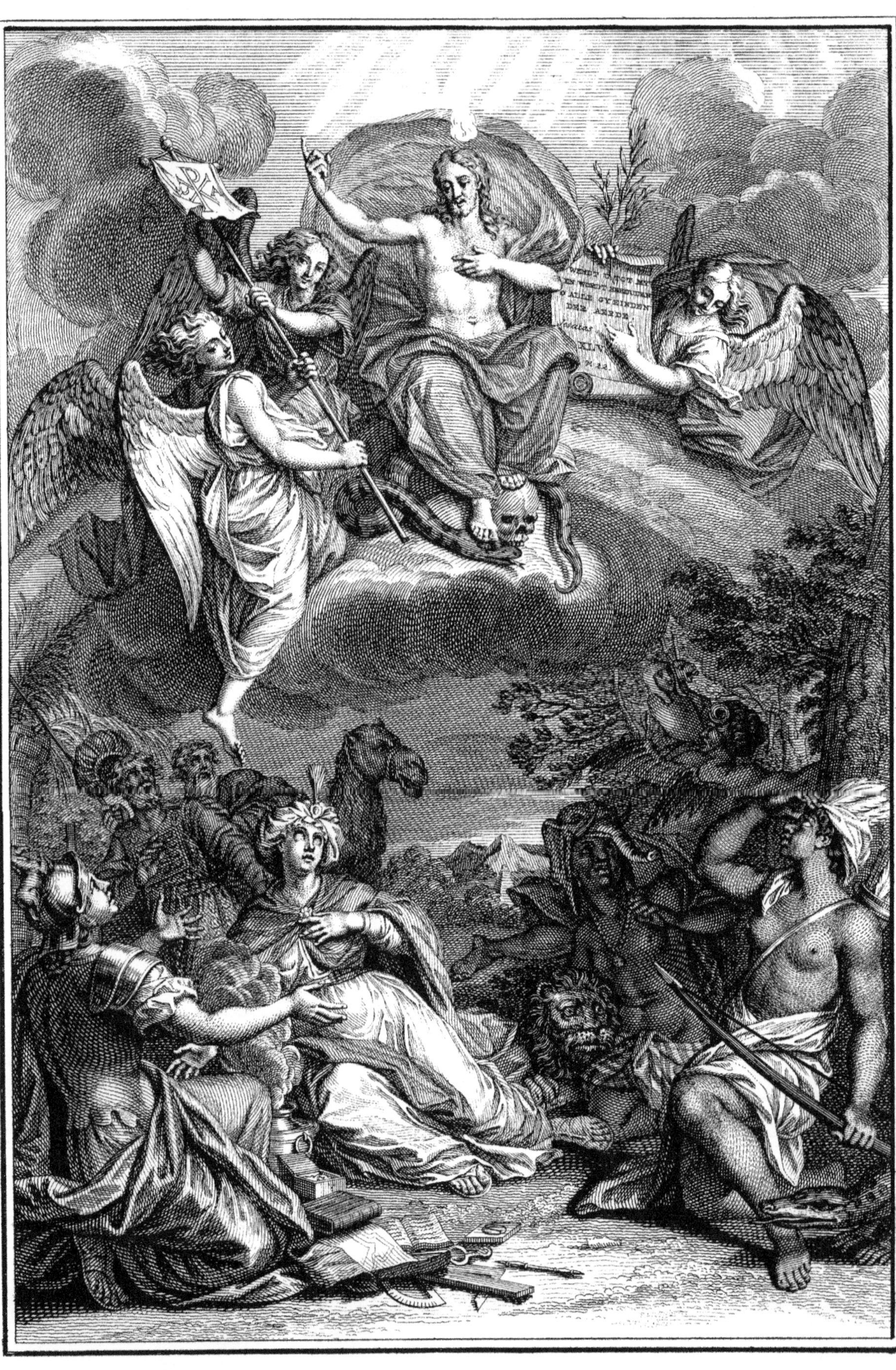

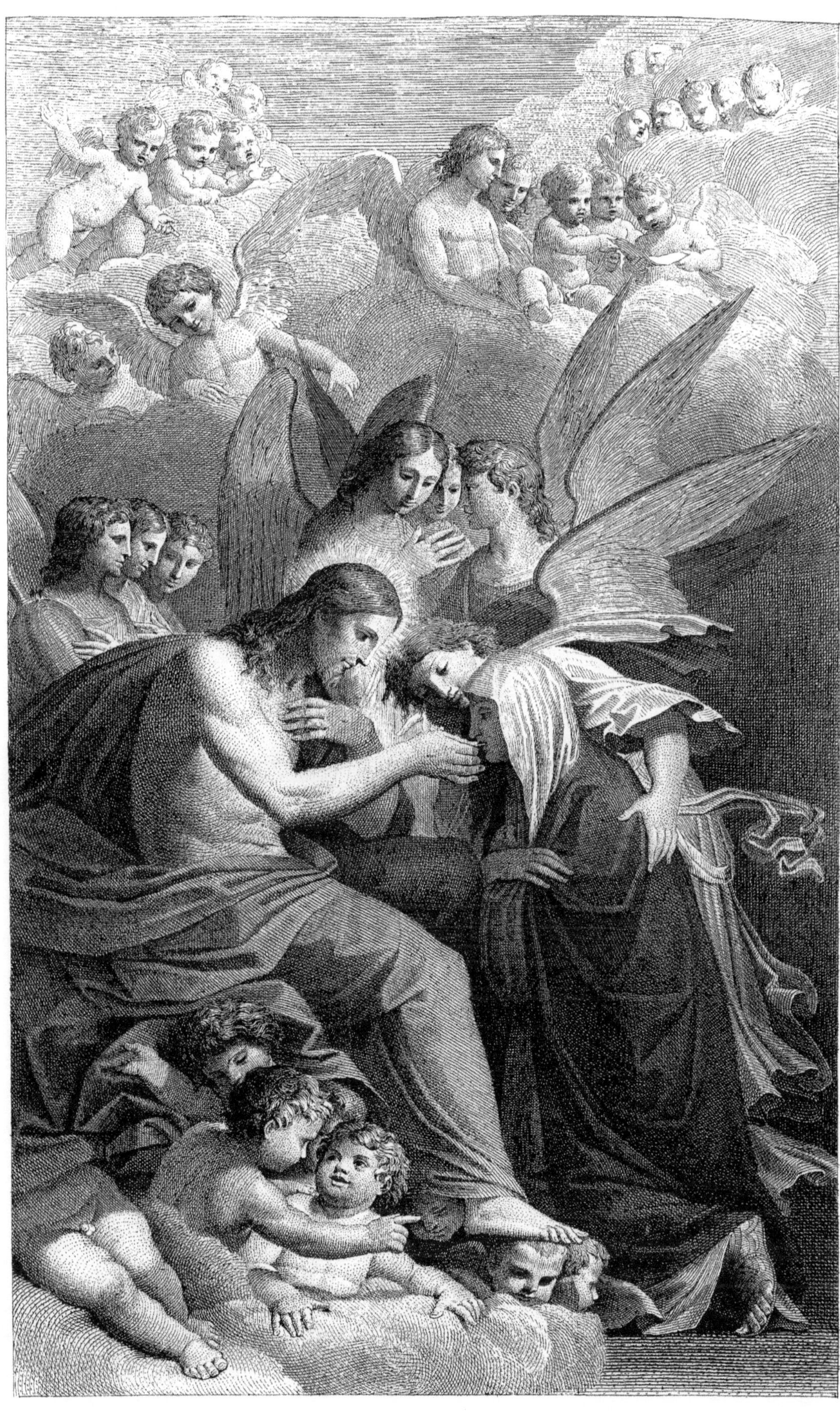

41

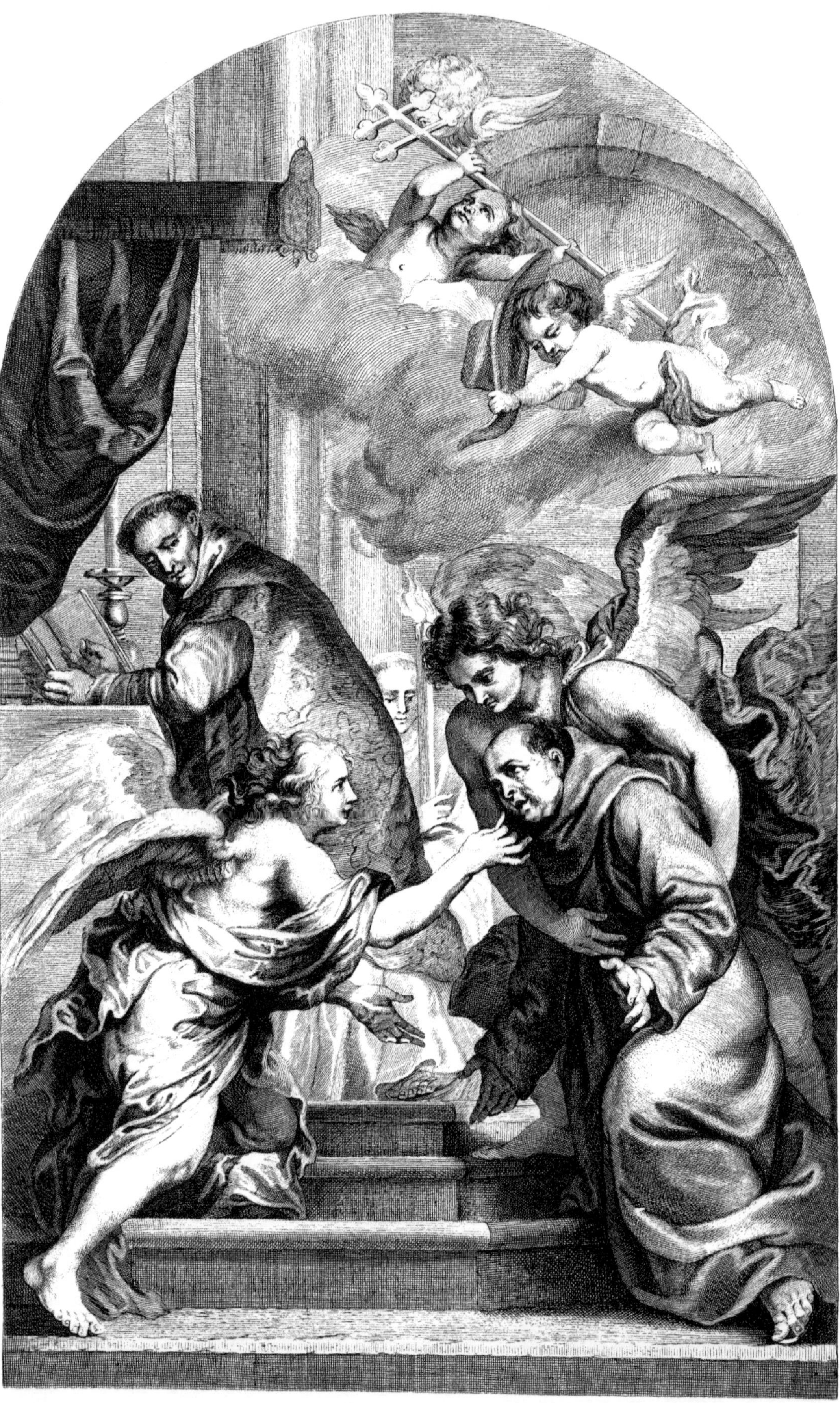

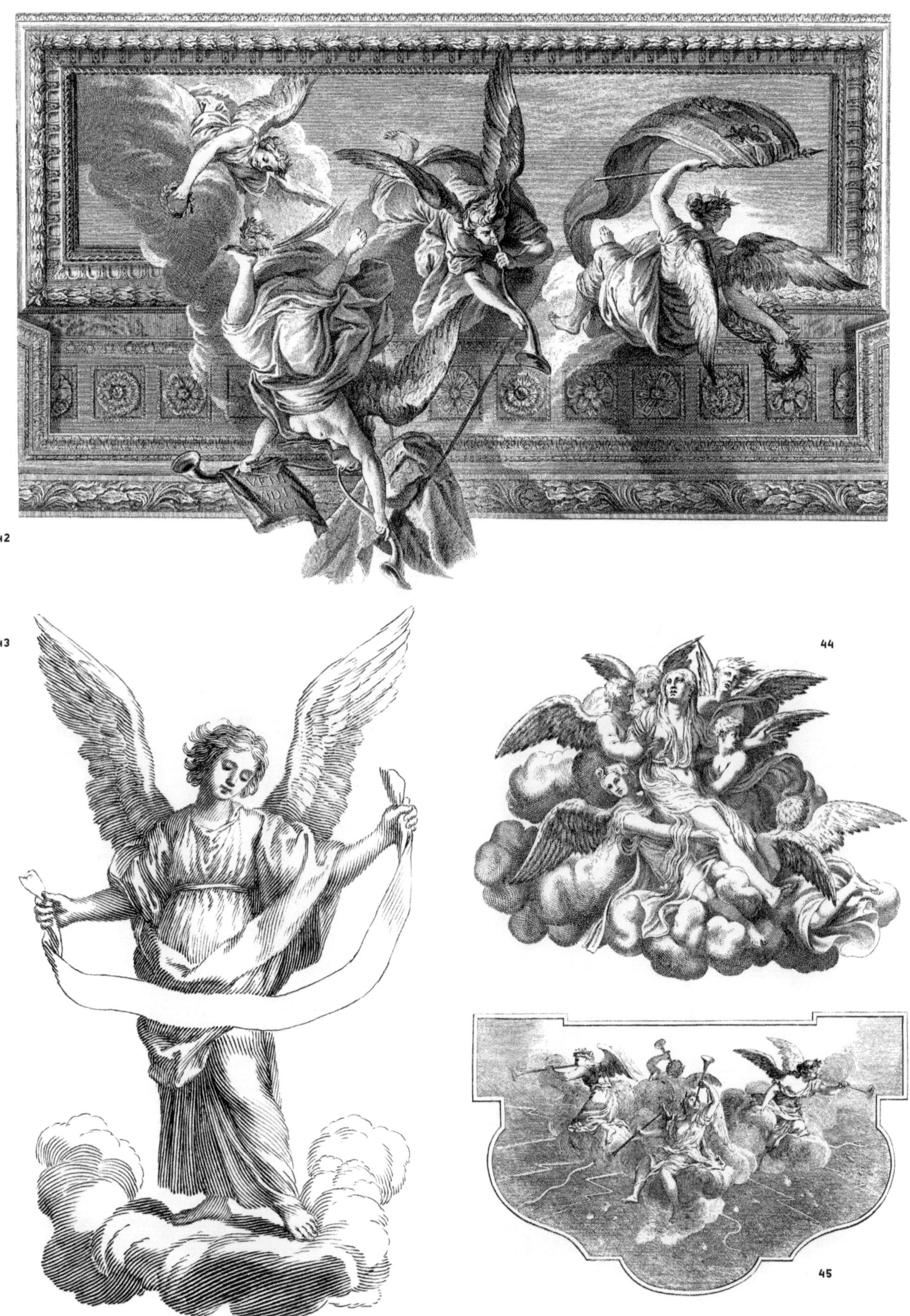

46

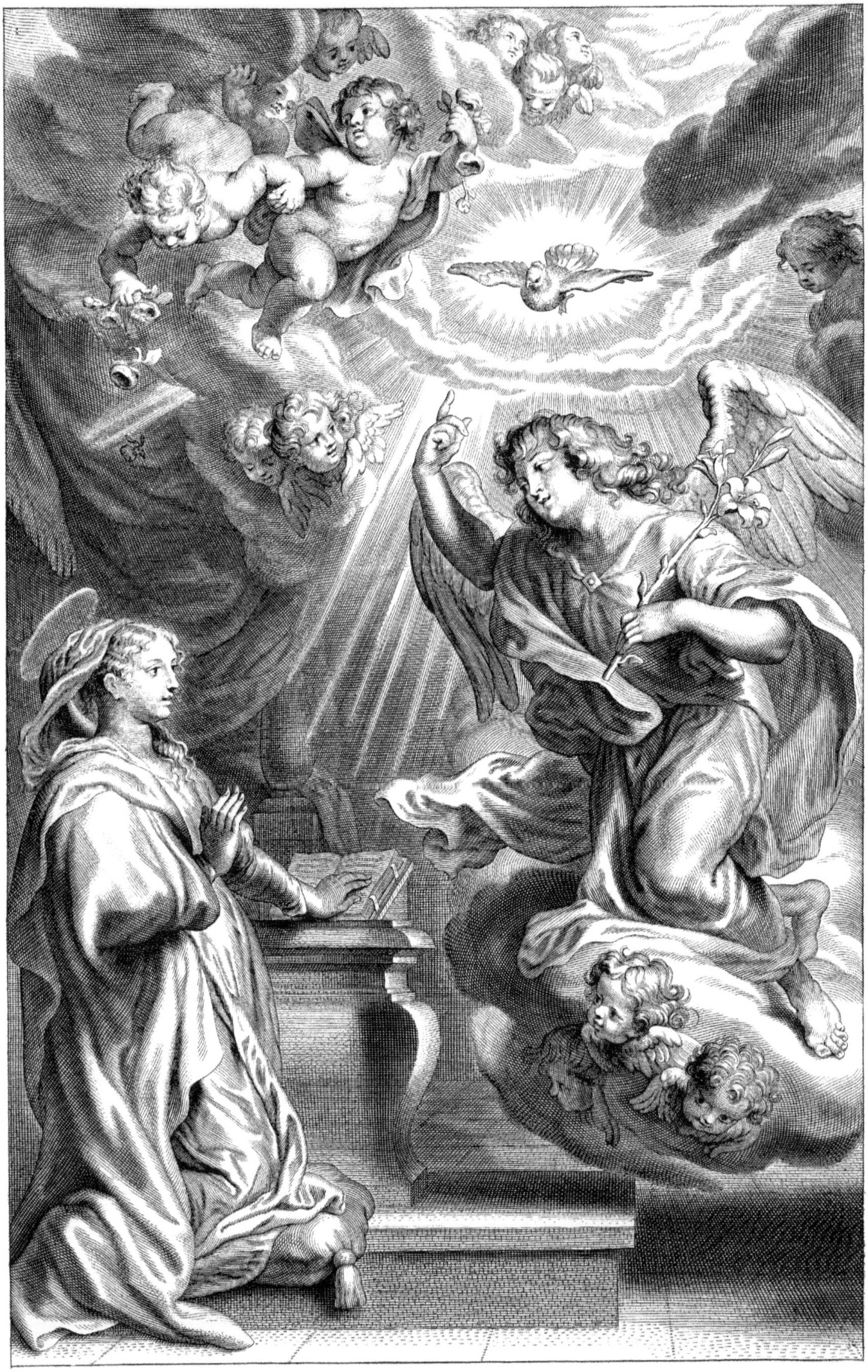

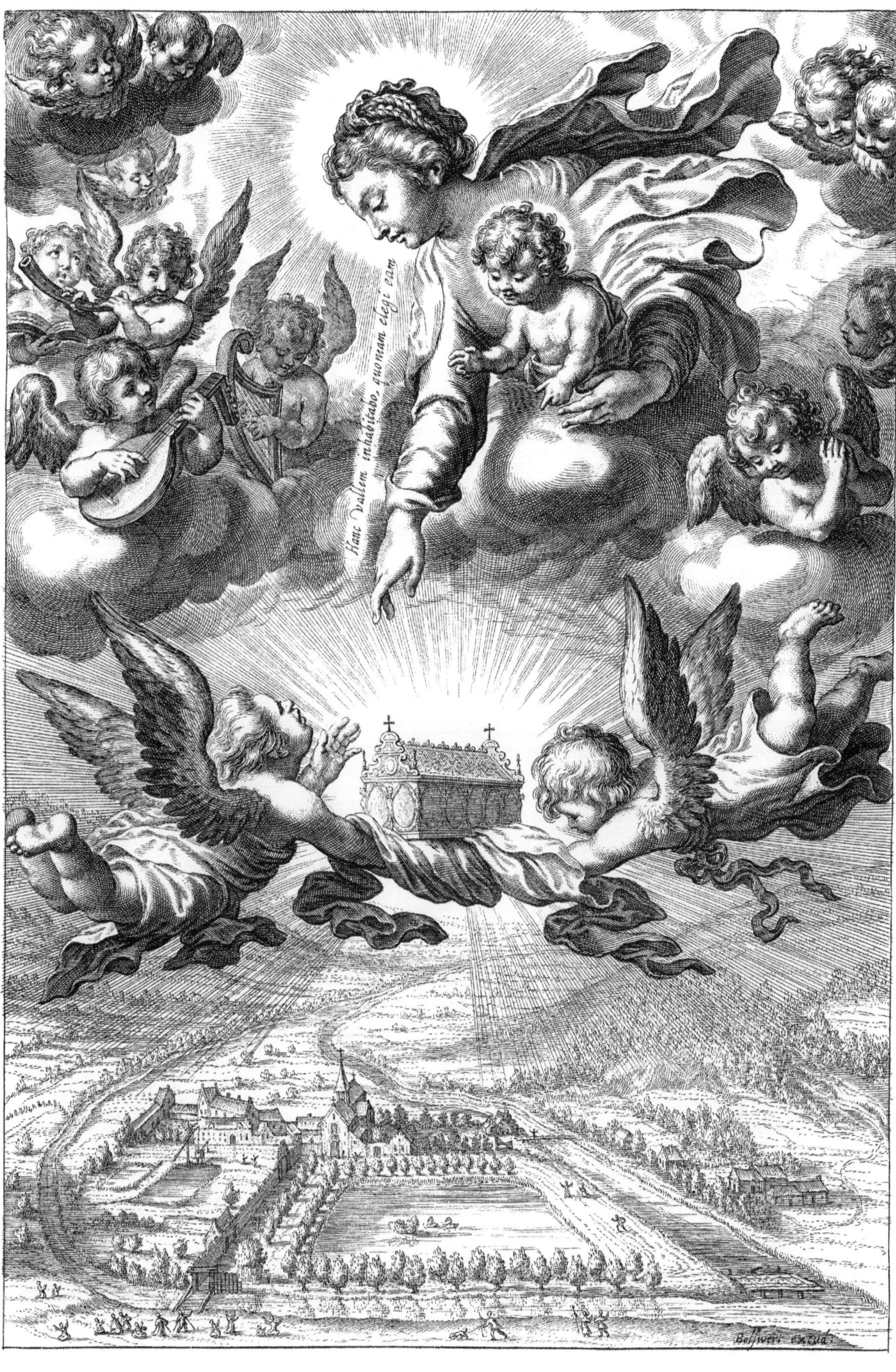
Hanc volui in habitatio, quoniam elegi eam
Bolswert excud.

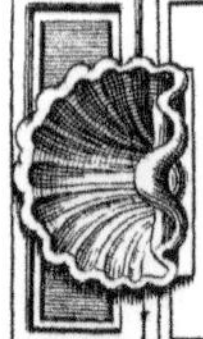

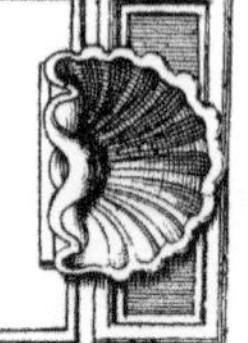

Petrus Berettinus Corton. delin.
G. Castellus incid.

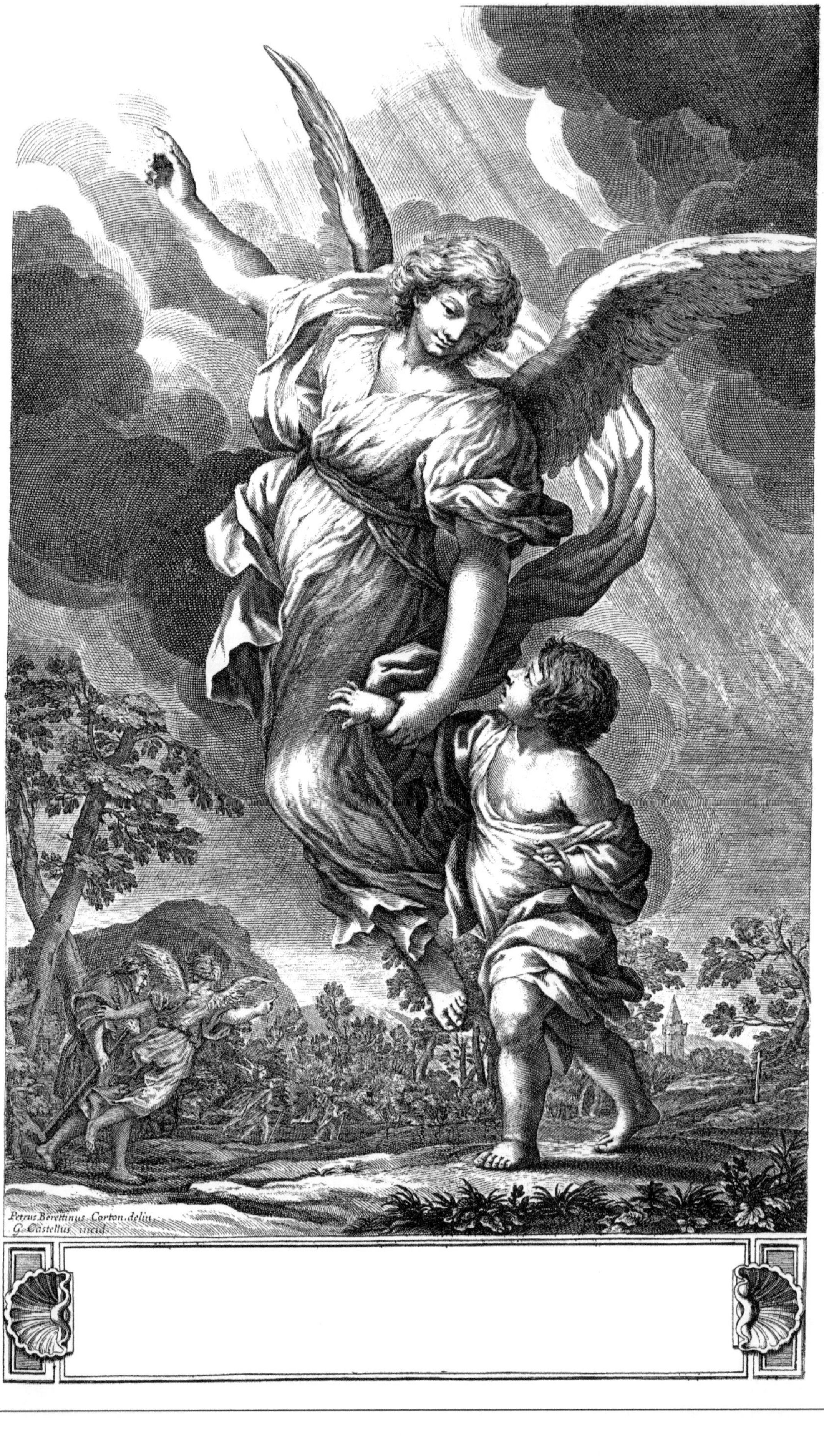

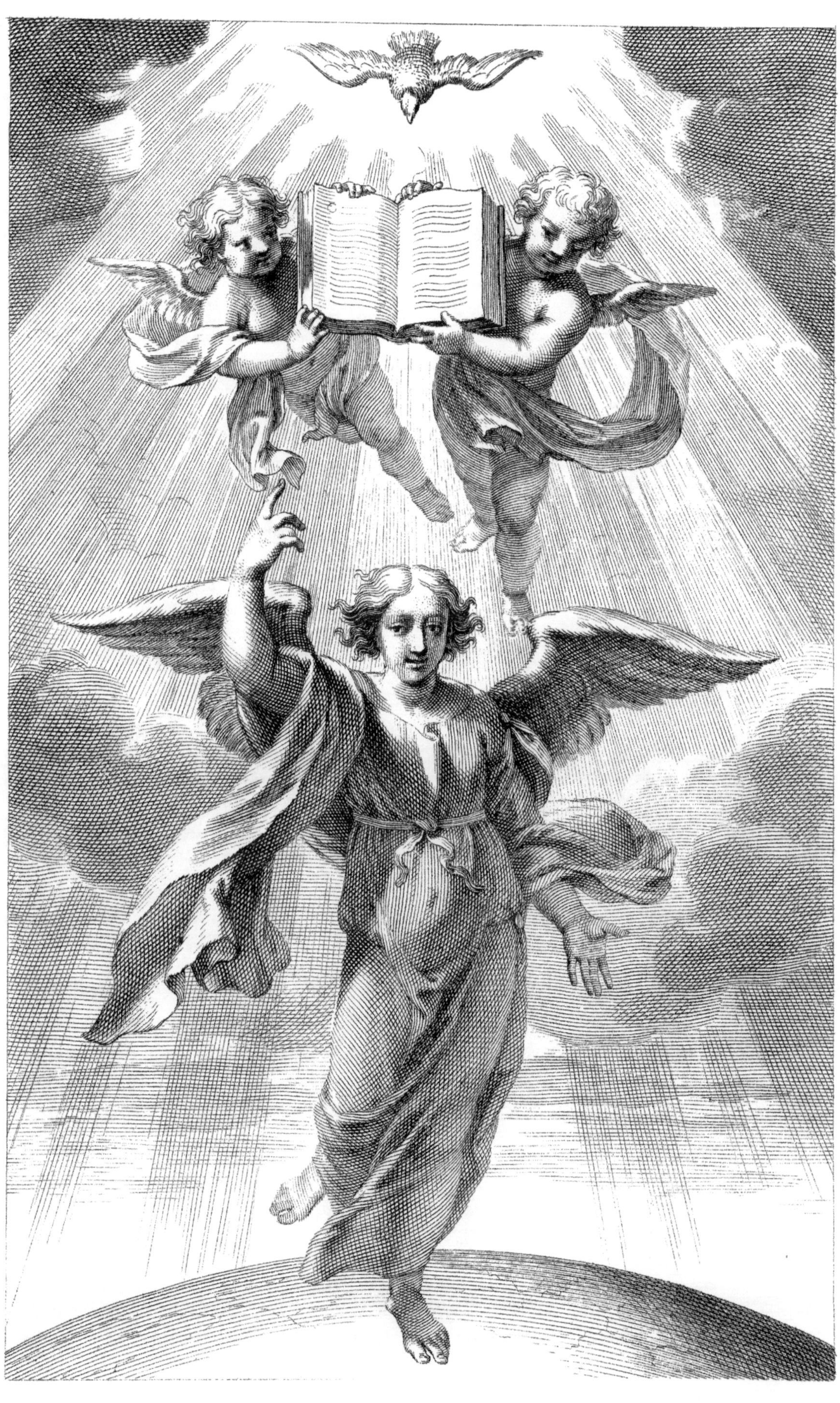

50

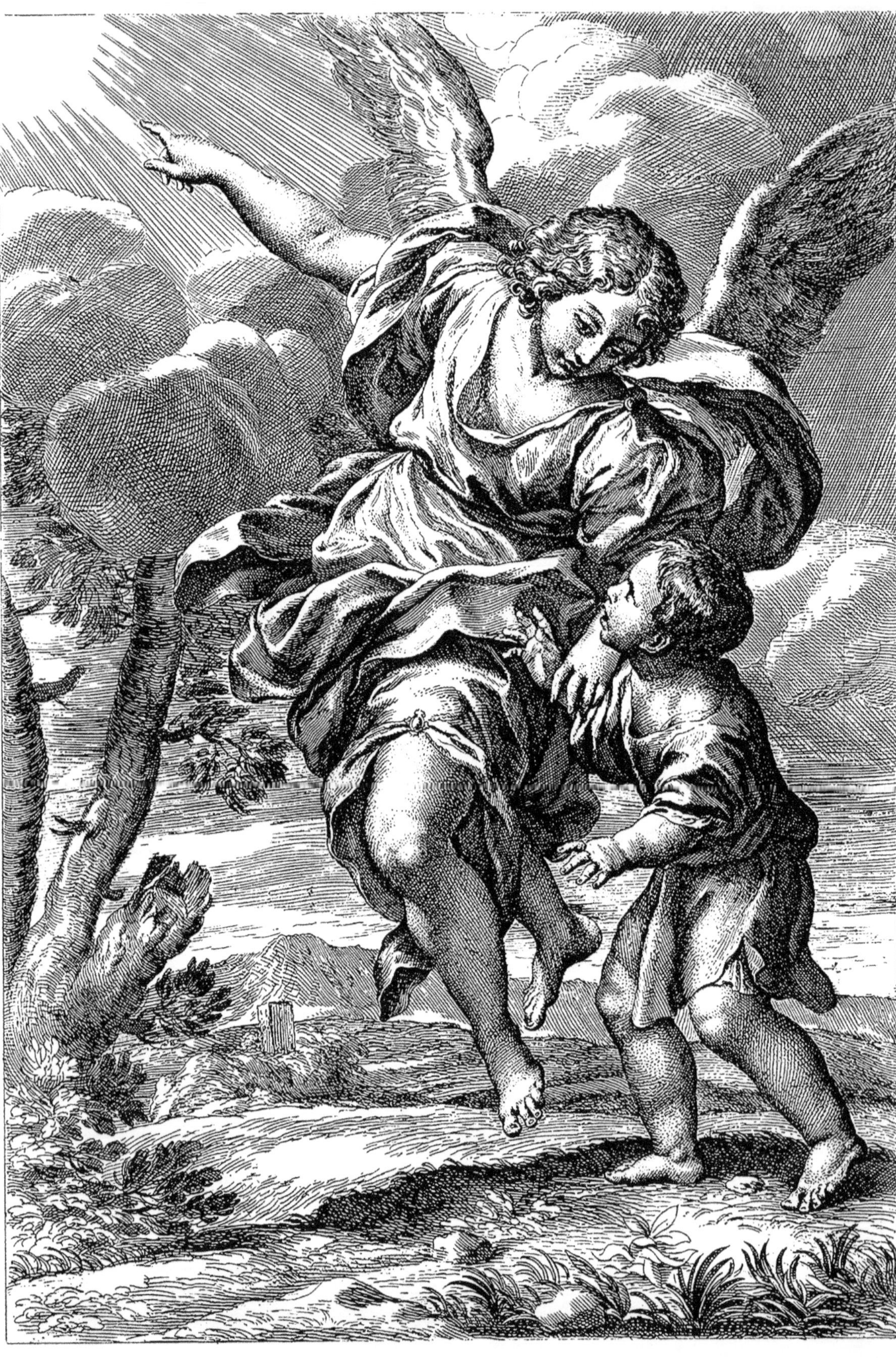

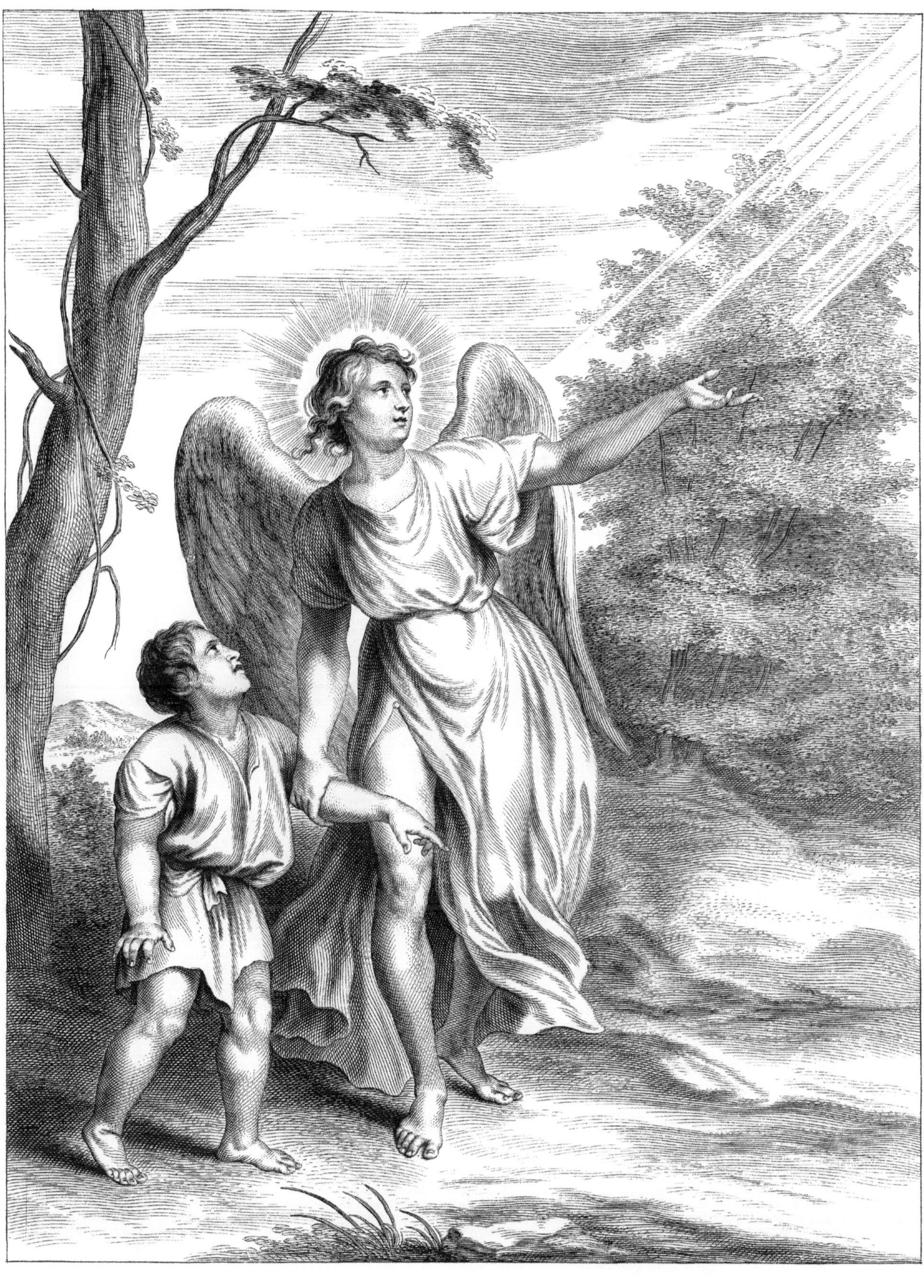

52

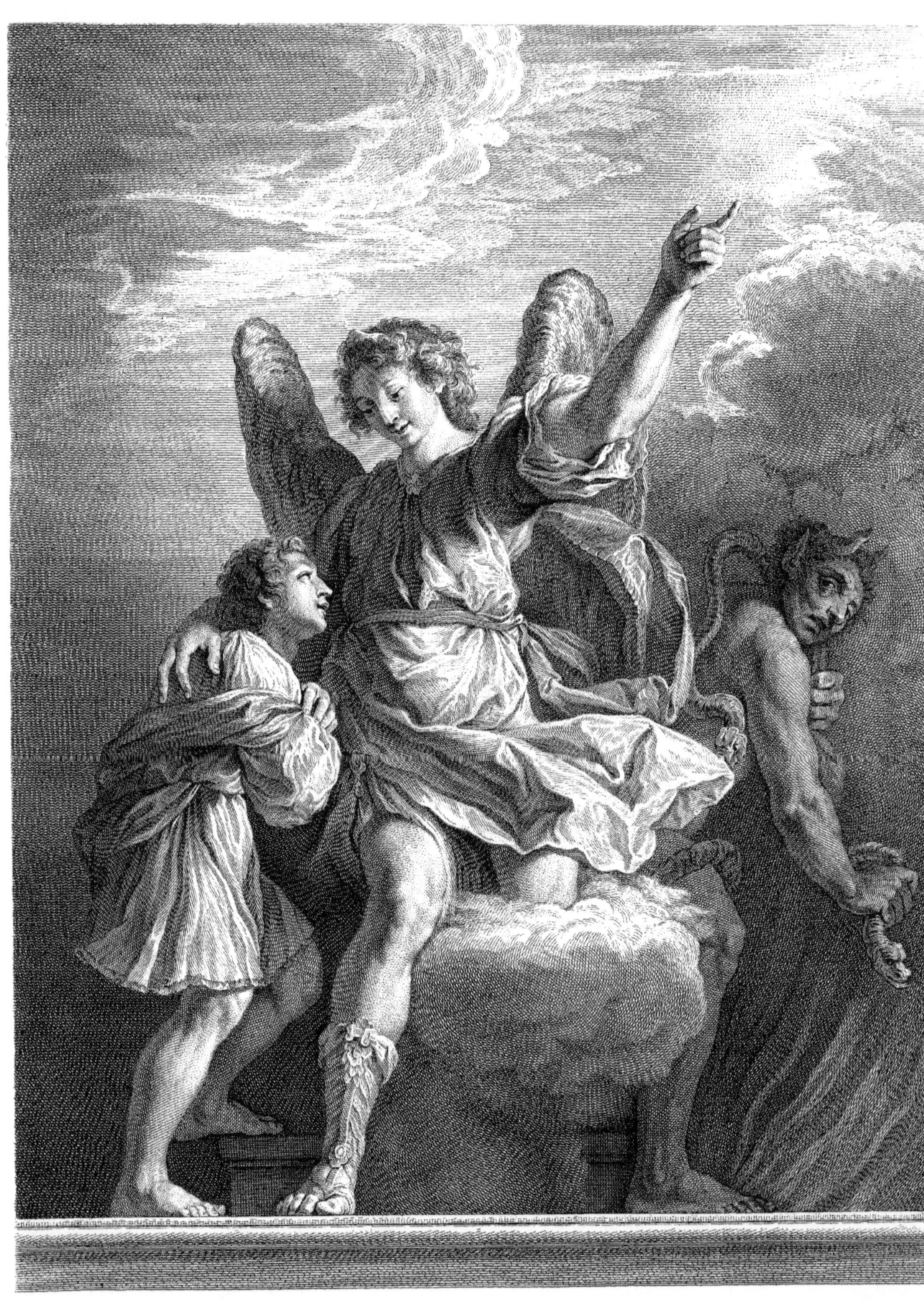

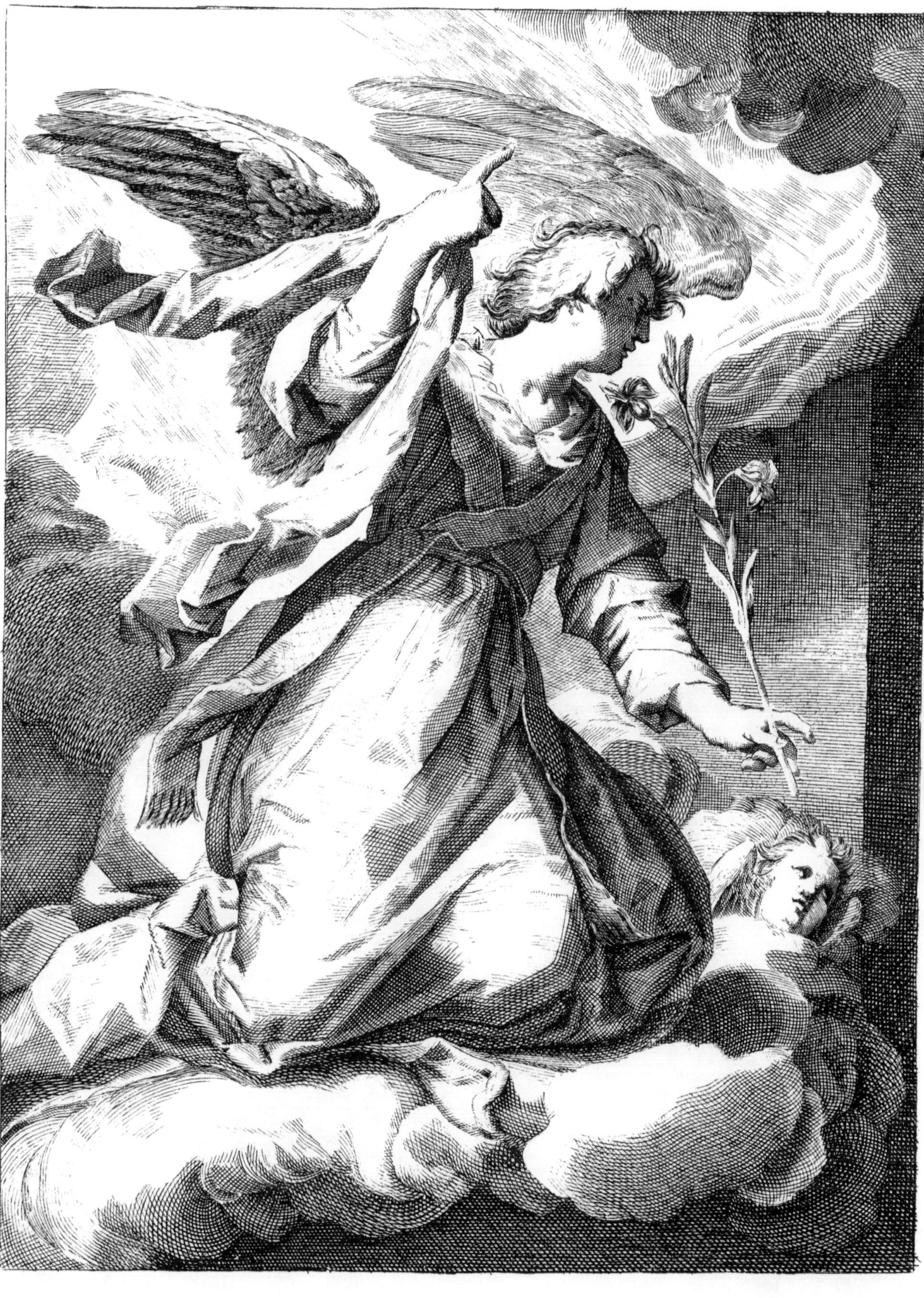

54

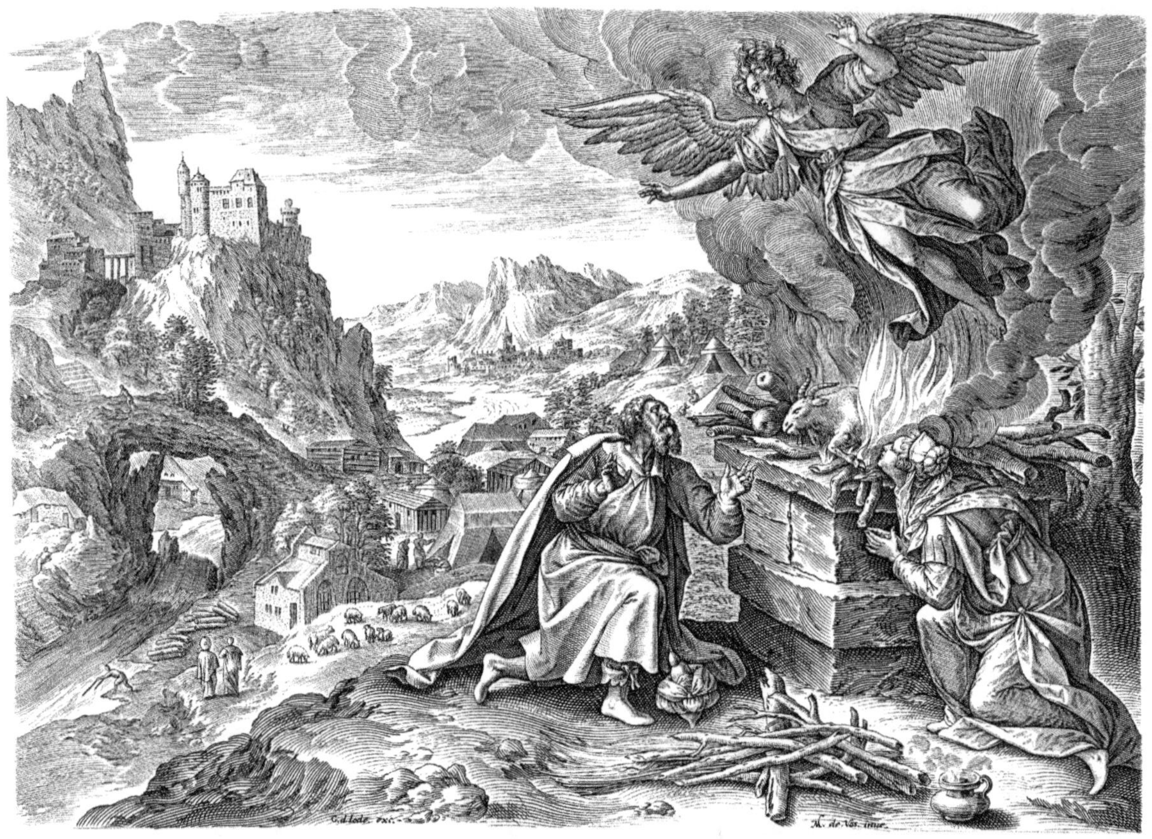

55

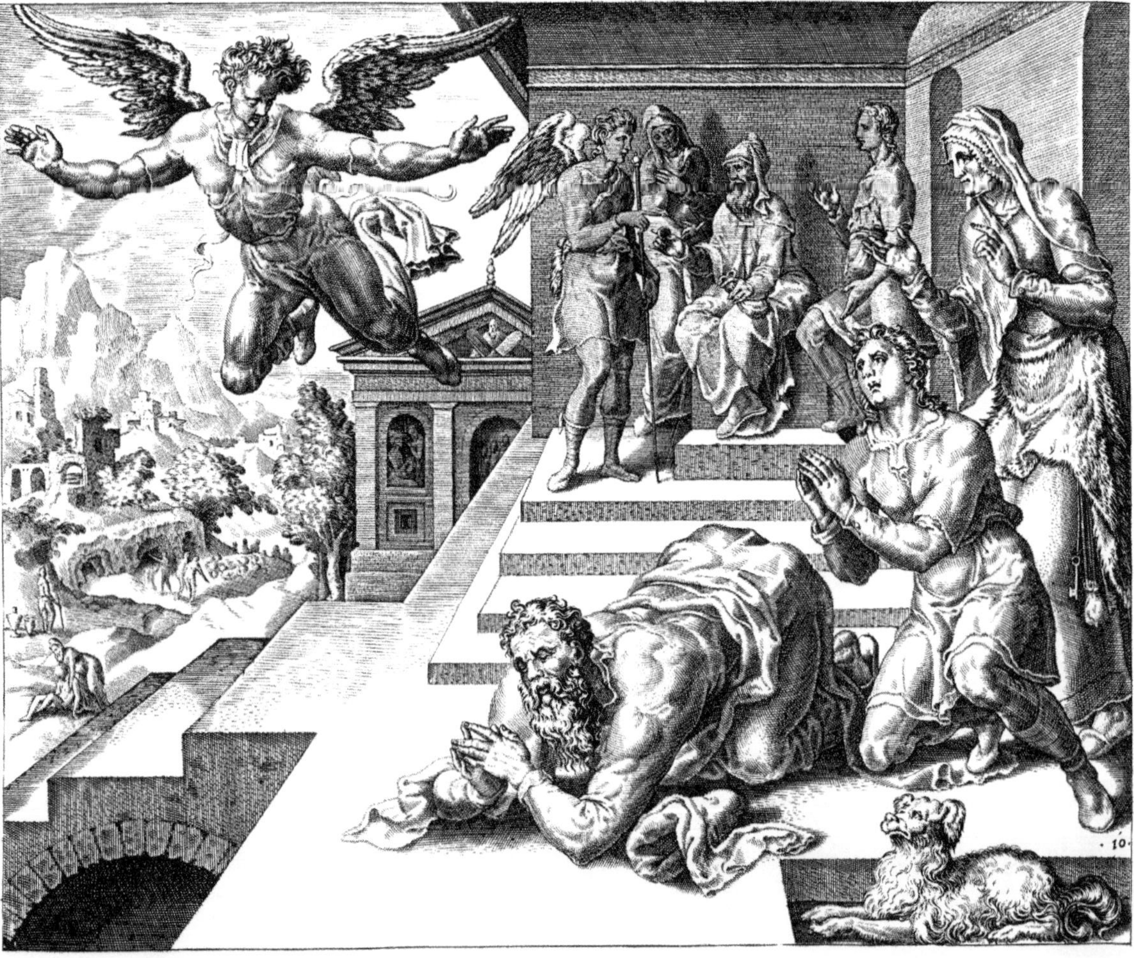

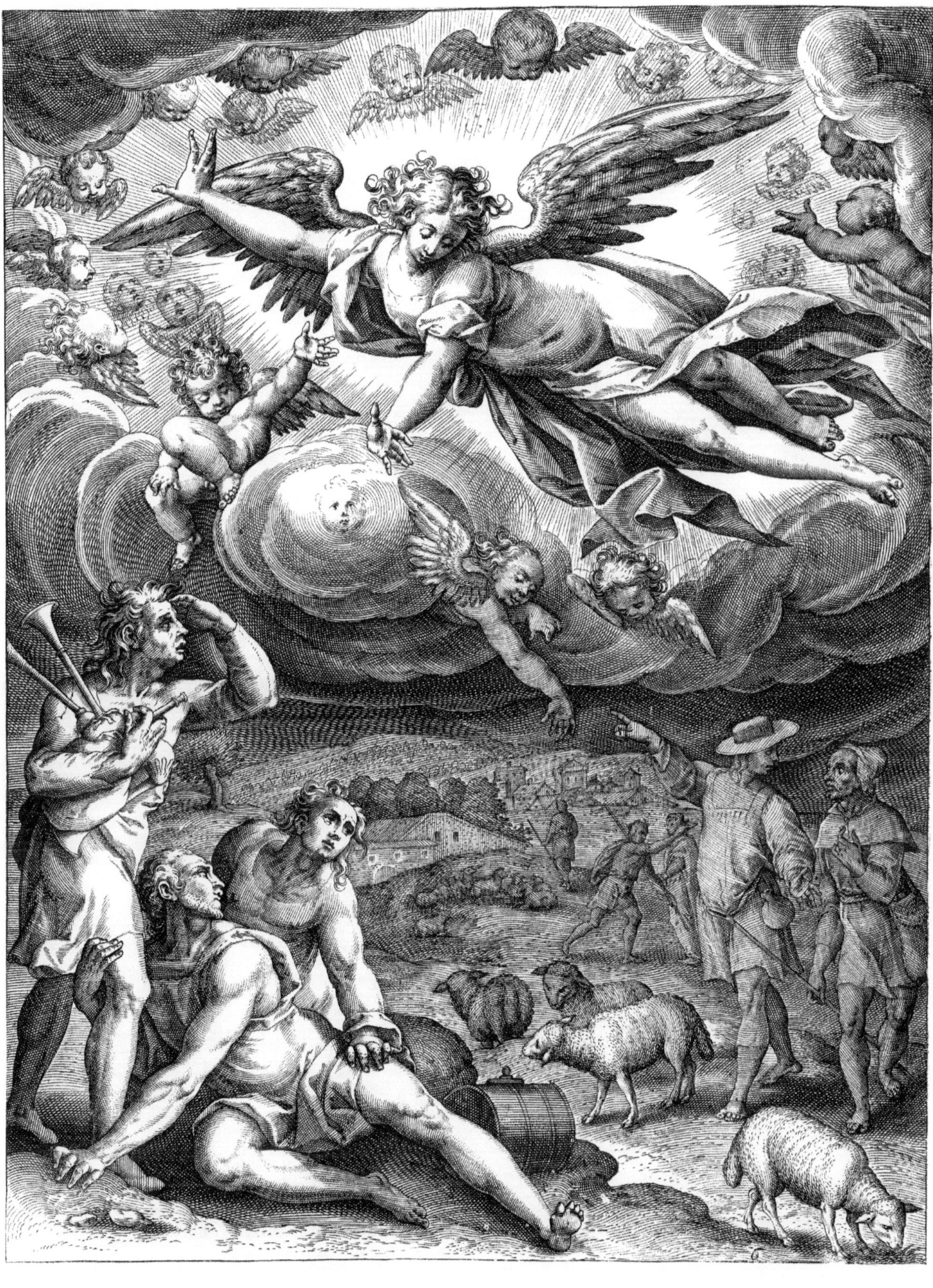

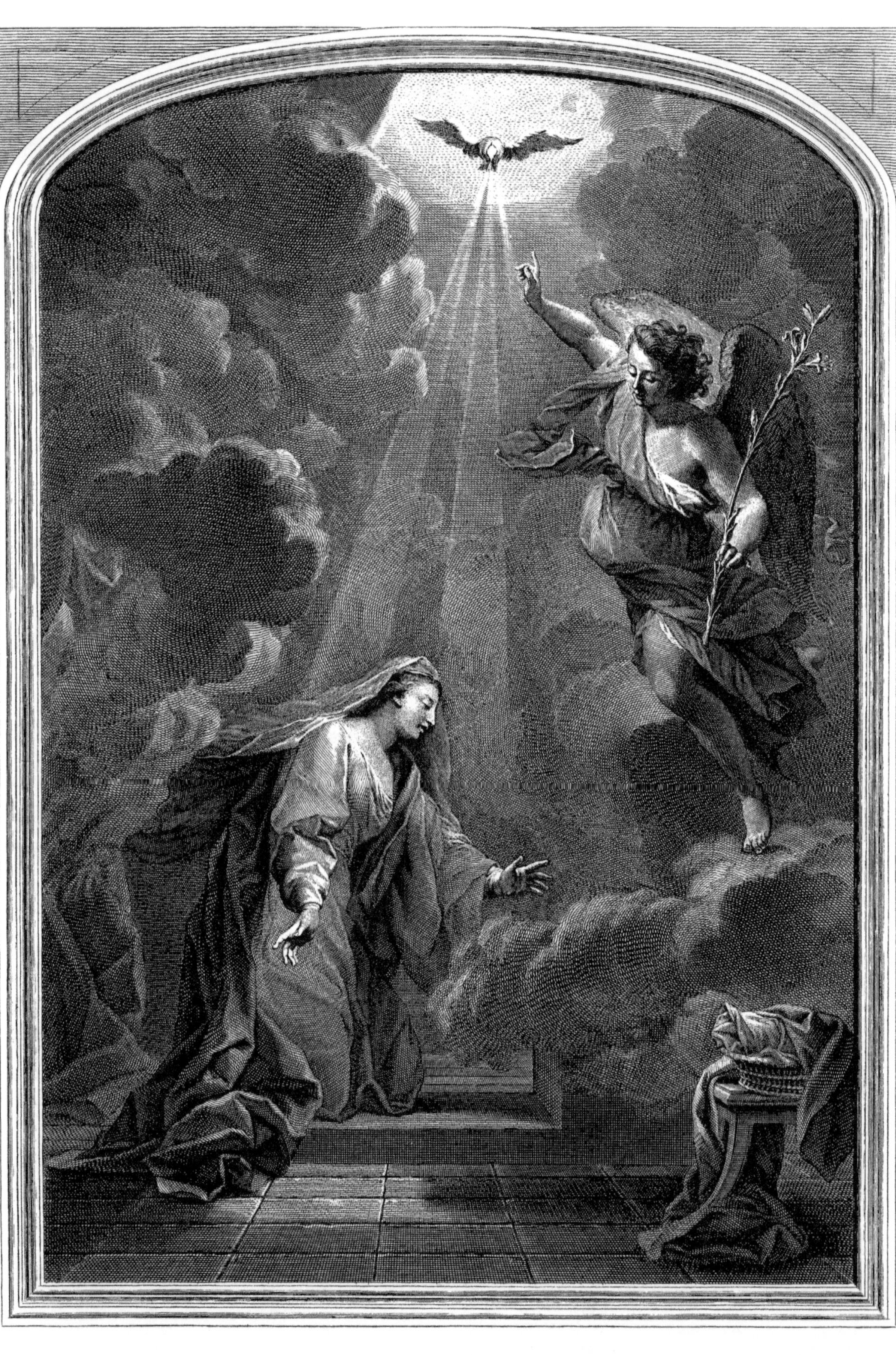

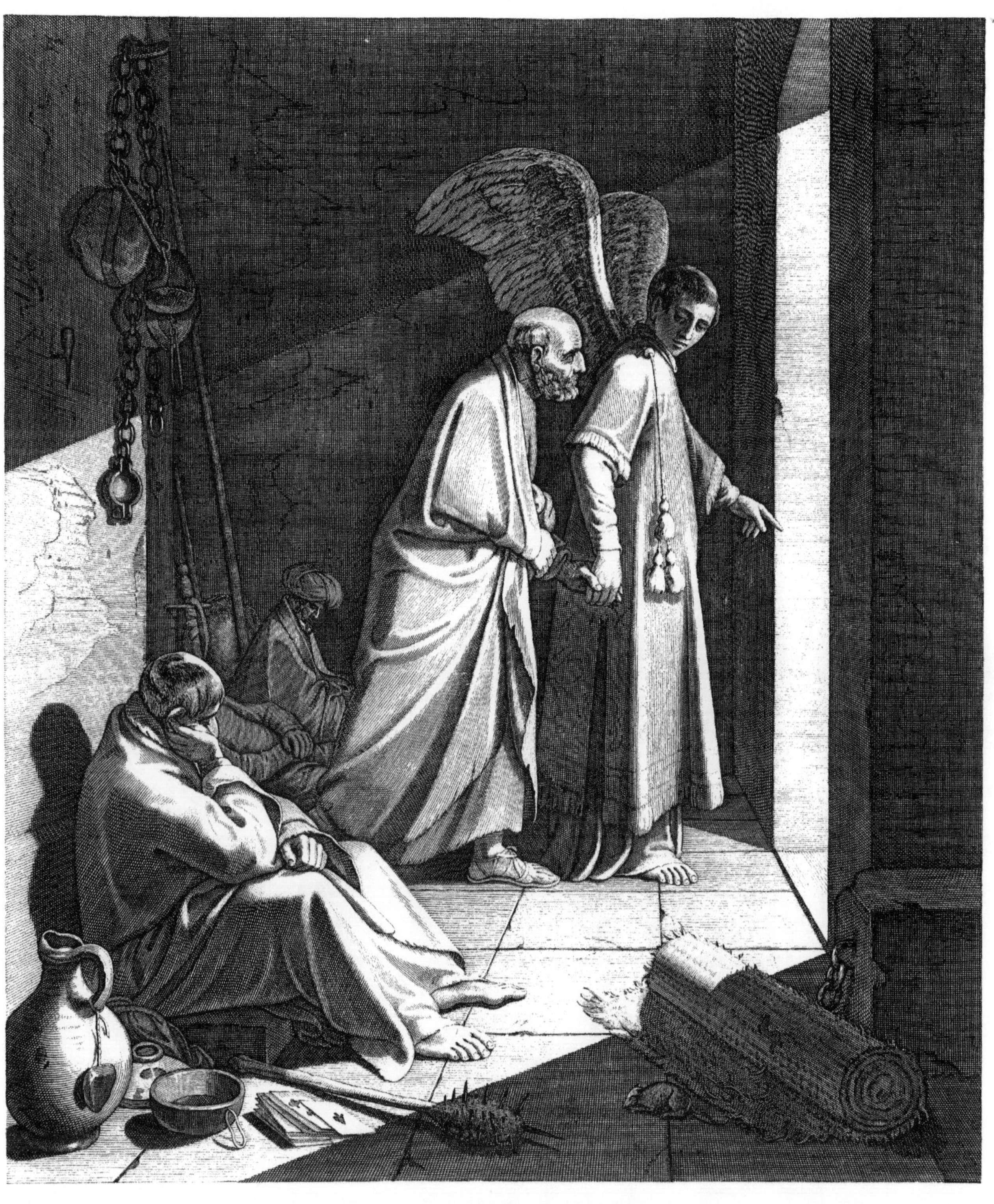

59

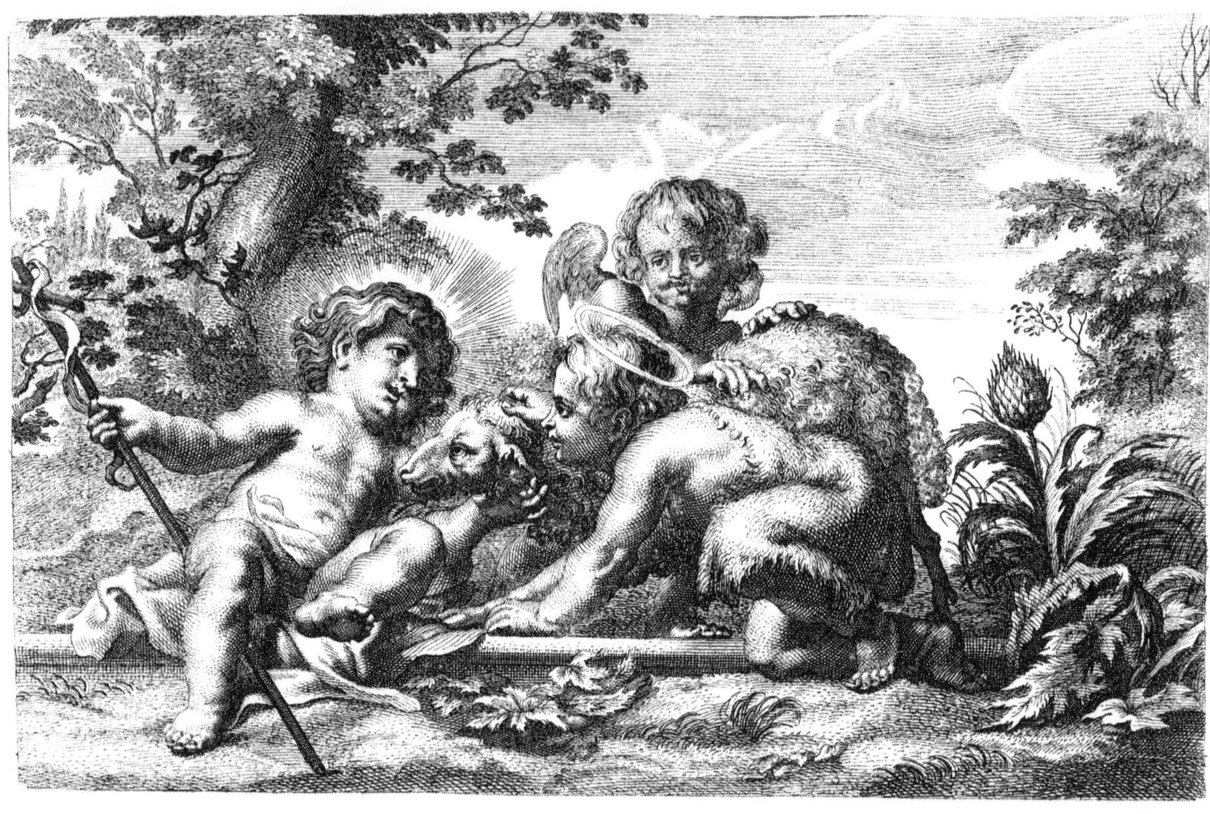

60

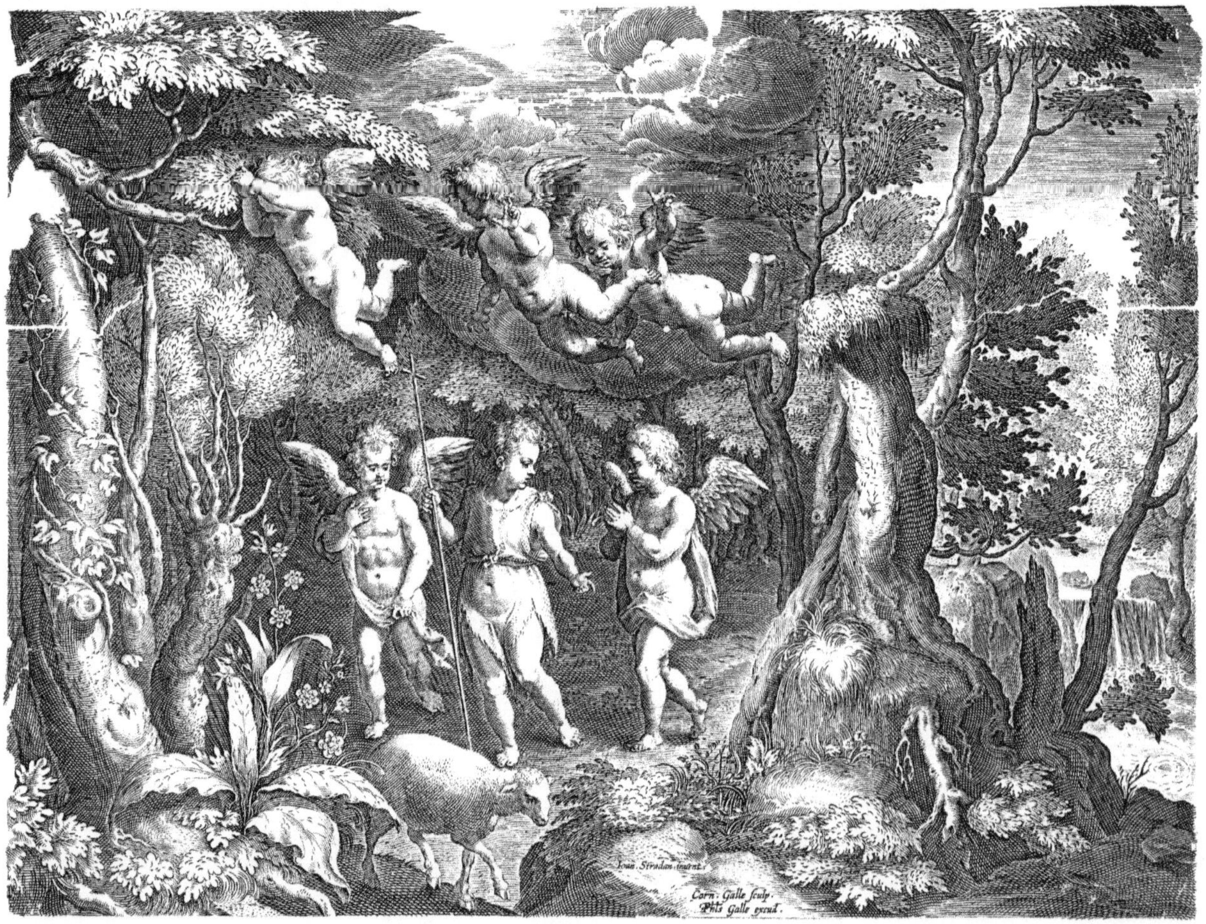

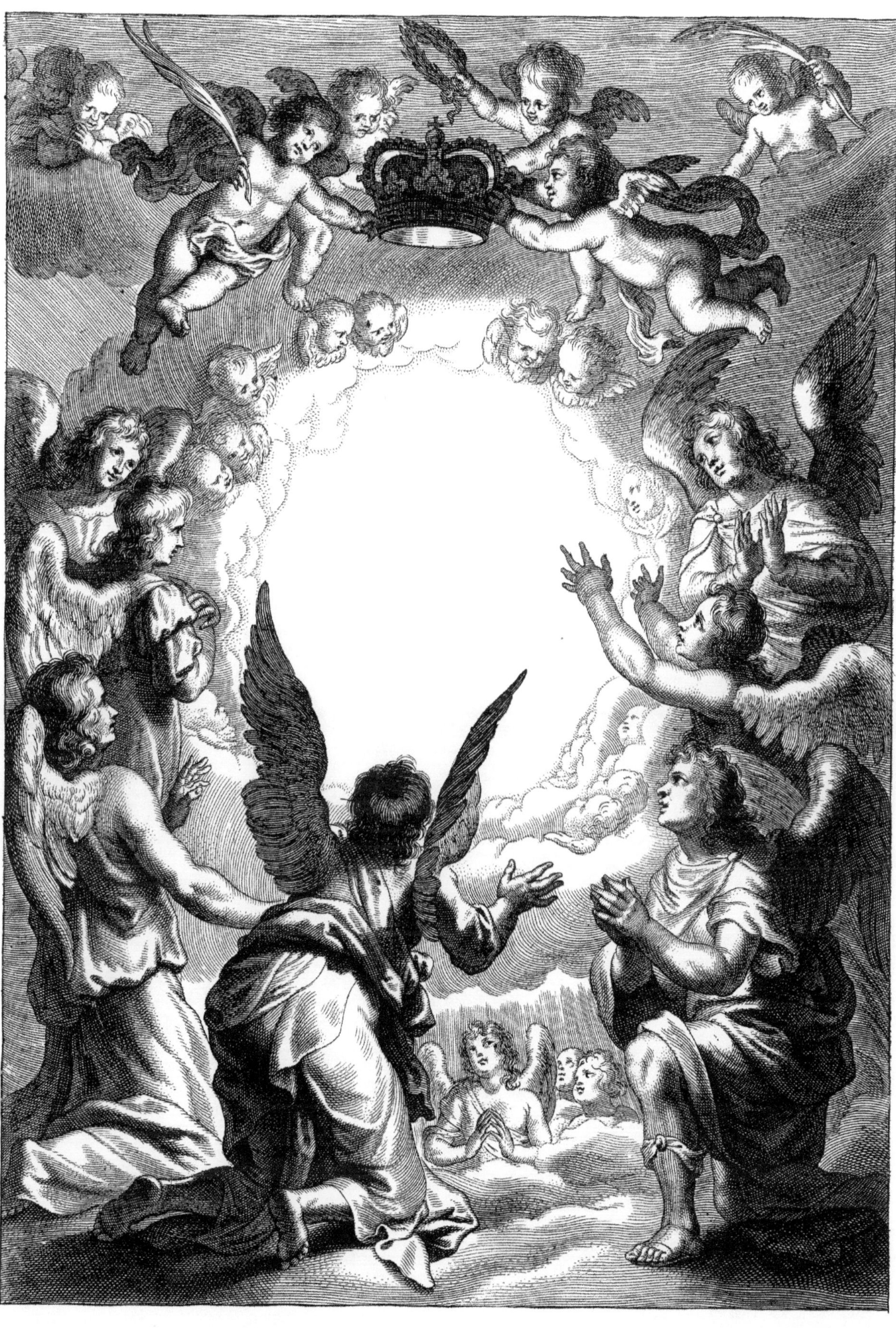

62

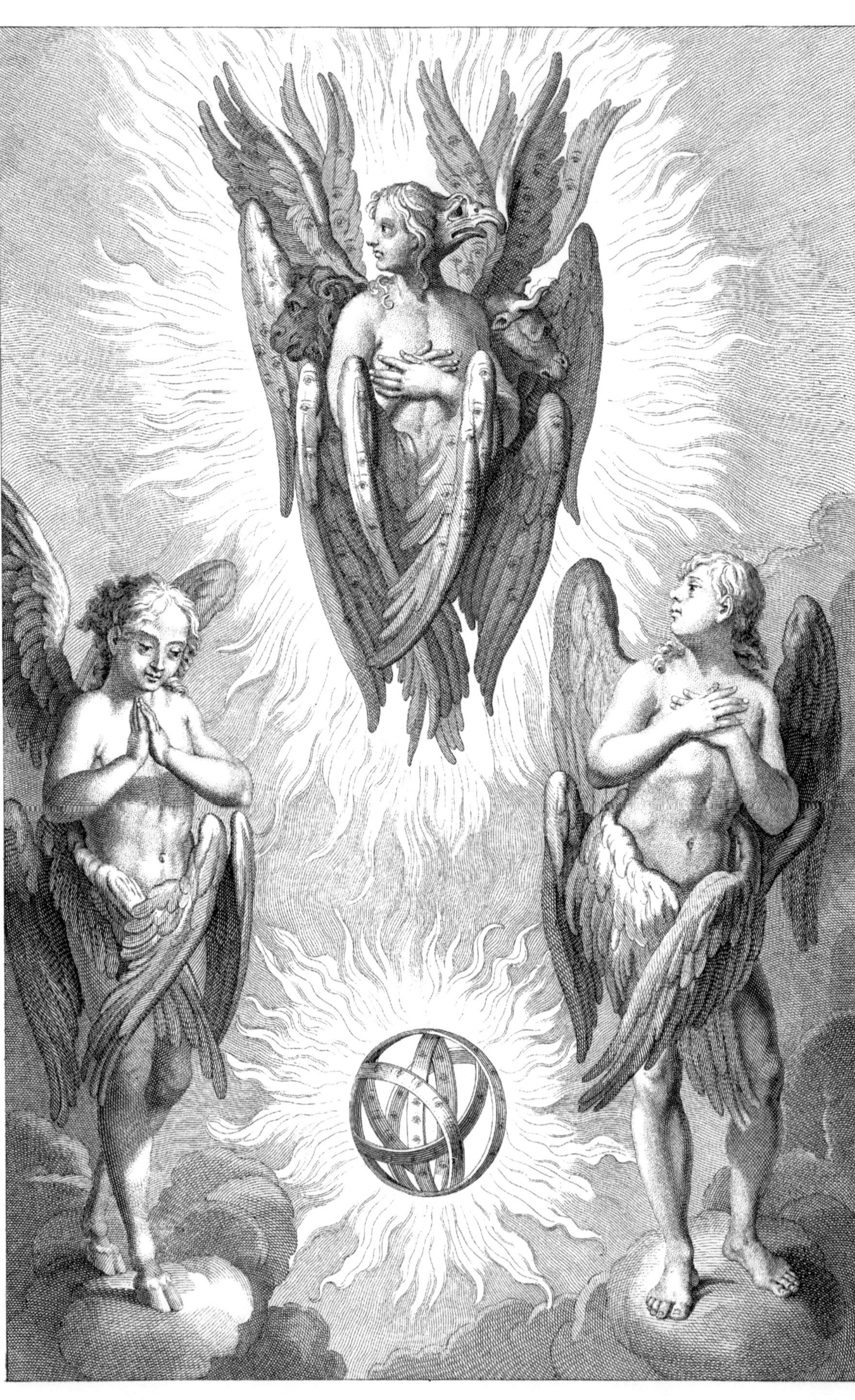

63

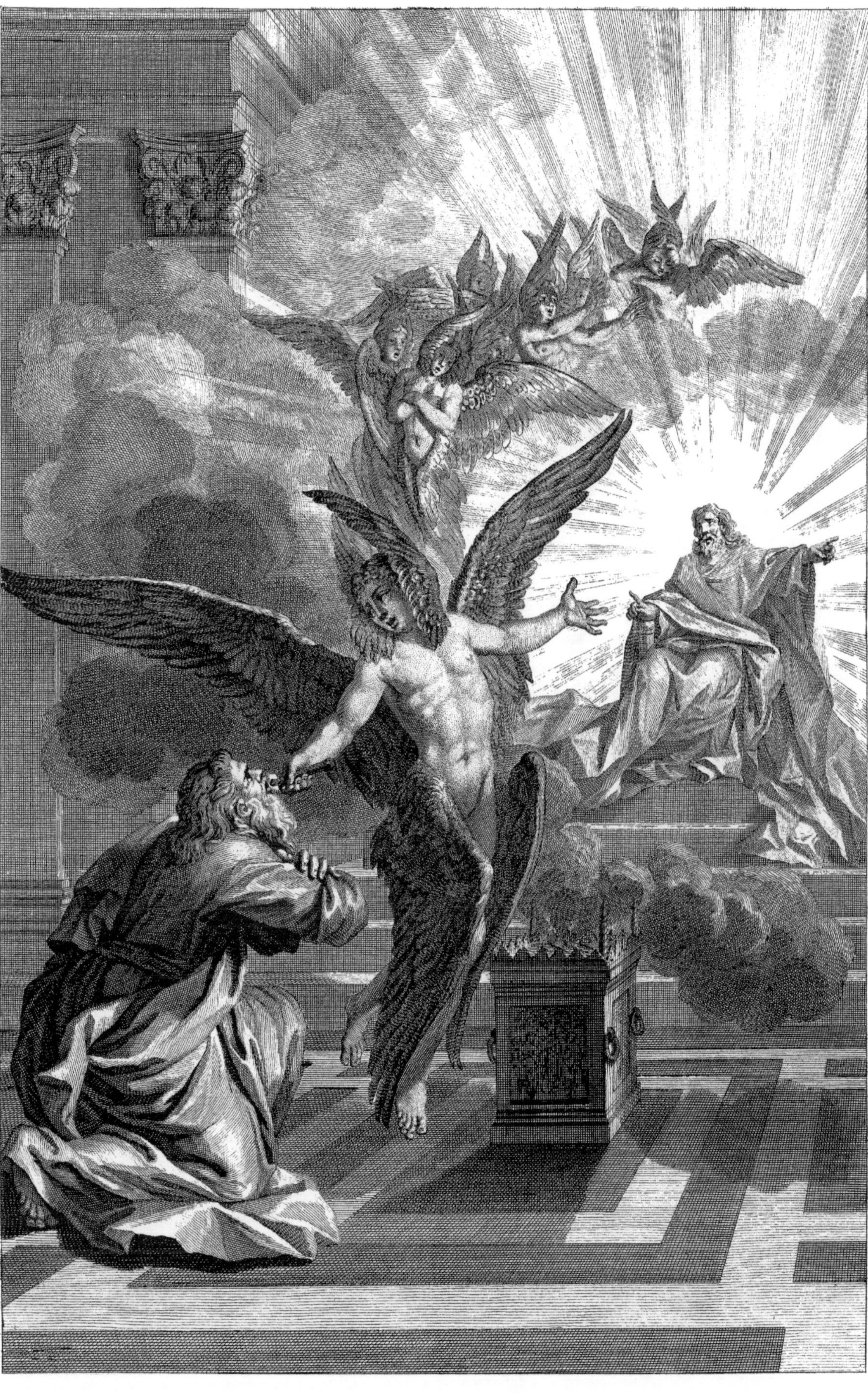

64

LA LOY.
I V
II VI
VII
III VIII
IV IX
X
LA
SAINTE
BIBLE
LE
SAINT
EVANGILE.
N Berchem. Invent.
Mathan Sculp.

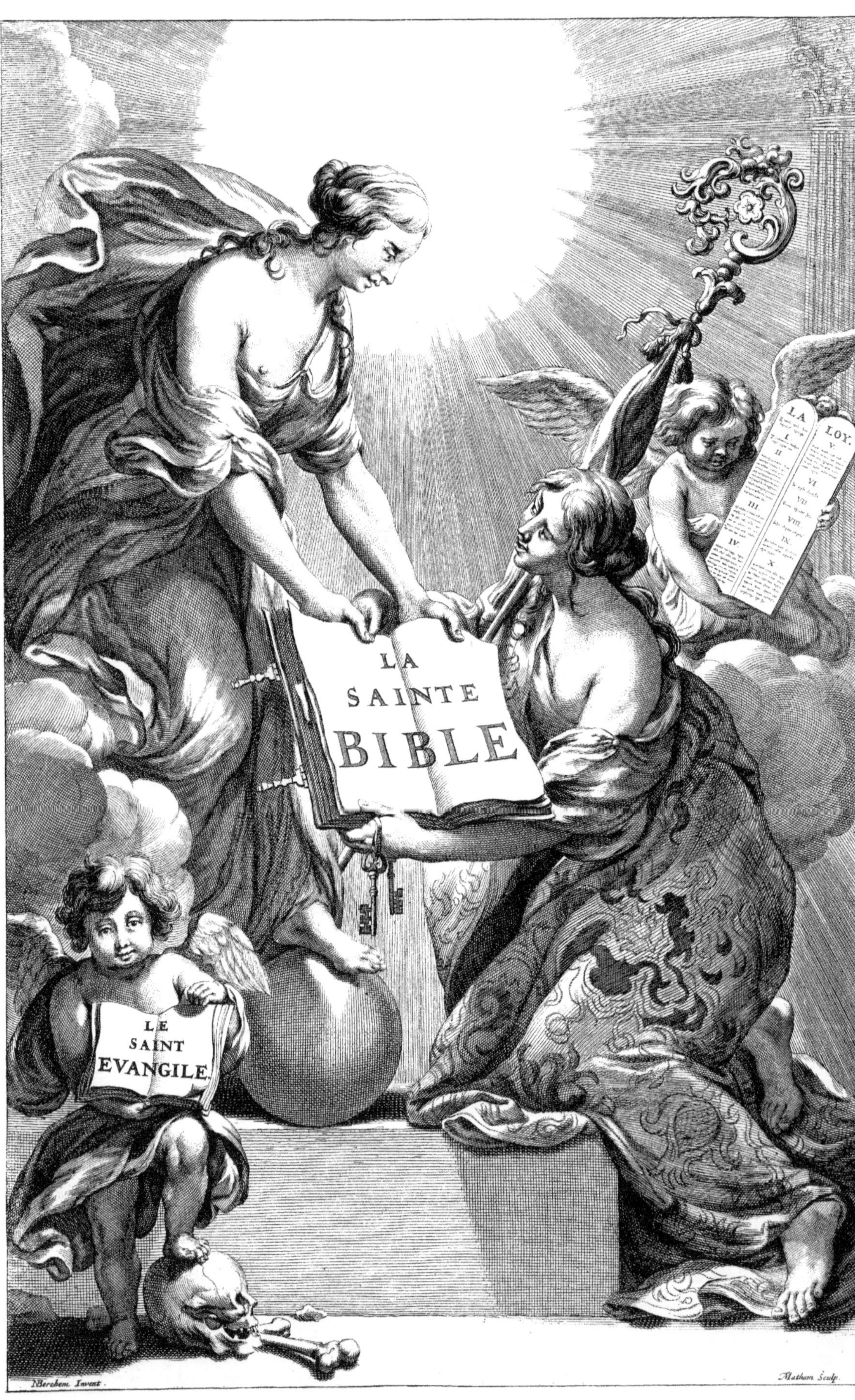

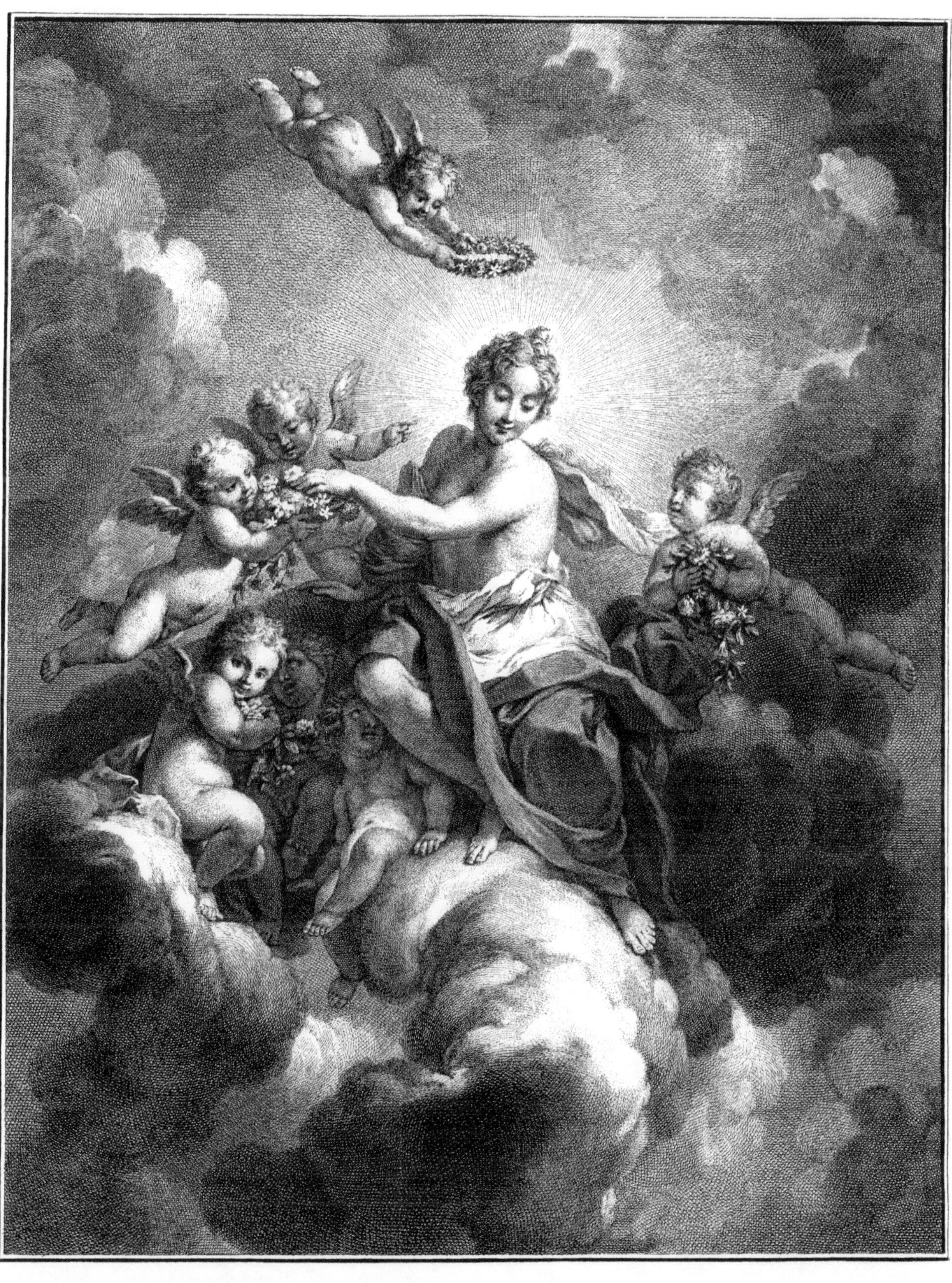

66

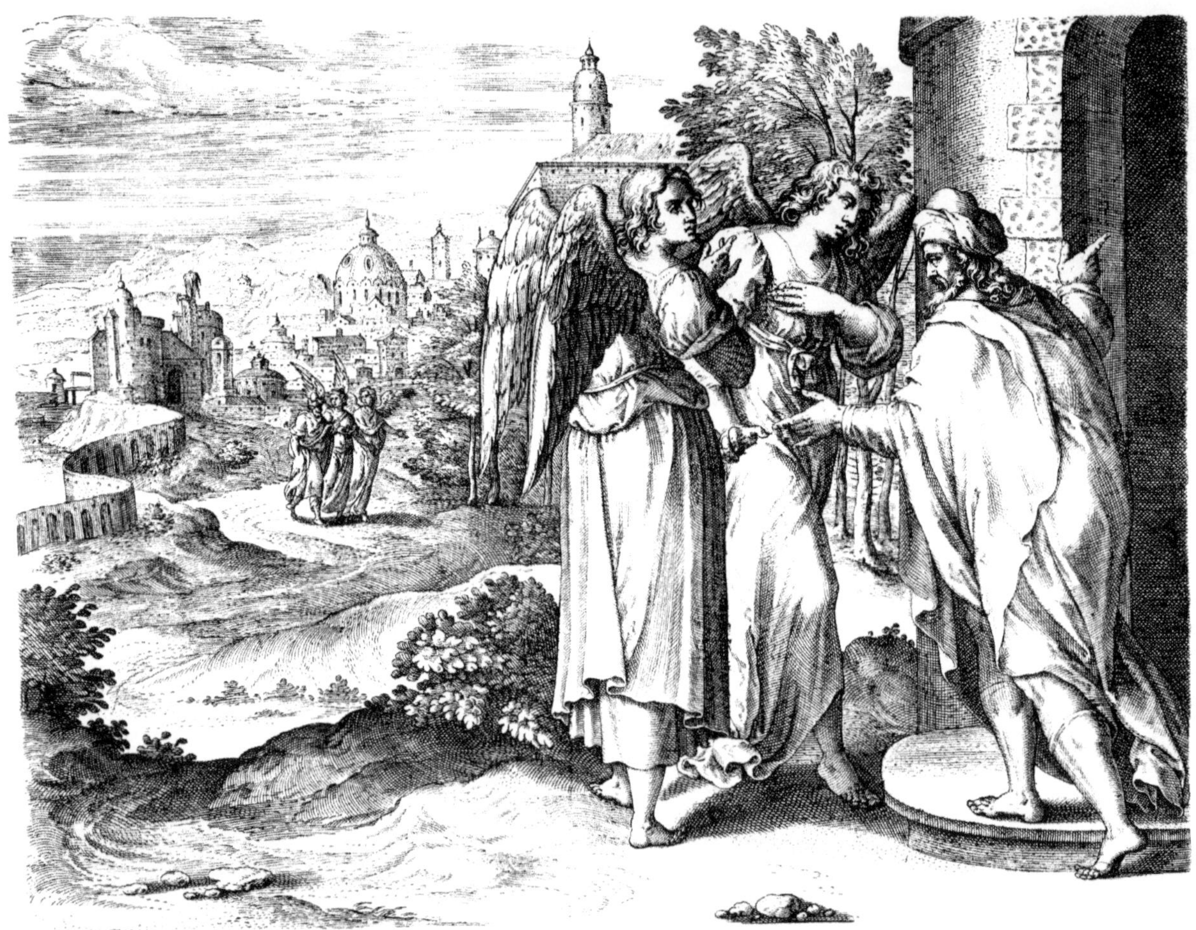

67

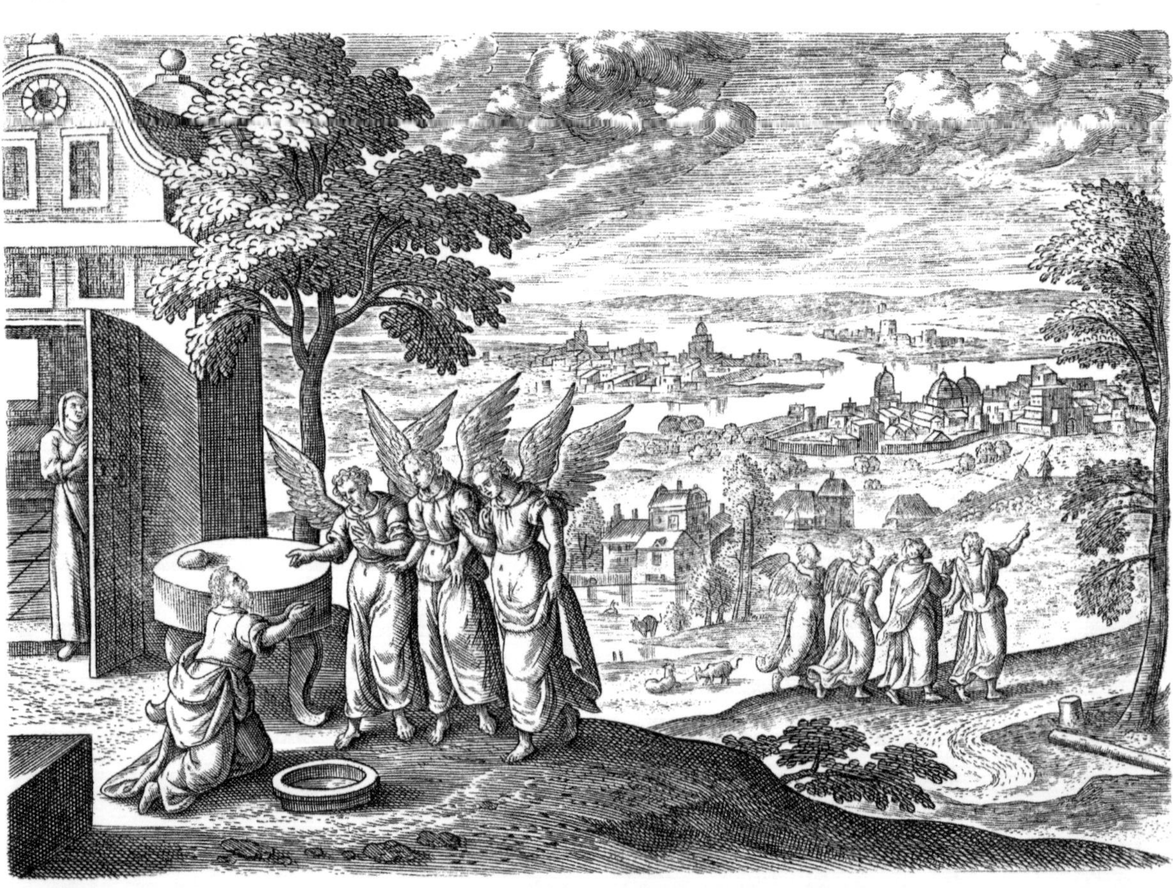

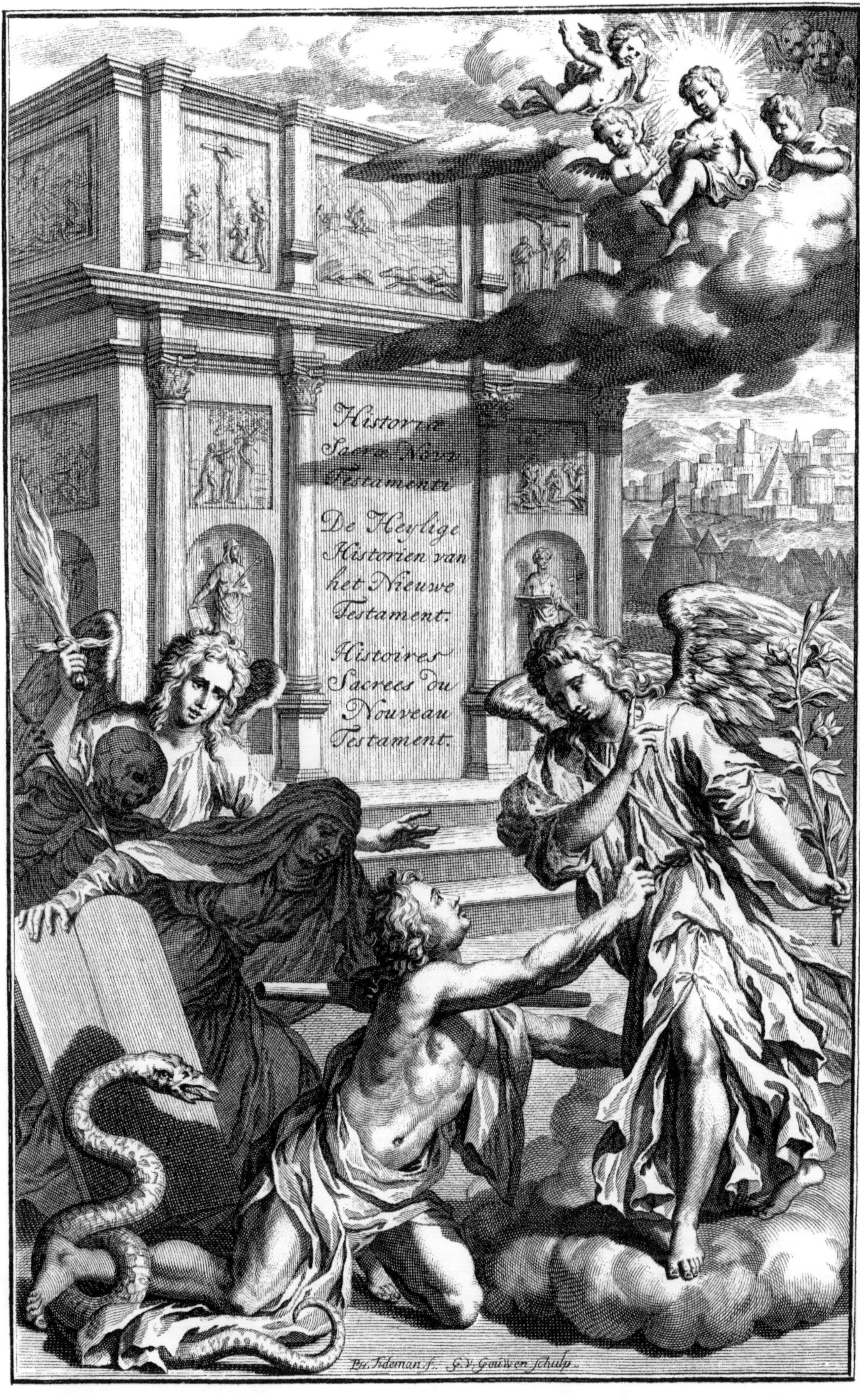
Historiæ
Sacræ Novi
Testamenti

De Heylige
Historien van
het Nieuwe
Testament.

Histoires
Sacrees du
Nouveau
Testament.

Ph. Tideman f.   G. v. Gouwen sculp.

69

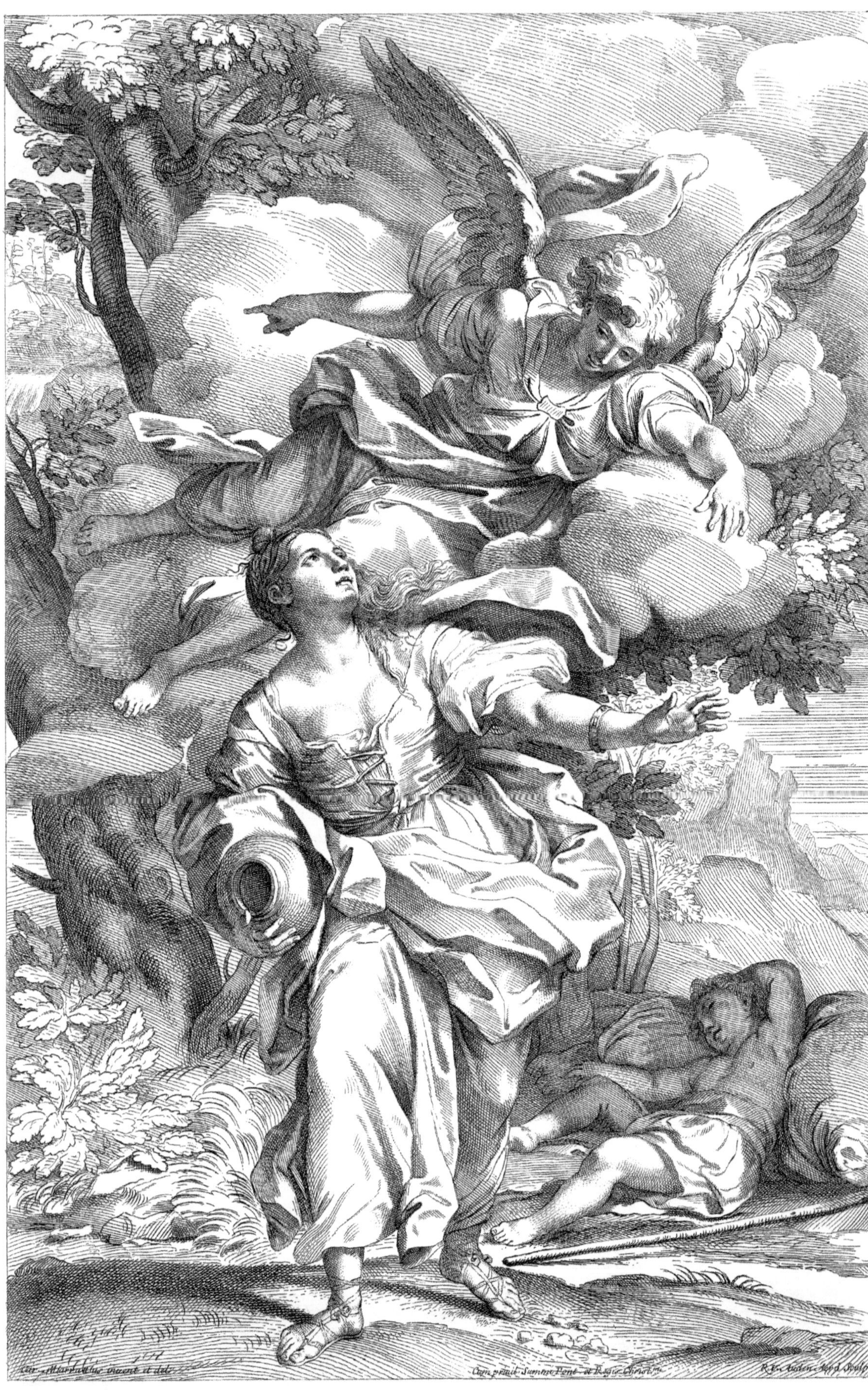

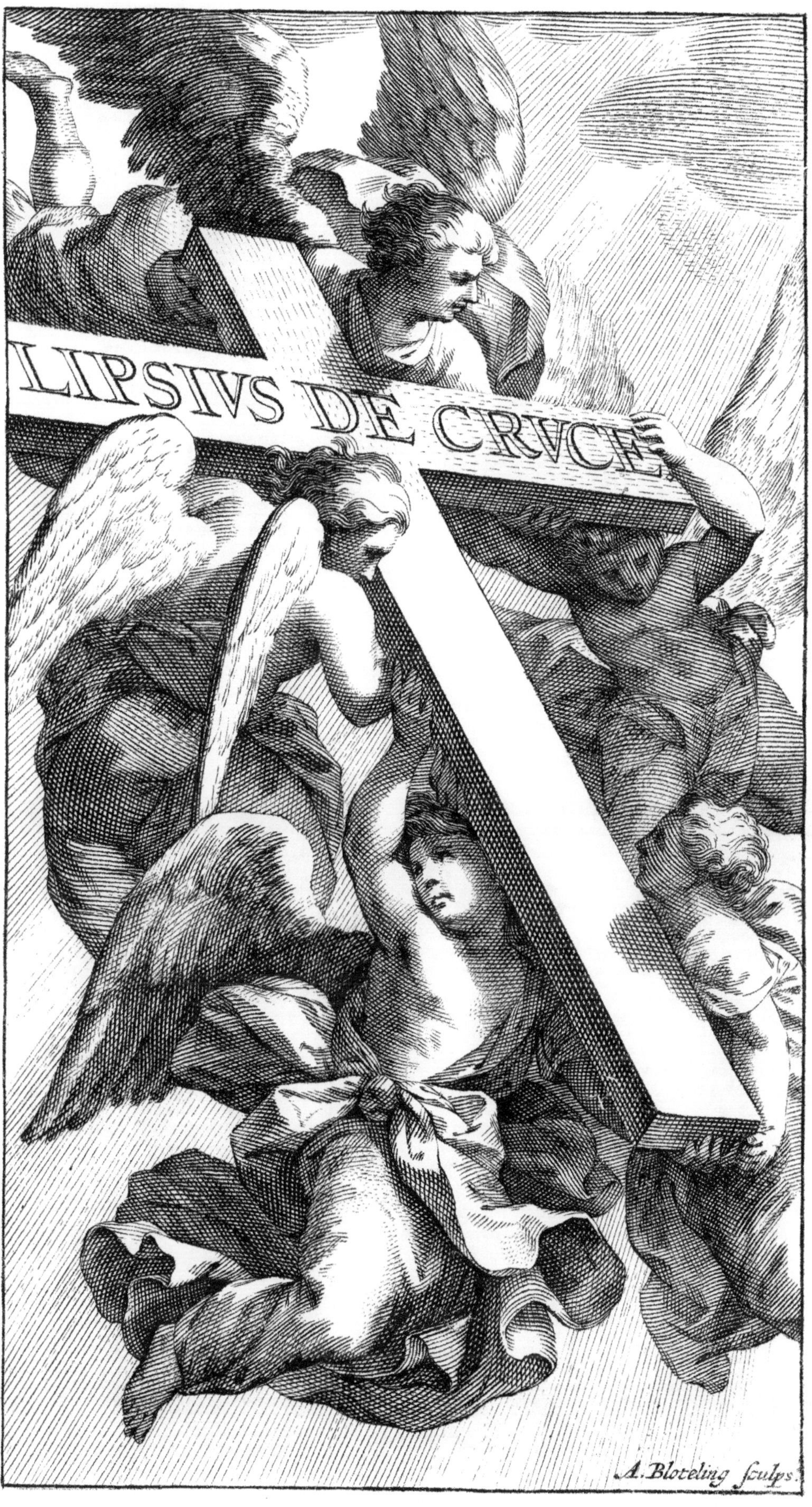
LIPSIVS DE CRVCE
A. Bloteling sculps.

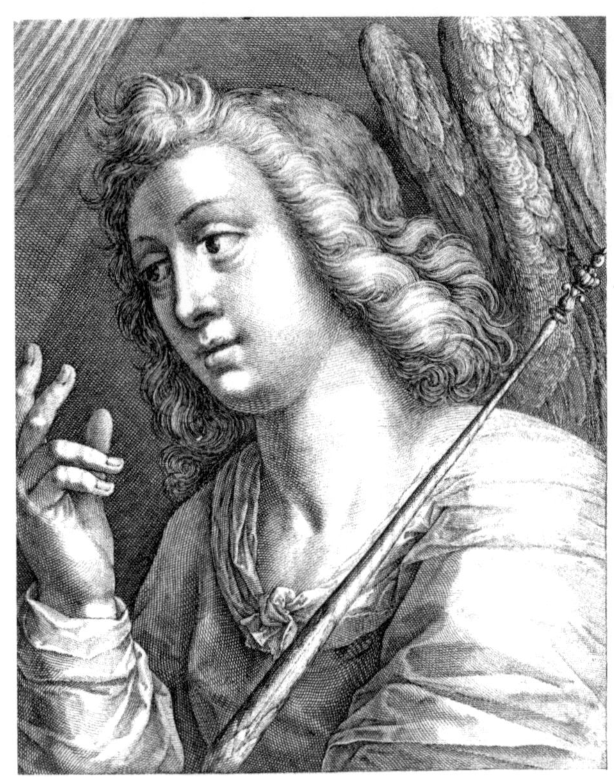

71

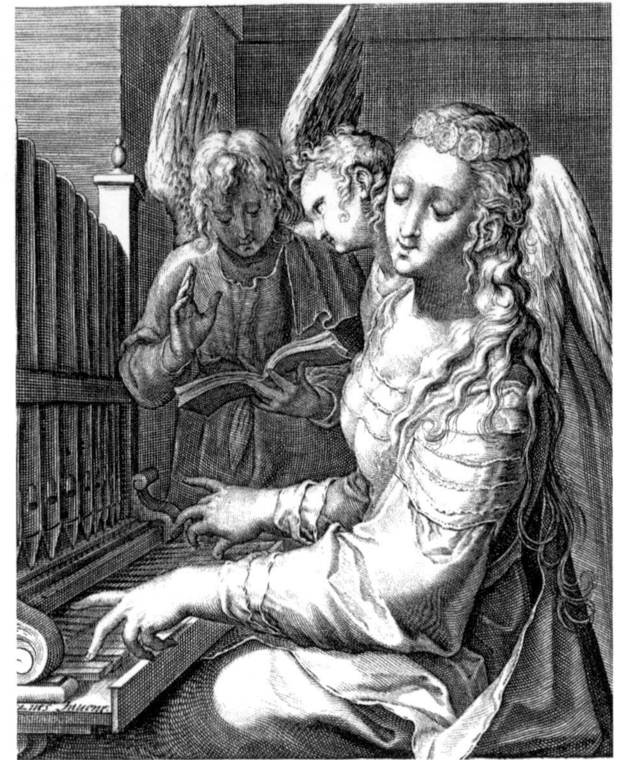

72

73

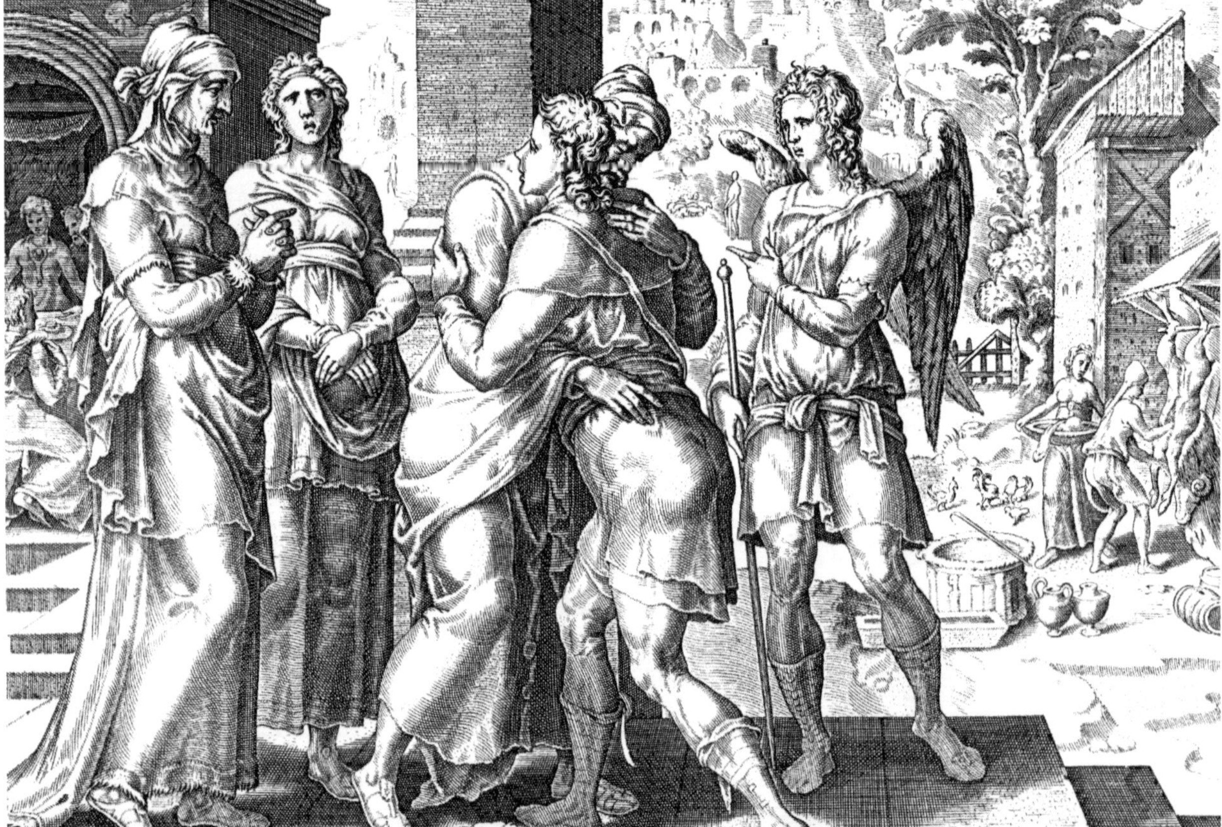

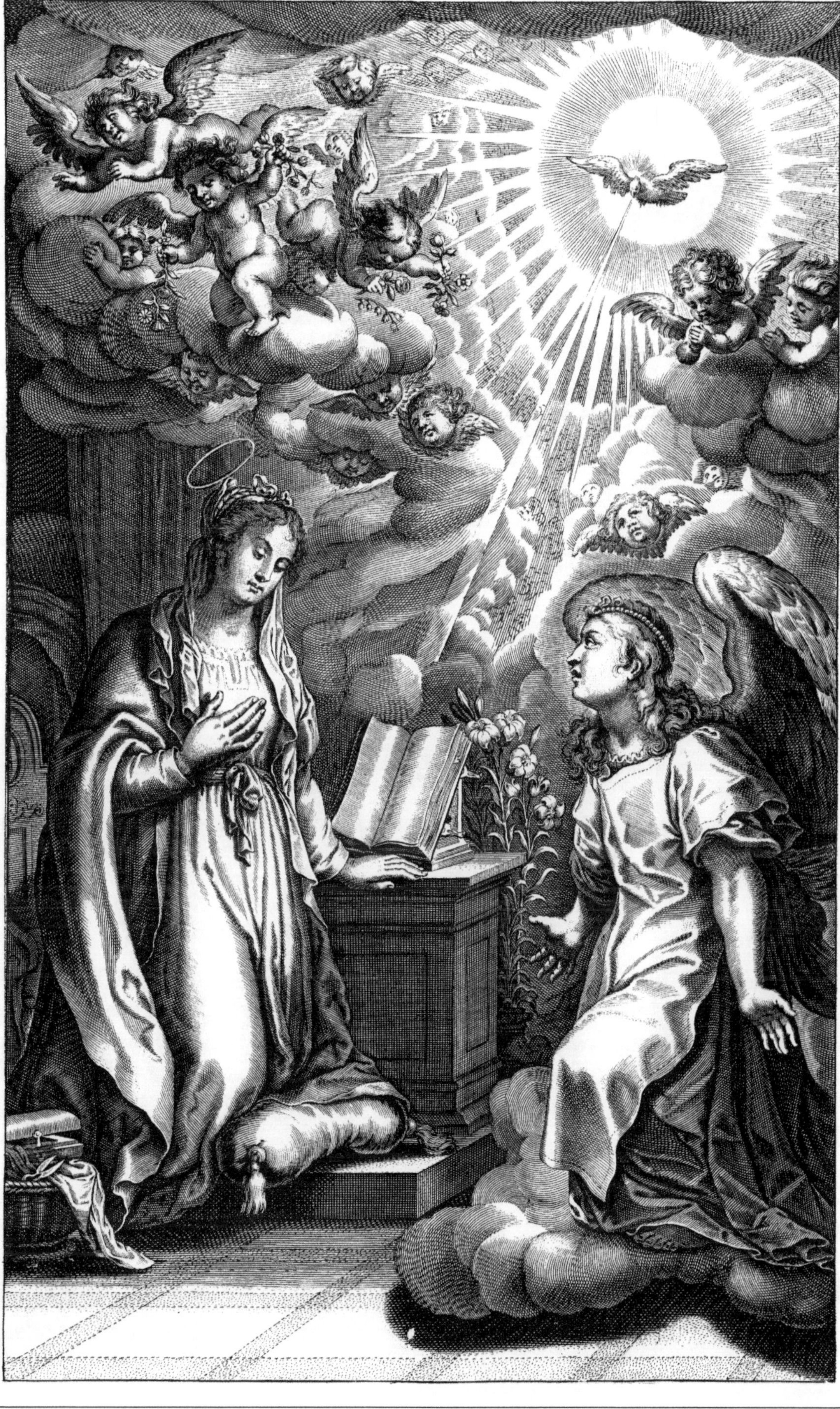

75

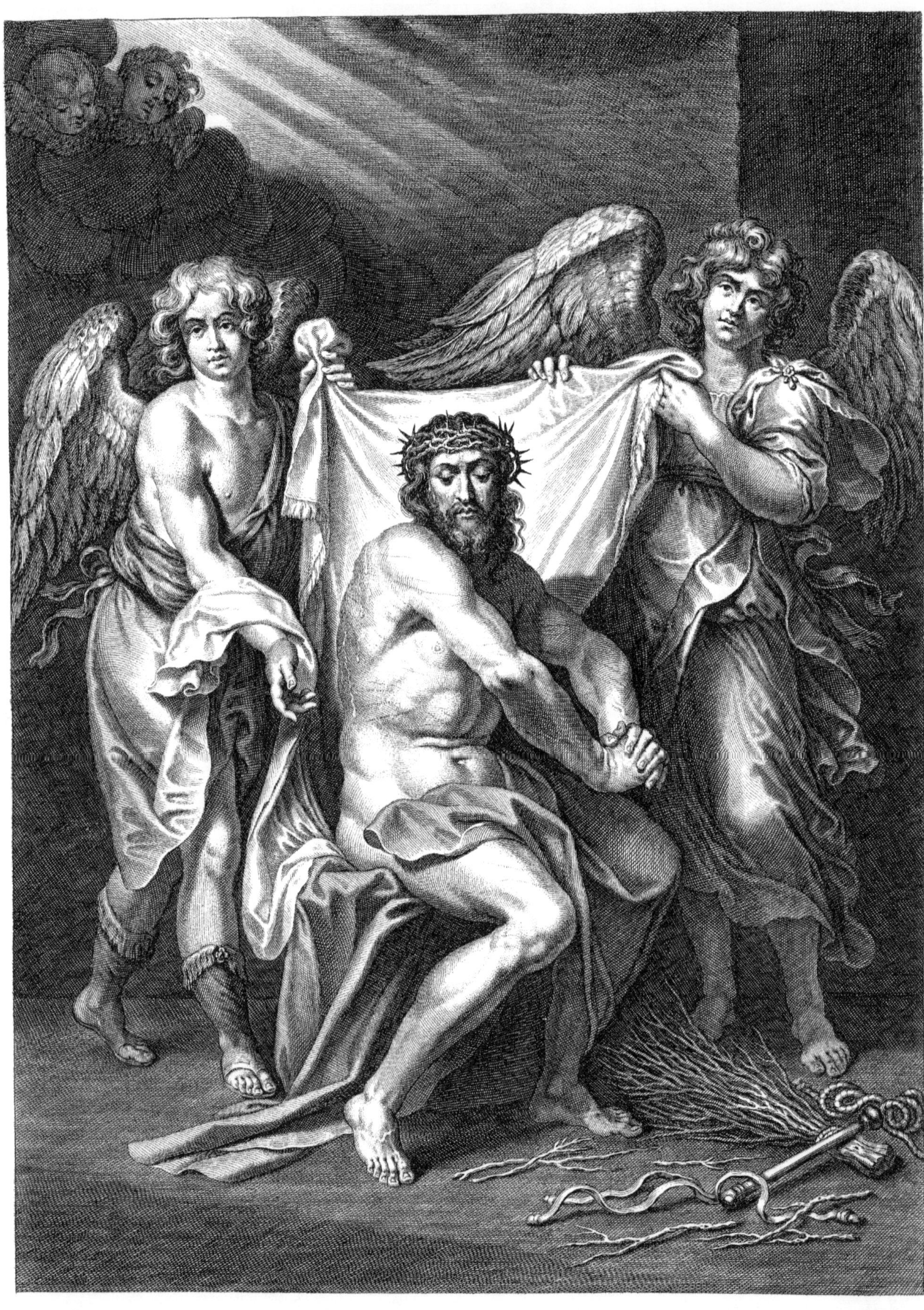

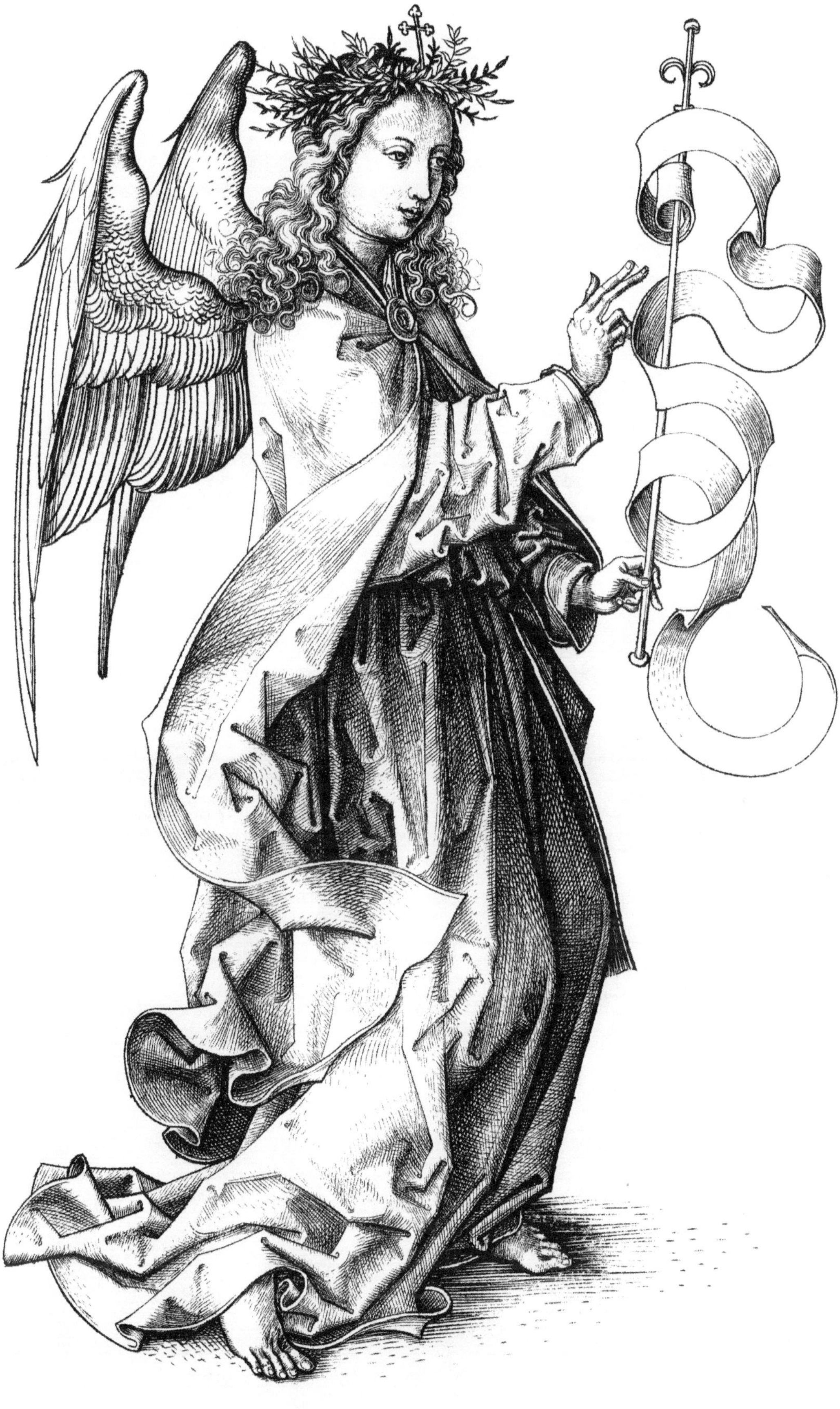

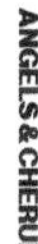

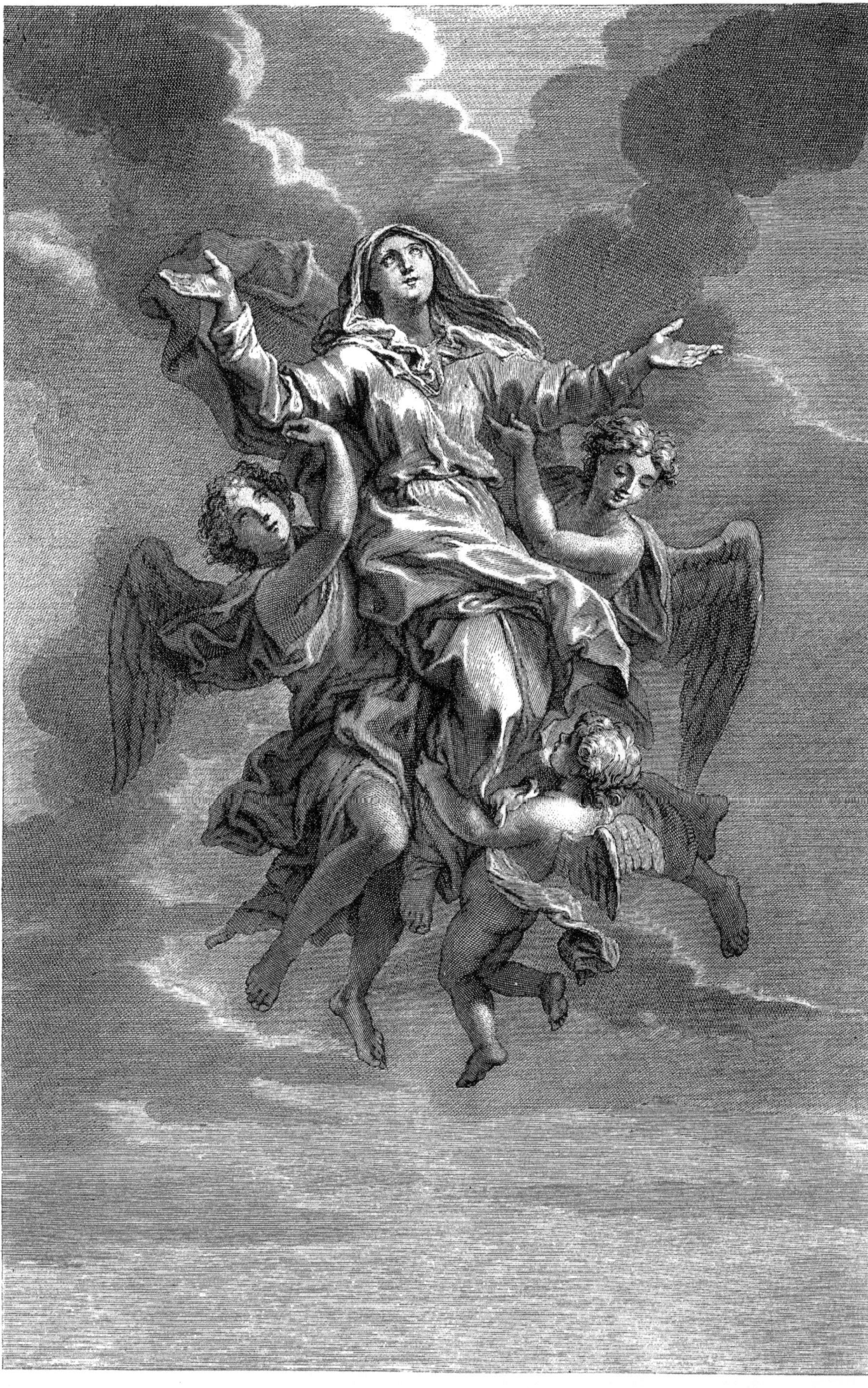

78

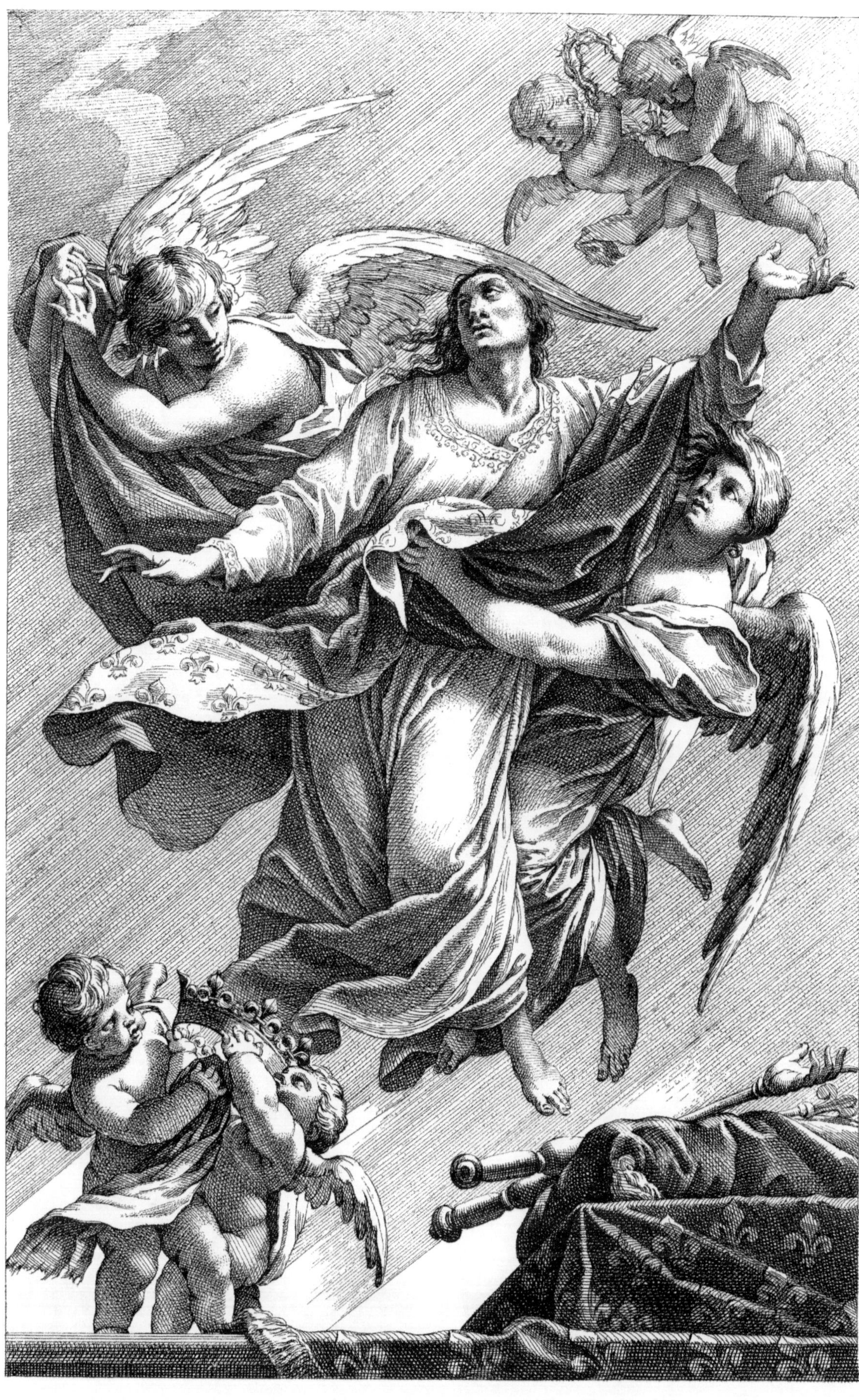

79

80

81

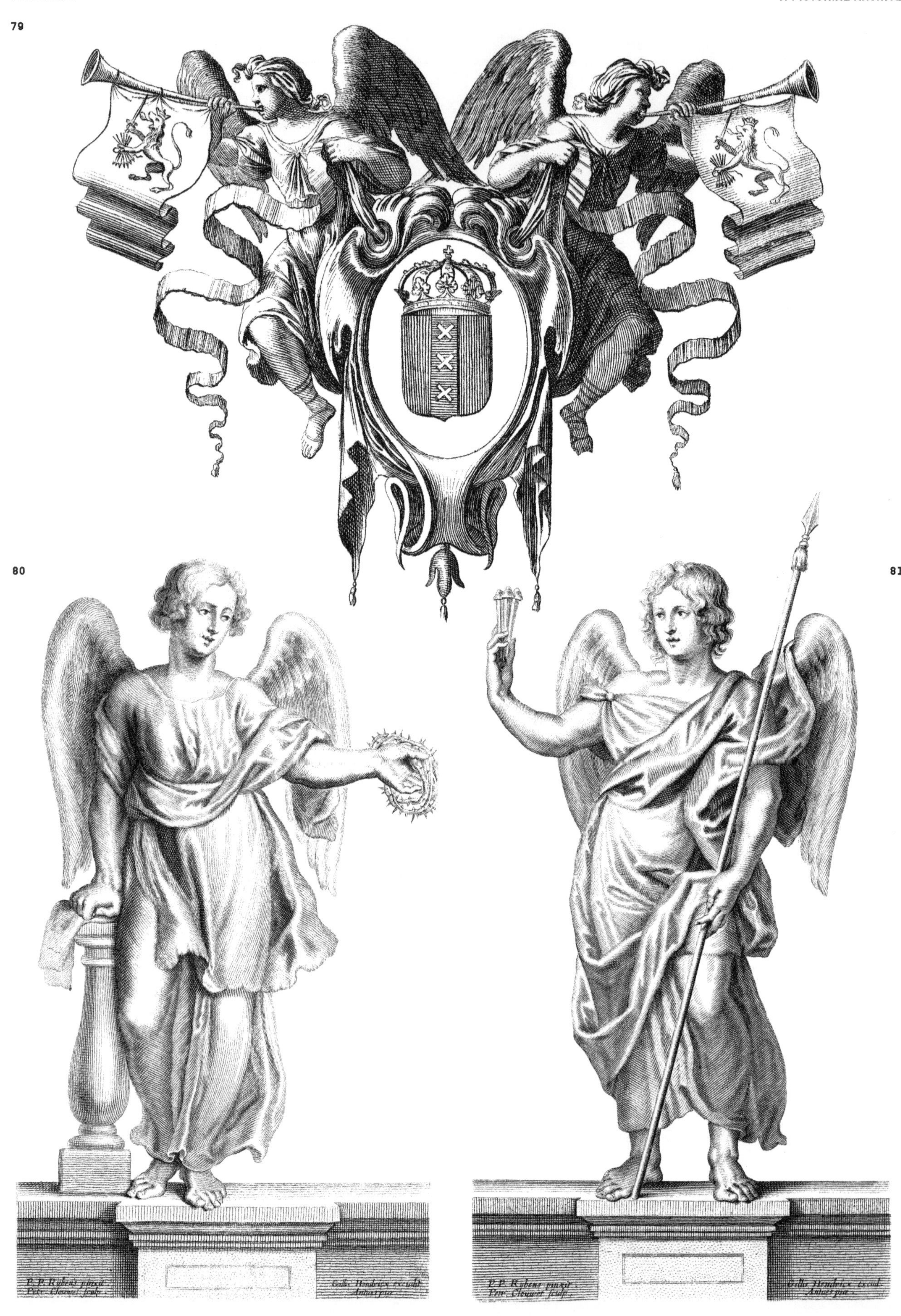

82

83

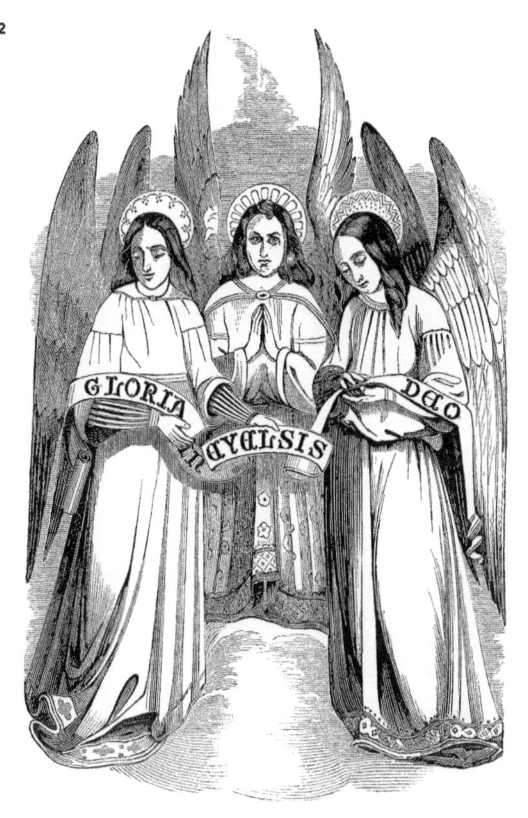

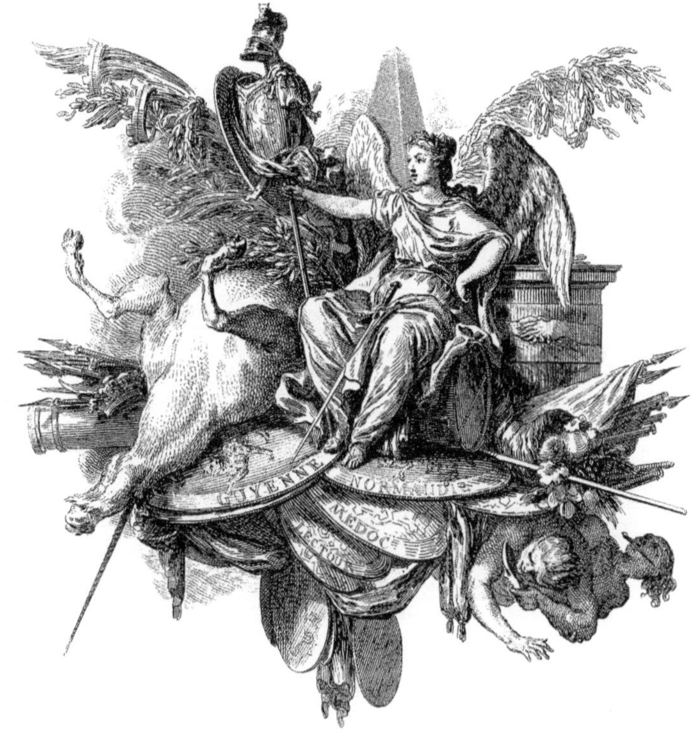

84

85

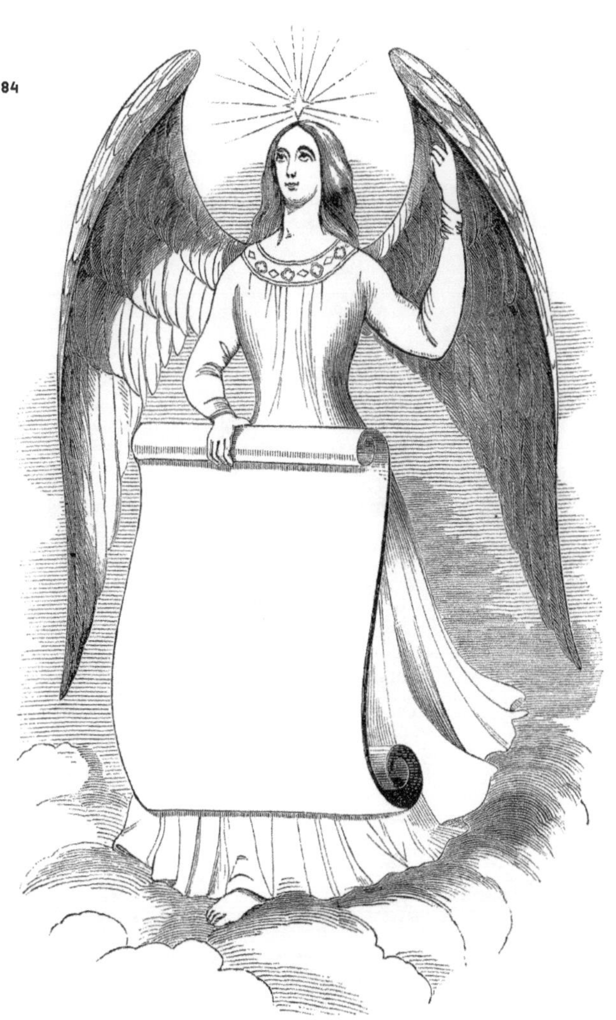

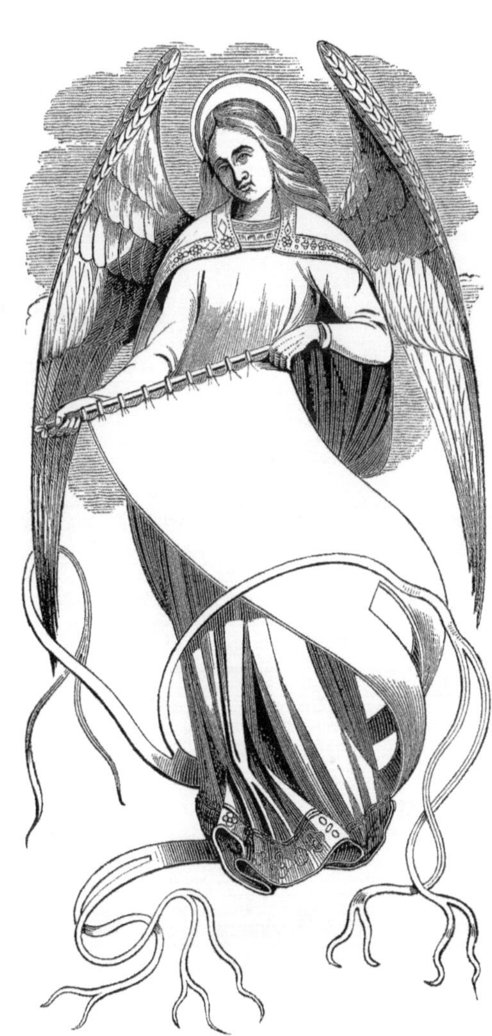

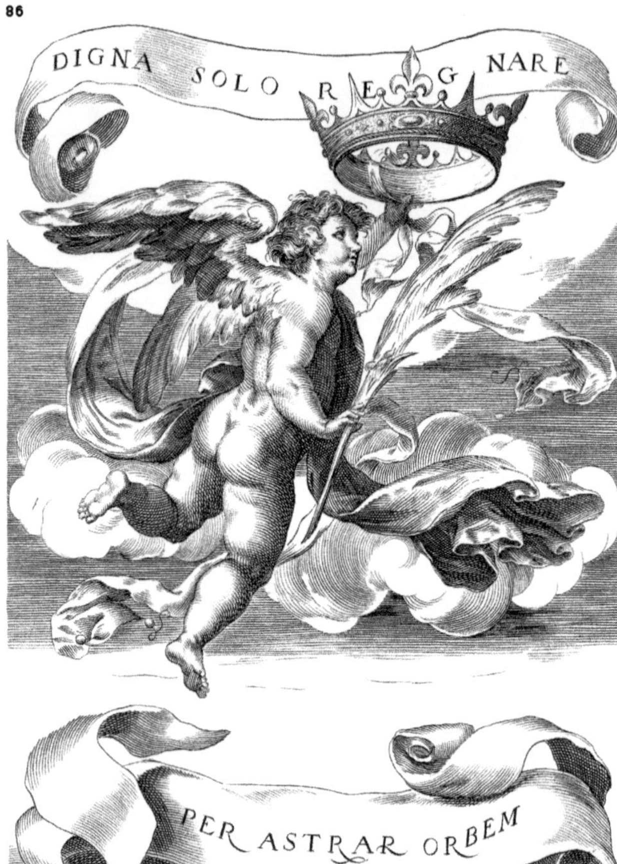

DIGNA SOLO REGNARE
PER ASTRAR ORBEM

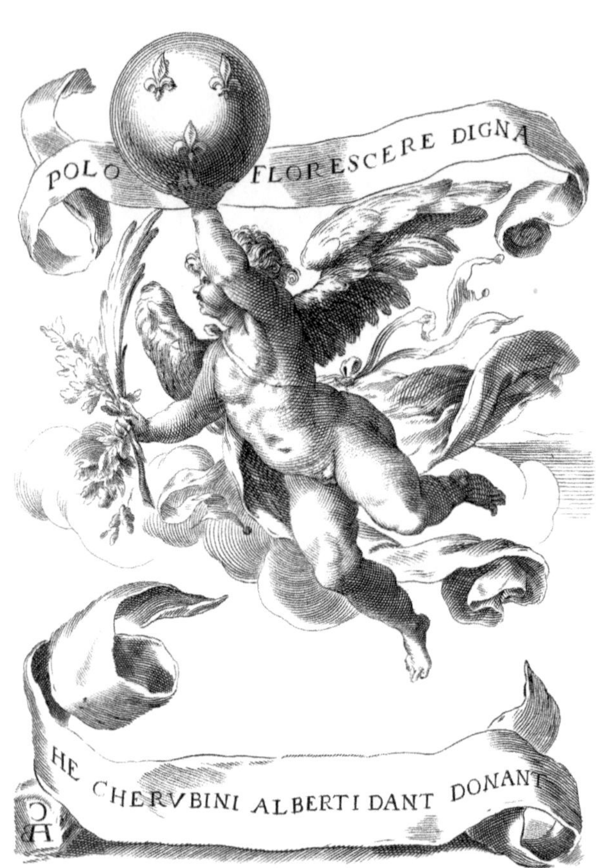

POLO FLORESCERE DIGNA
HE CHERVBINI ALBERTI DANT DONANT

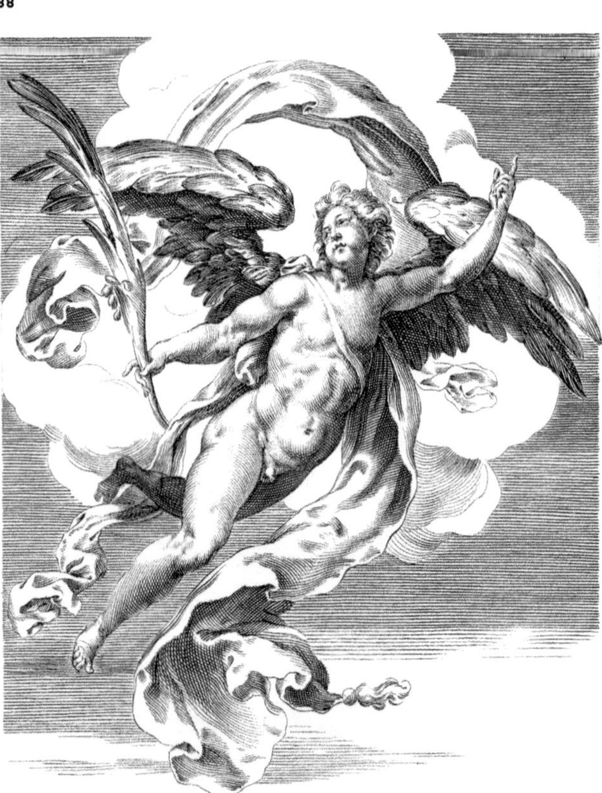

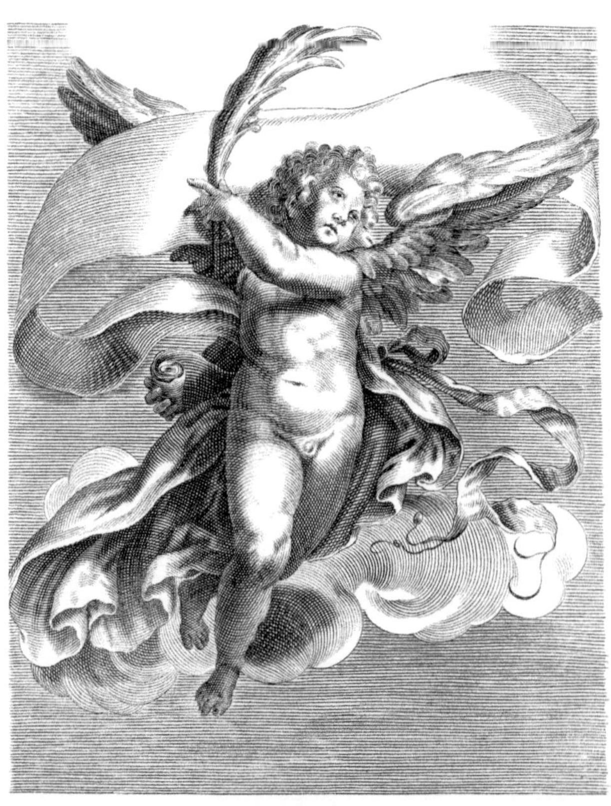

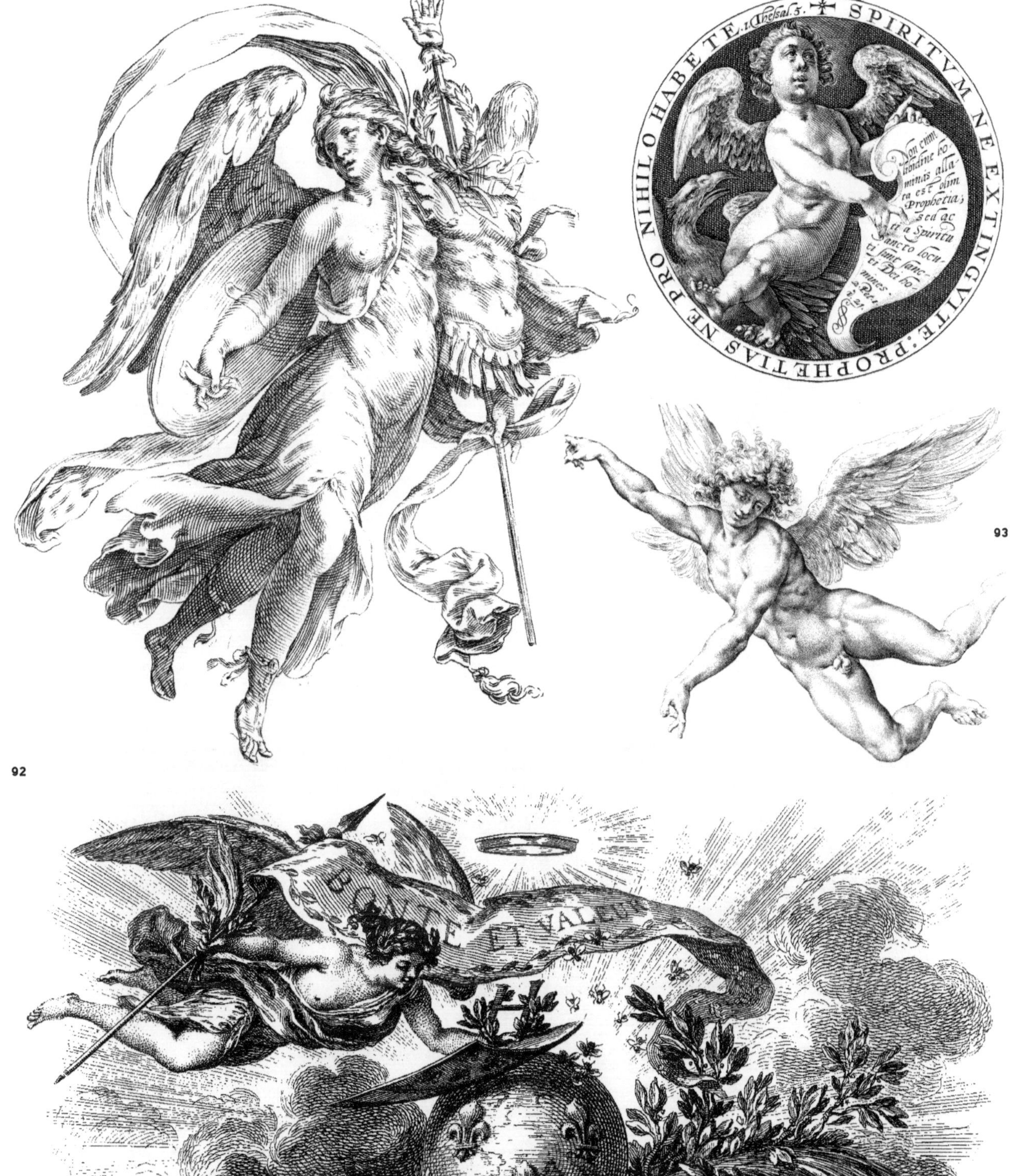

93

92

94

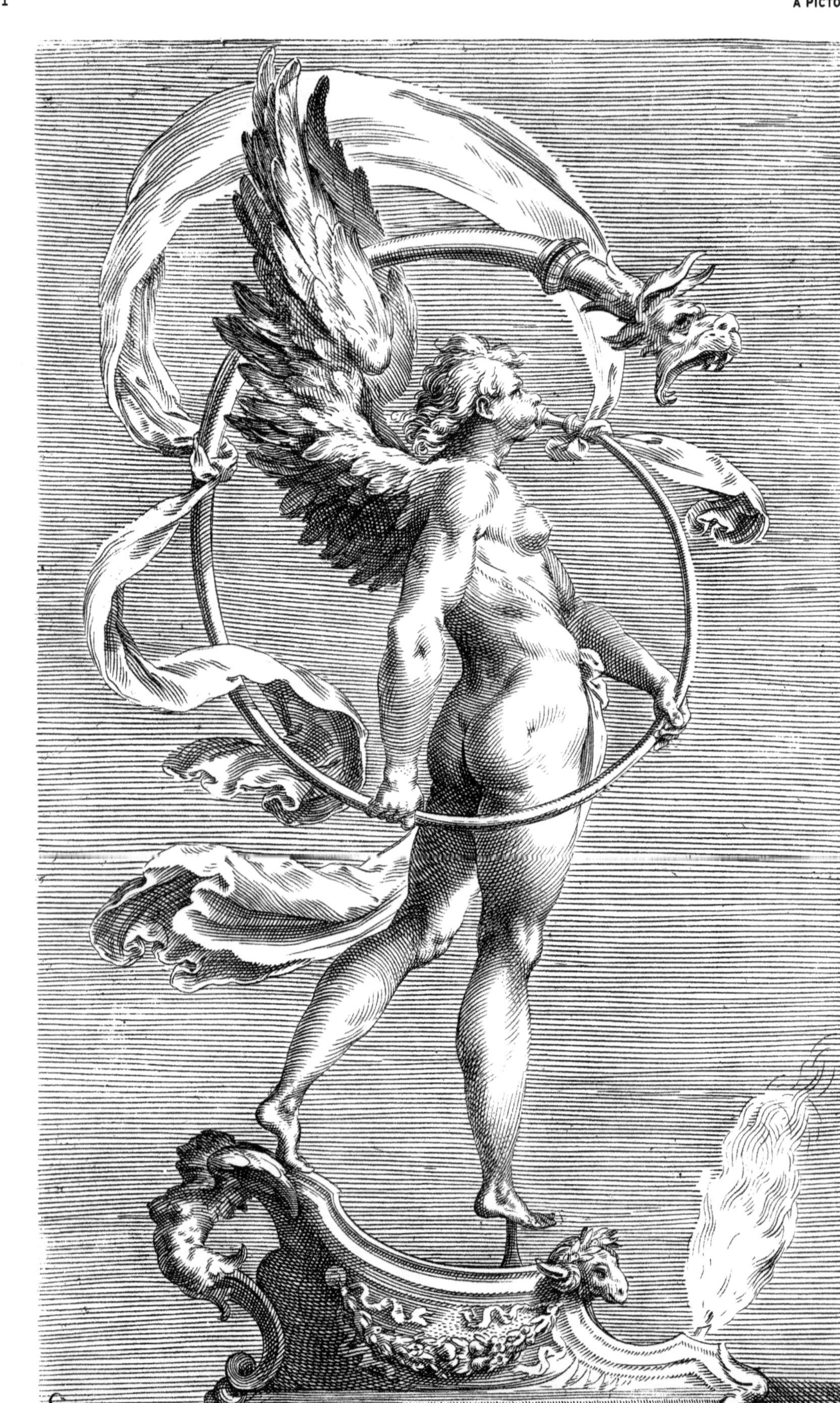

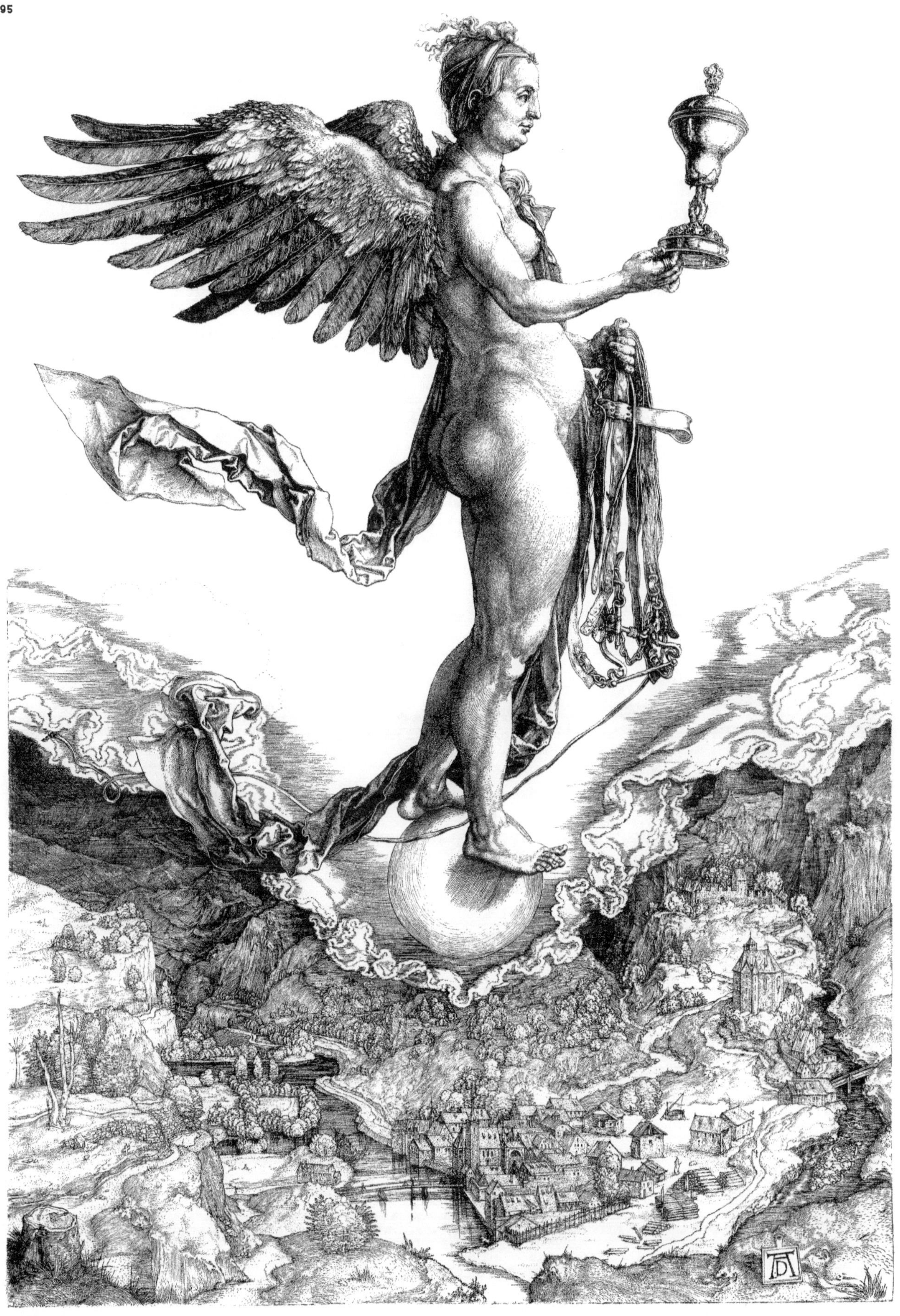

96

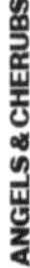

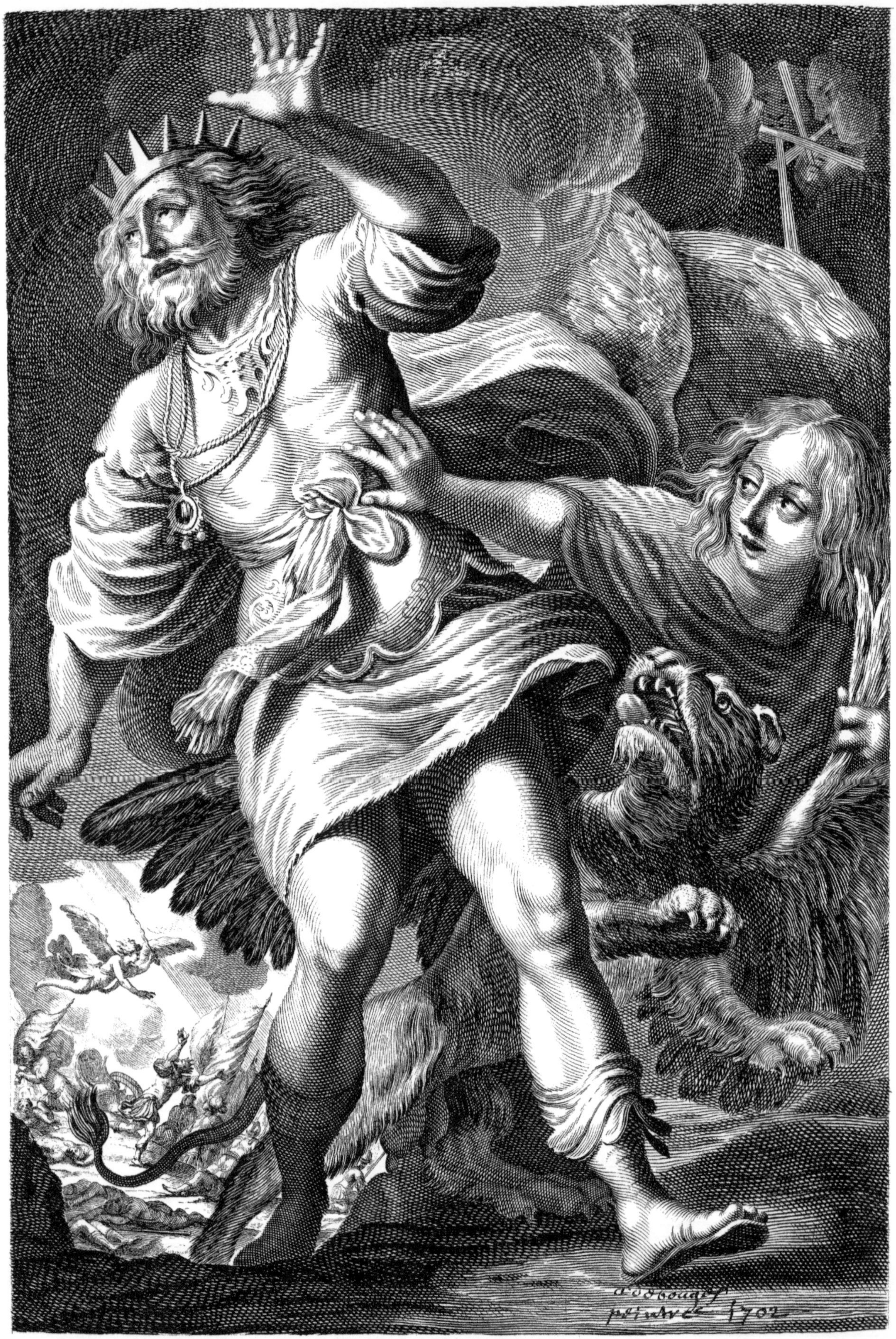

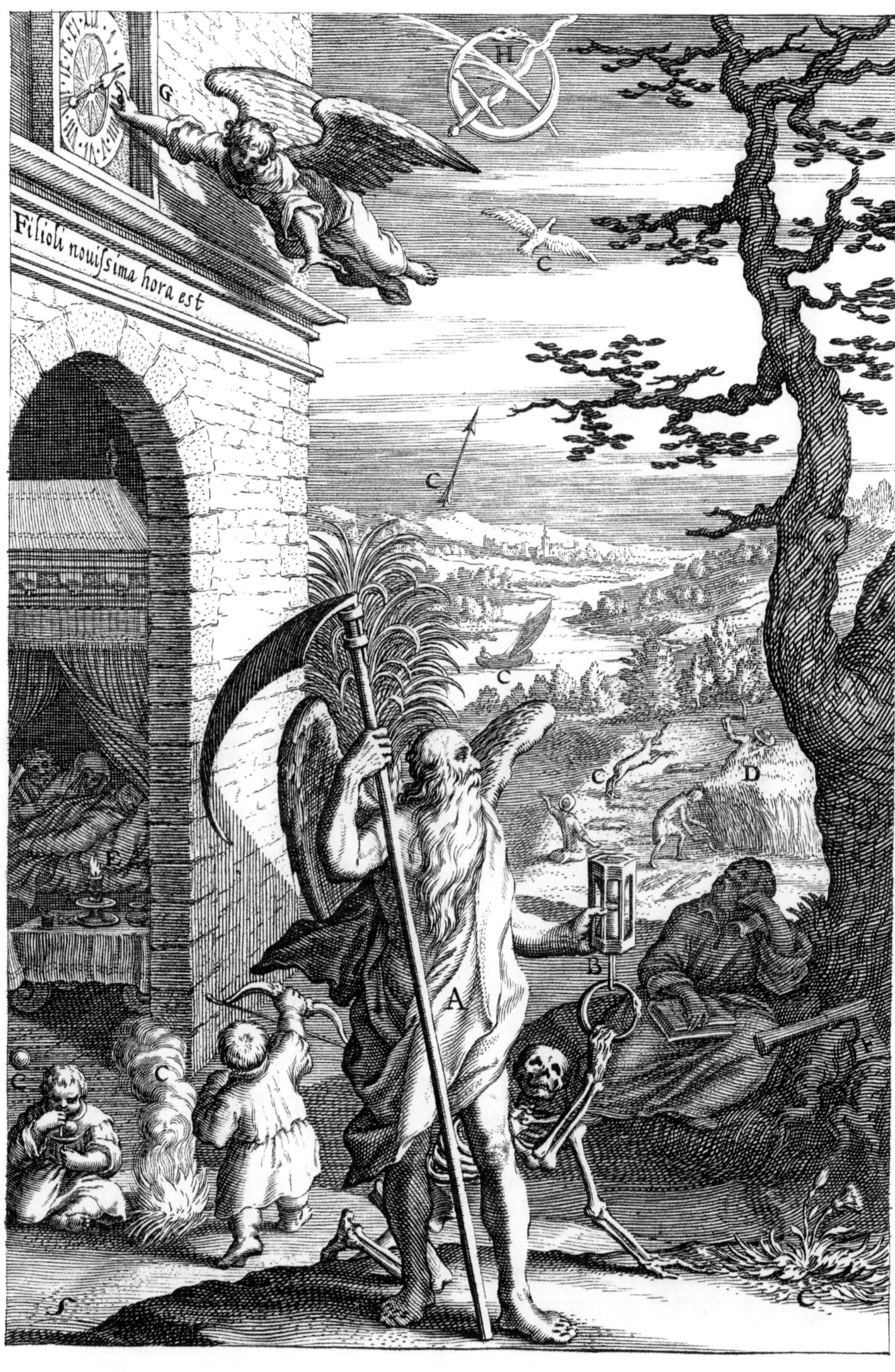
Filioli nouiſsima hora est

98

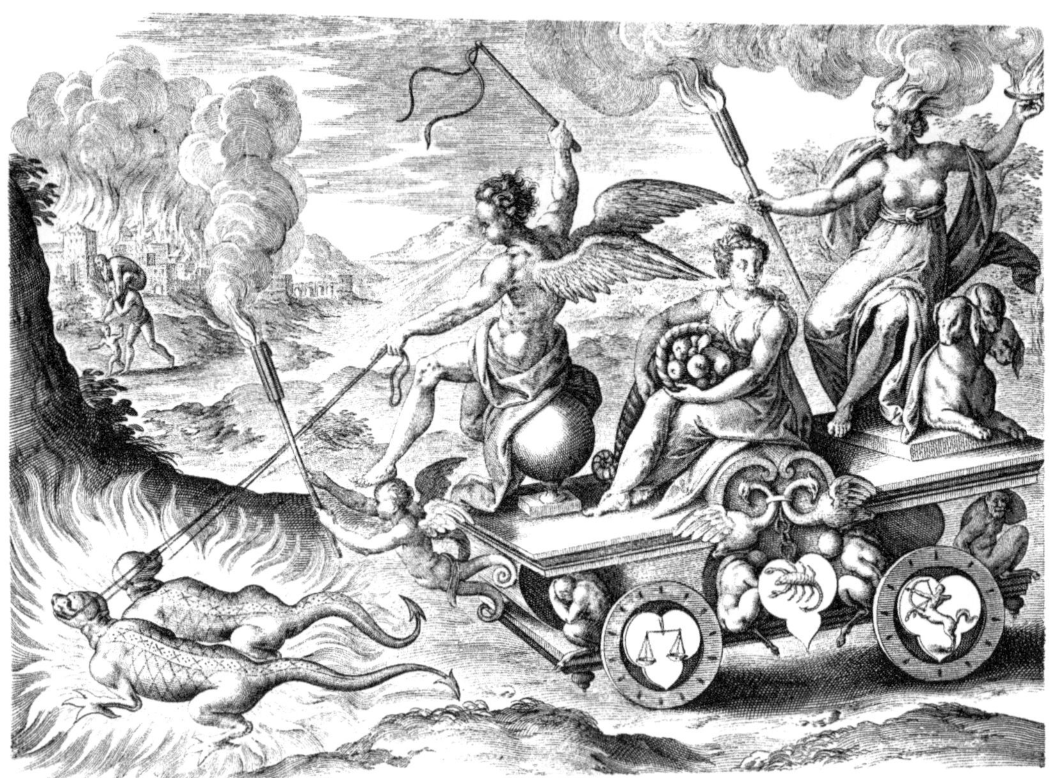

99

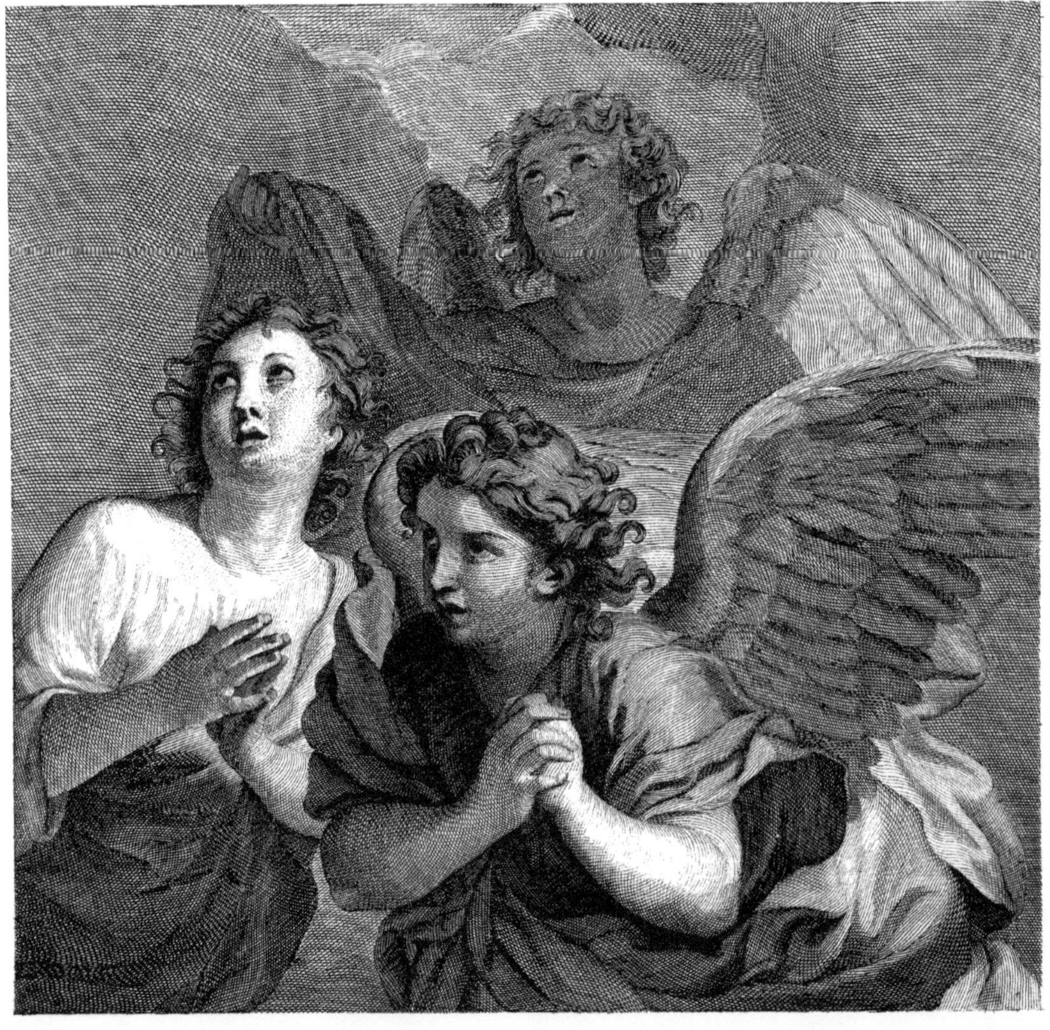

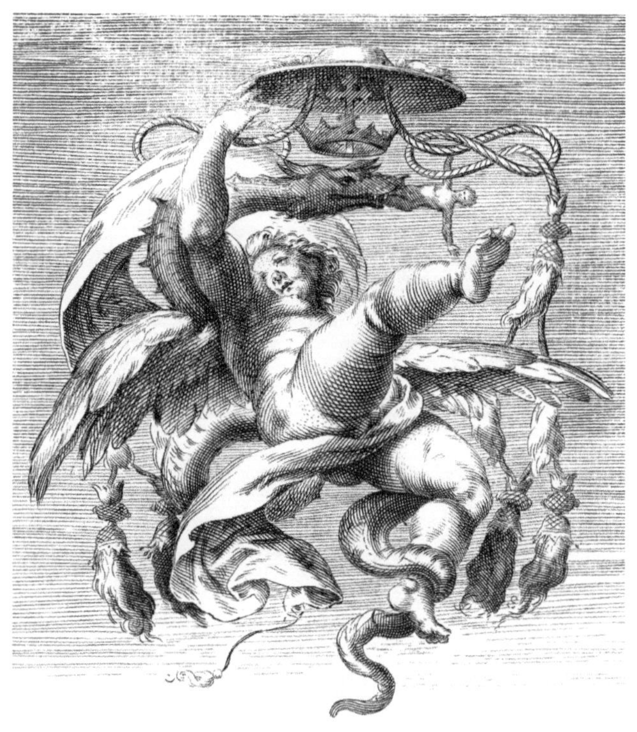

101

100

102

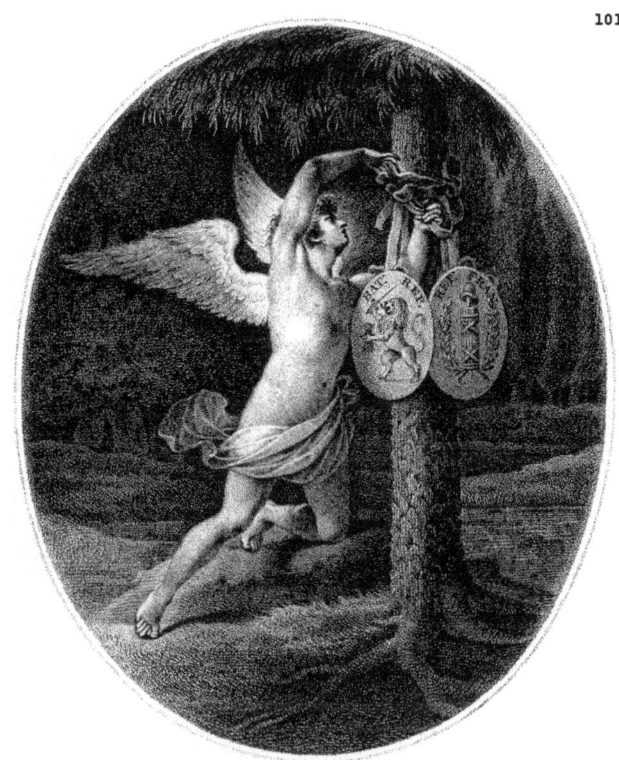

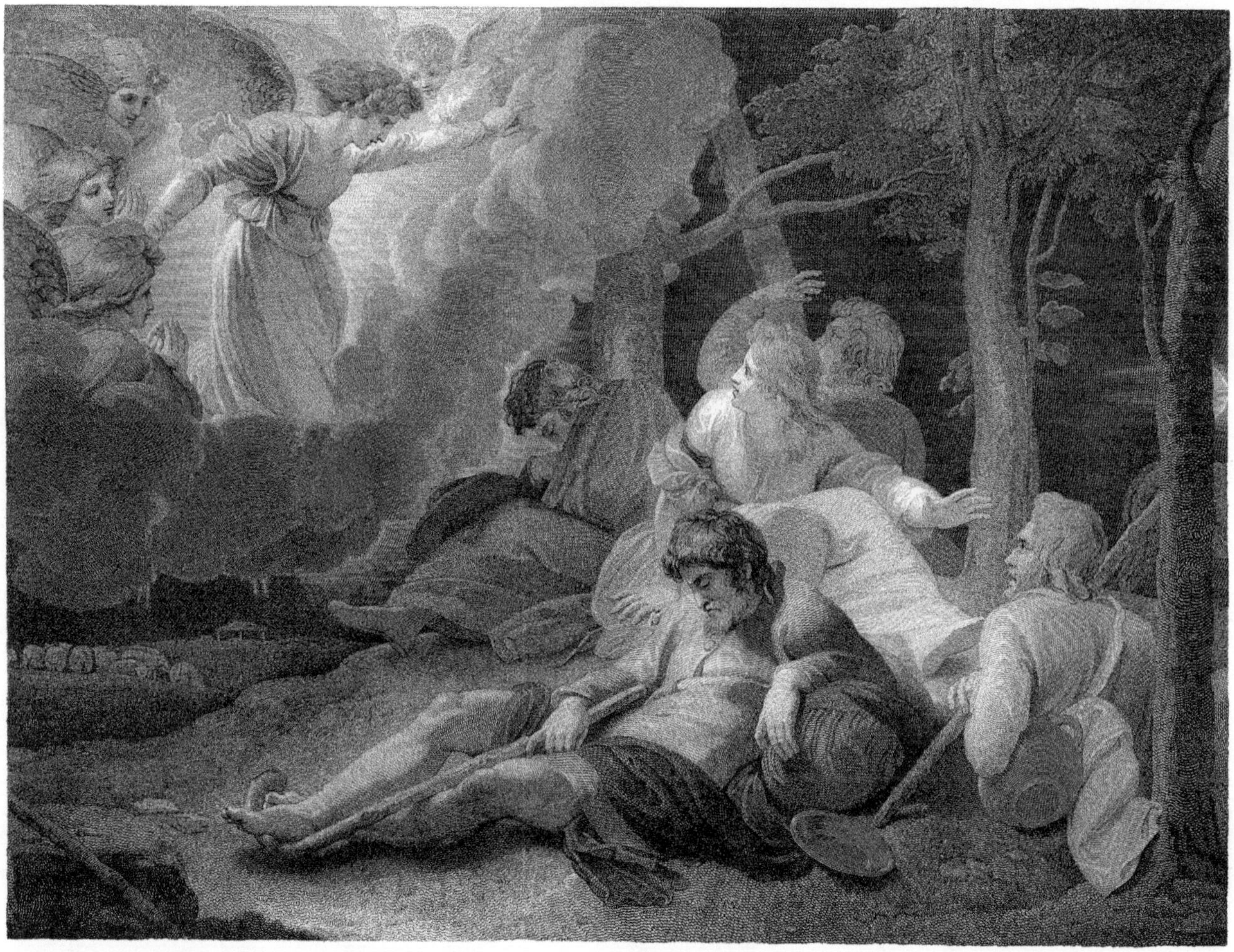

103

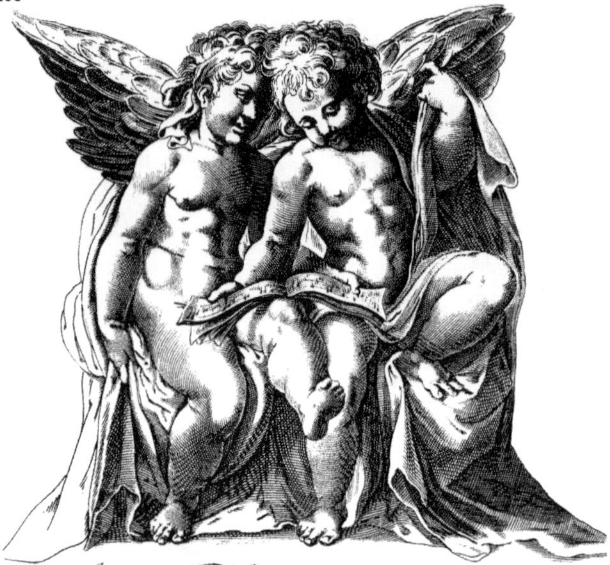

104

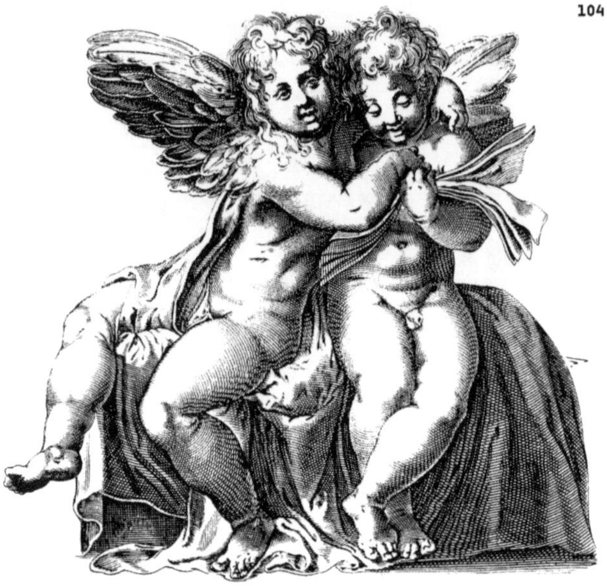

105

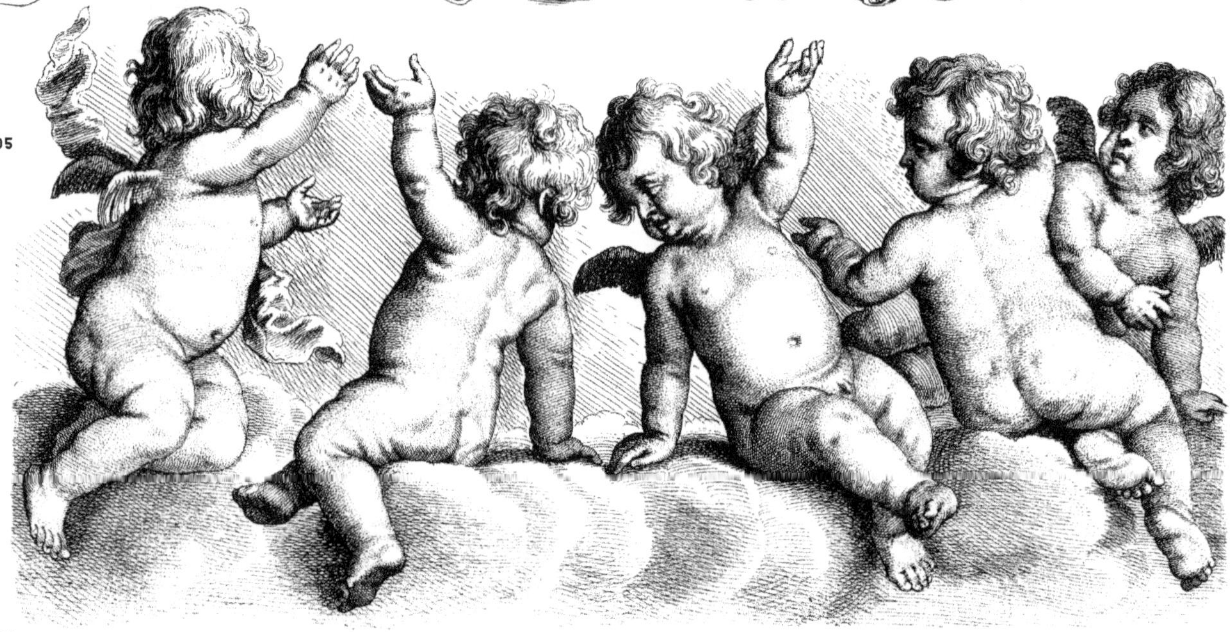

106

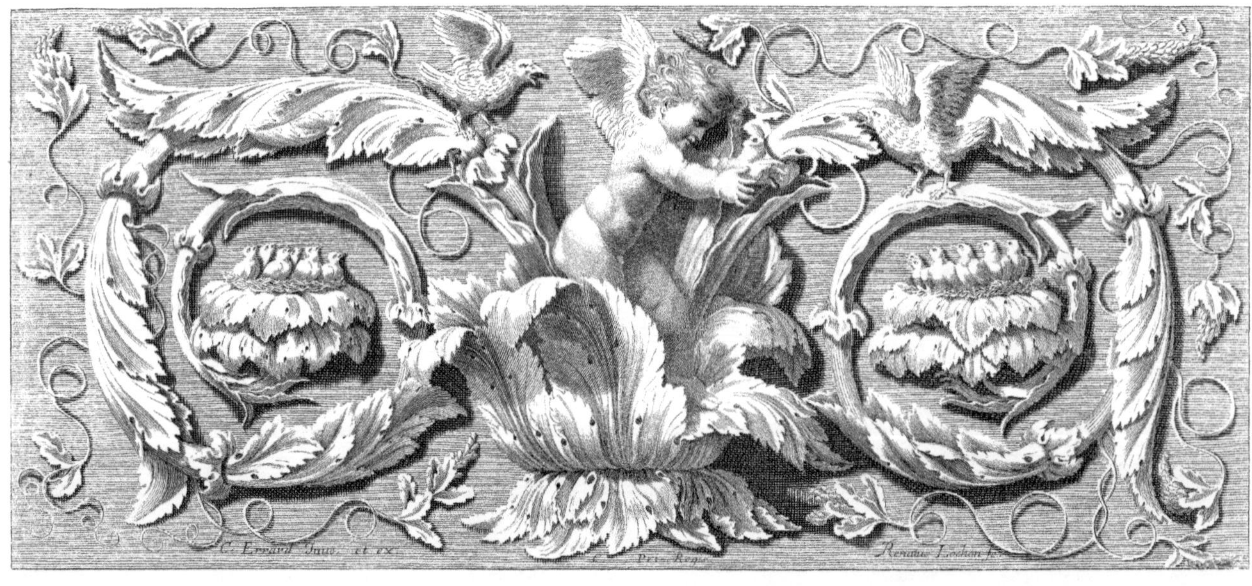

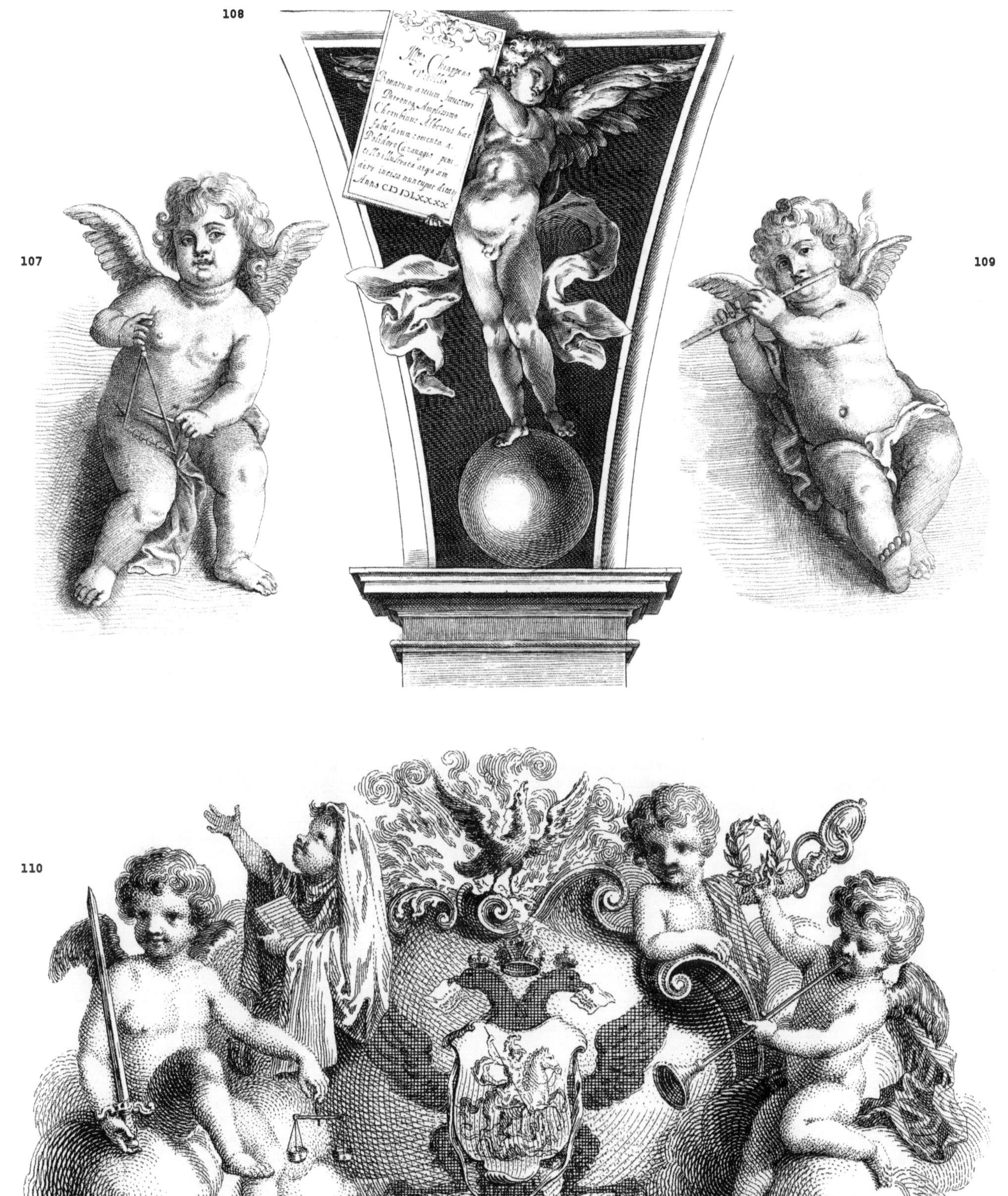

108

107

109

110

111

112

113

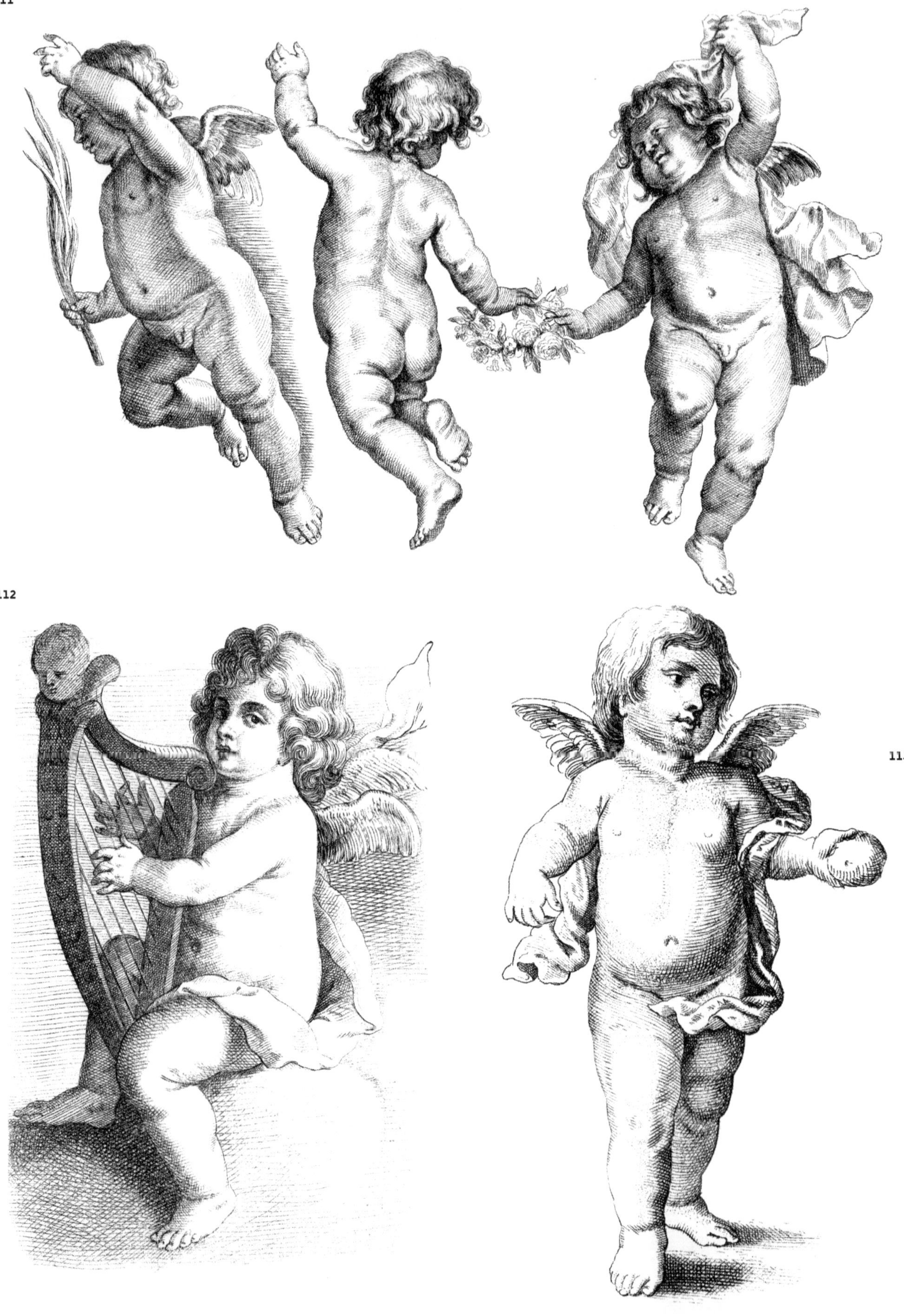

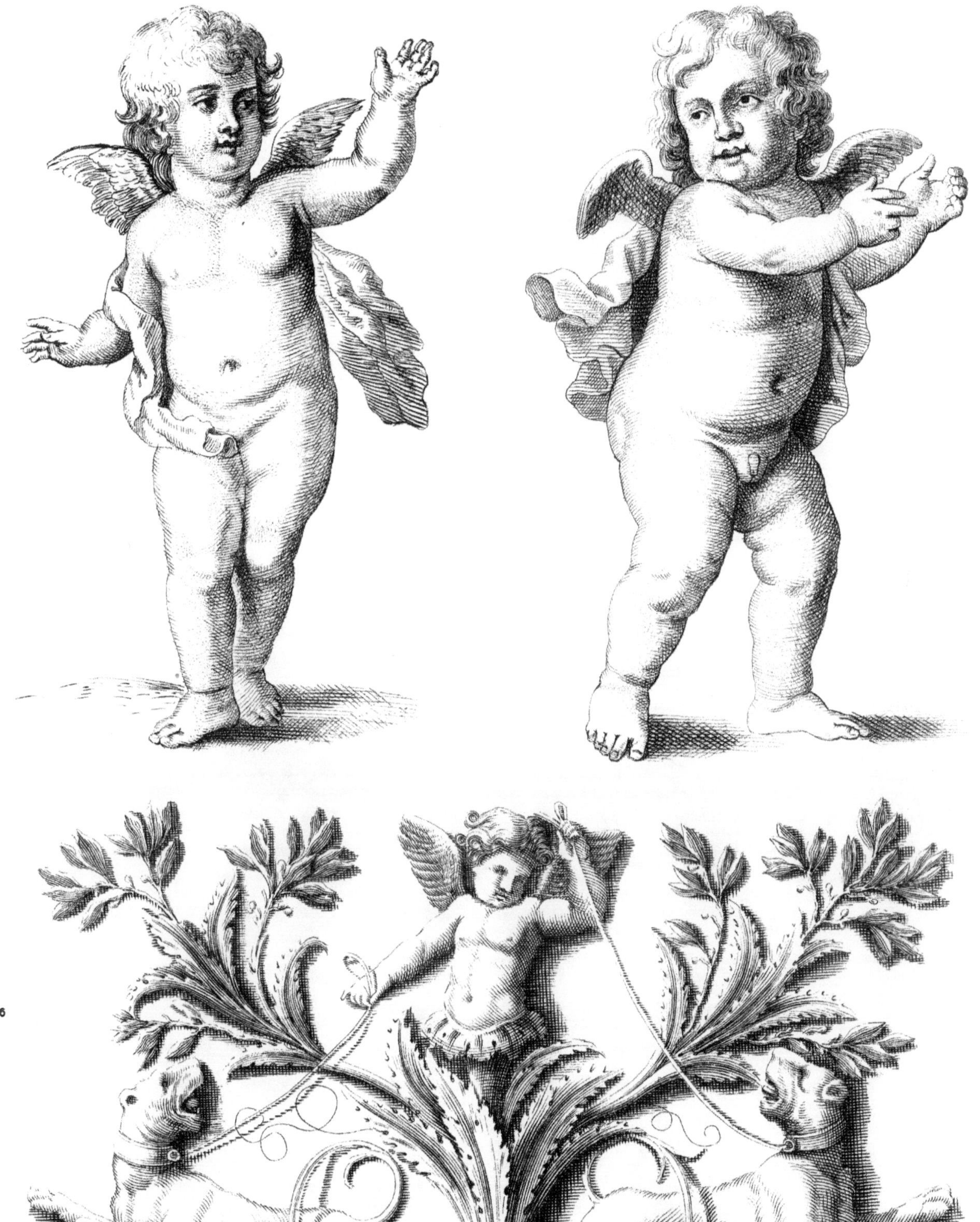

116

117

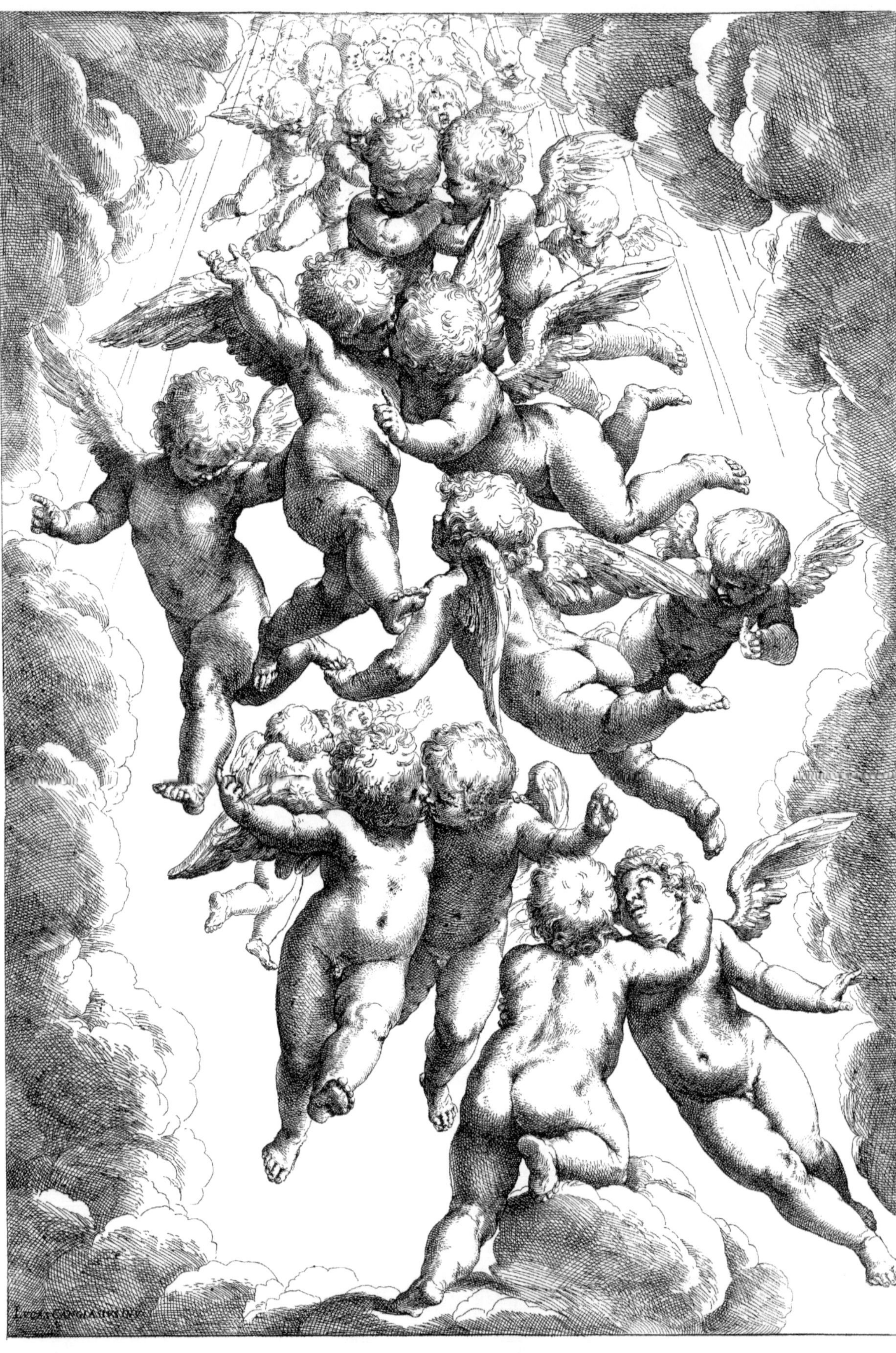

118

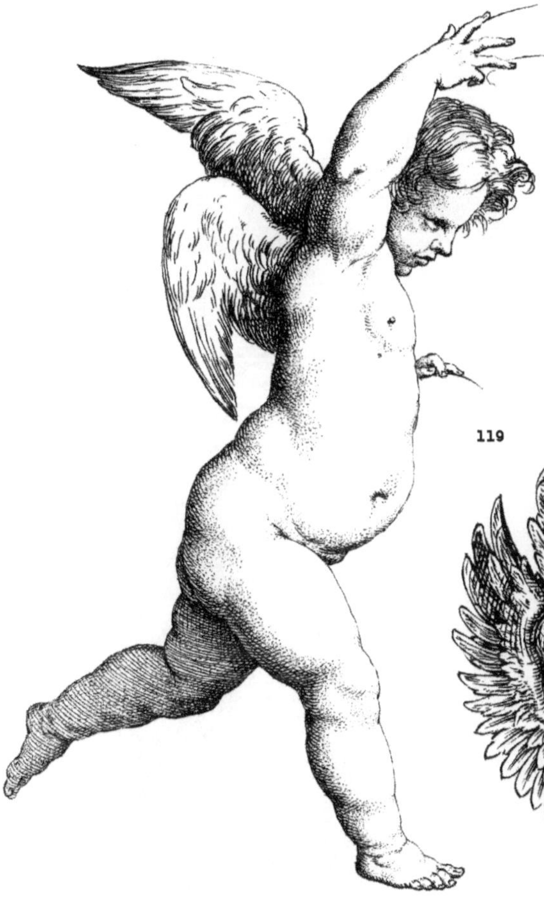

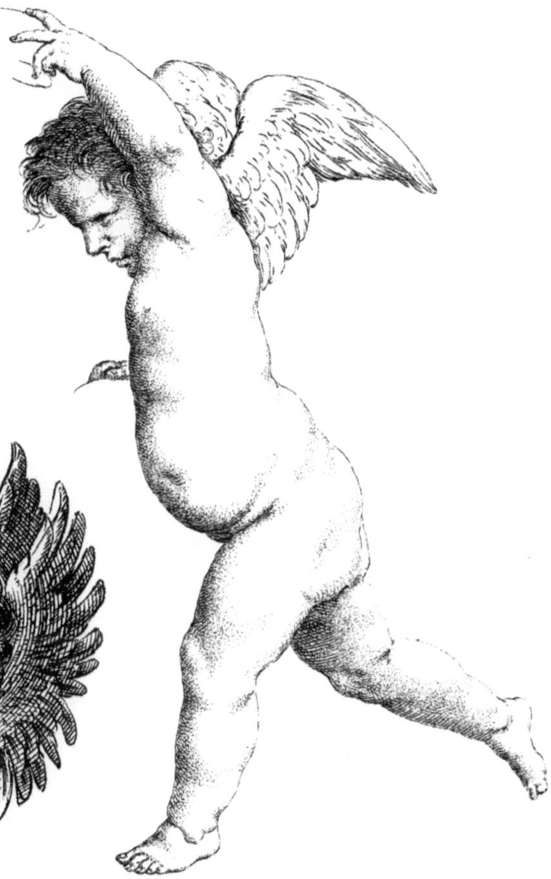

119

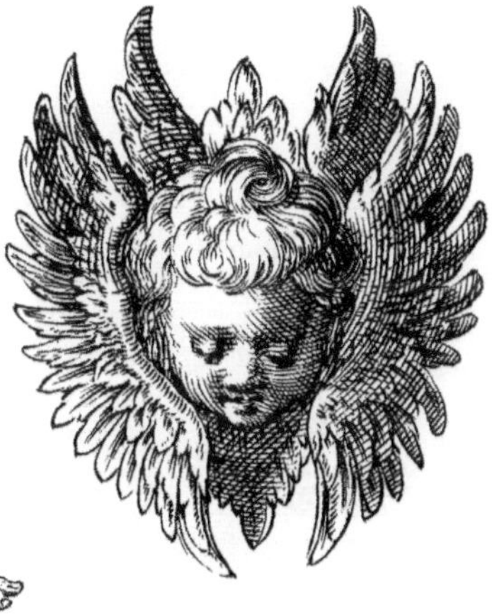

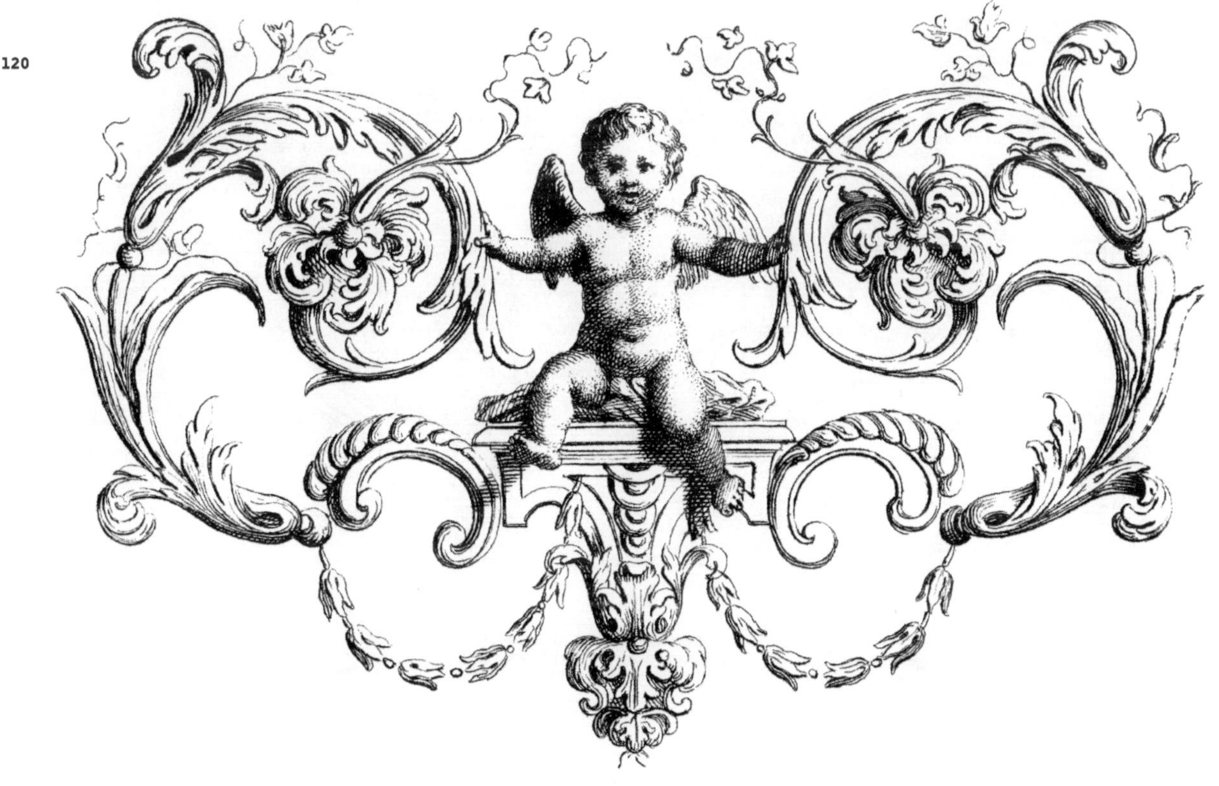

120

121

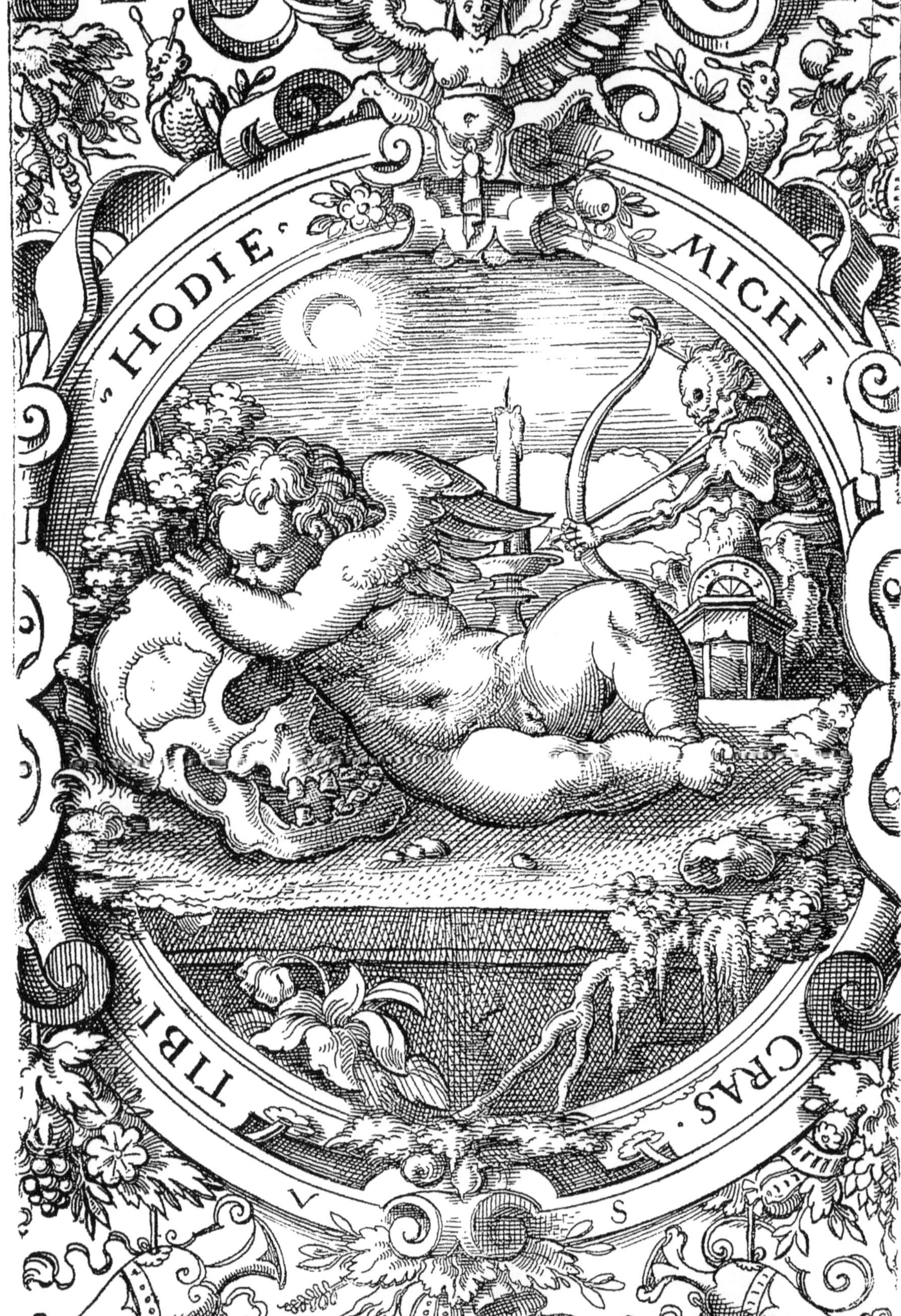

122

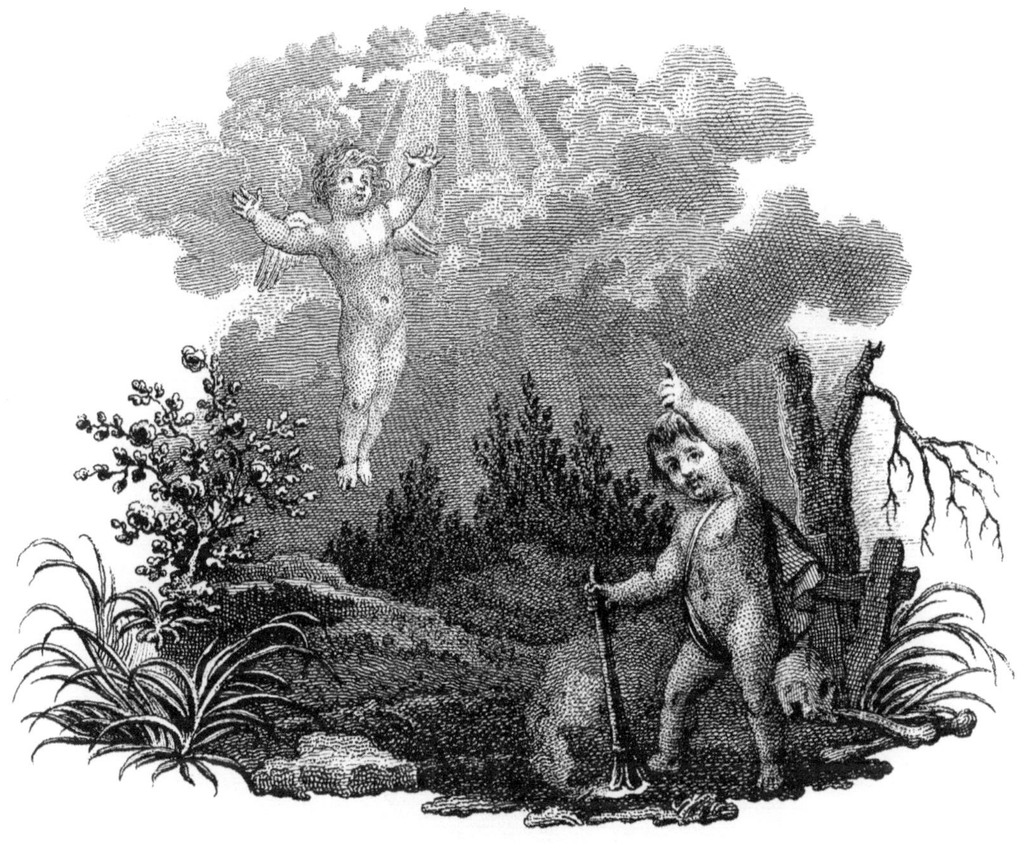

123

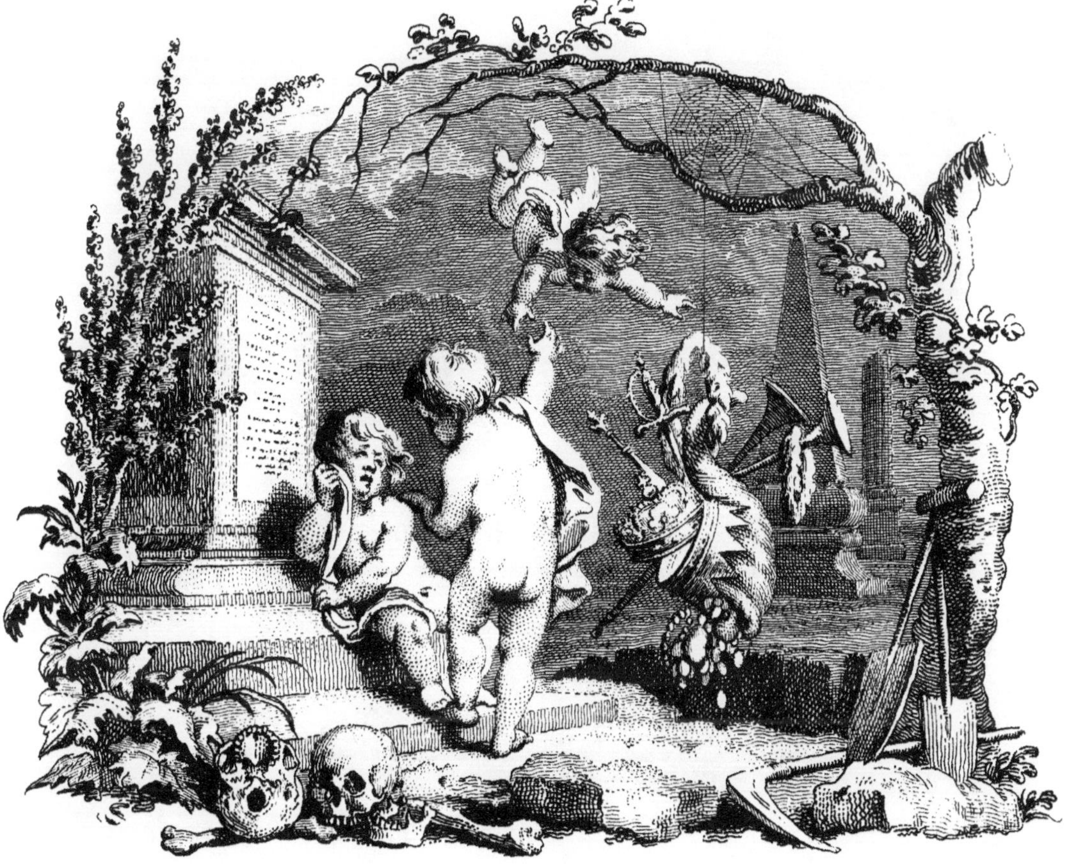

124

125

126

127

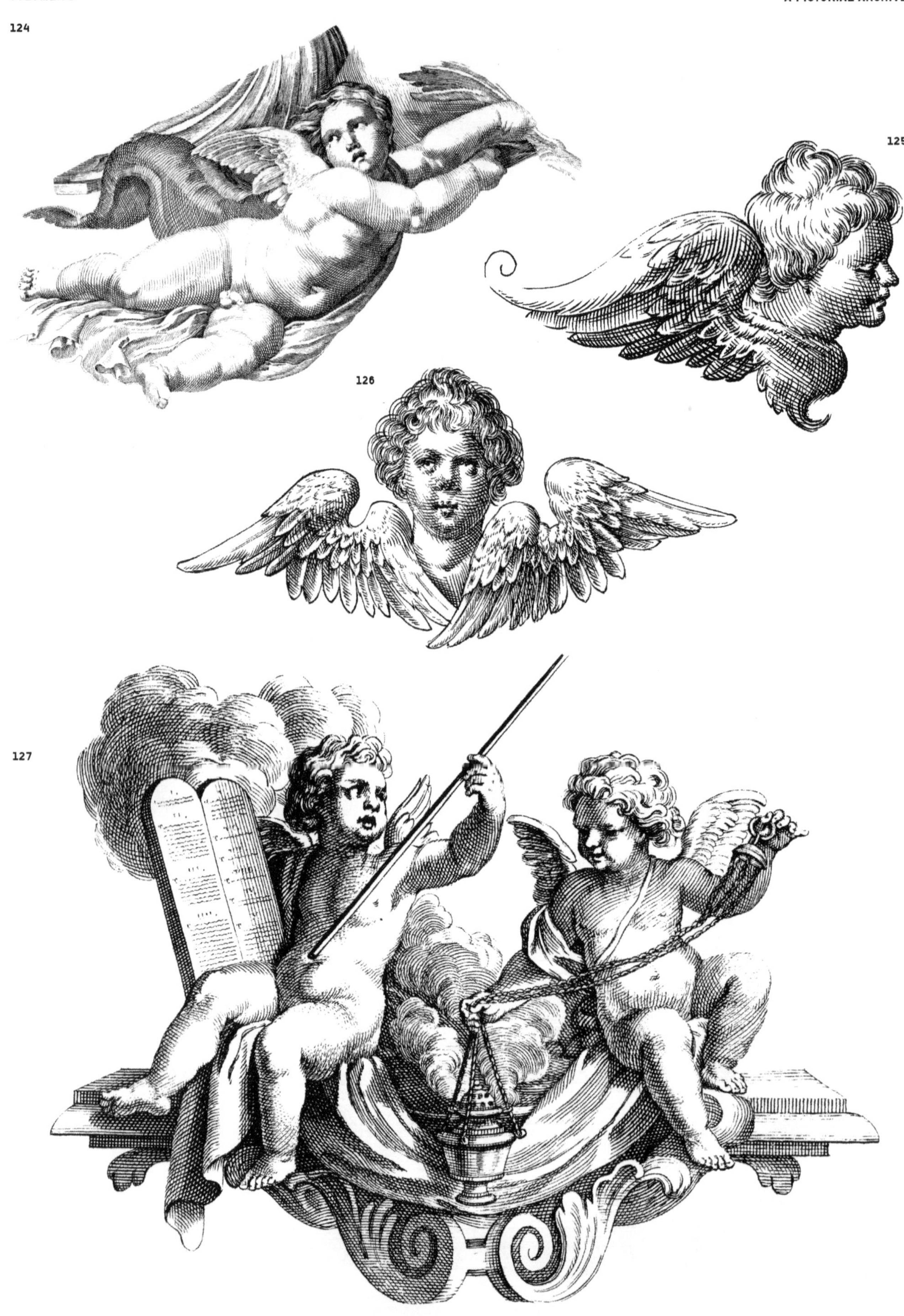

128

129

130

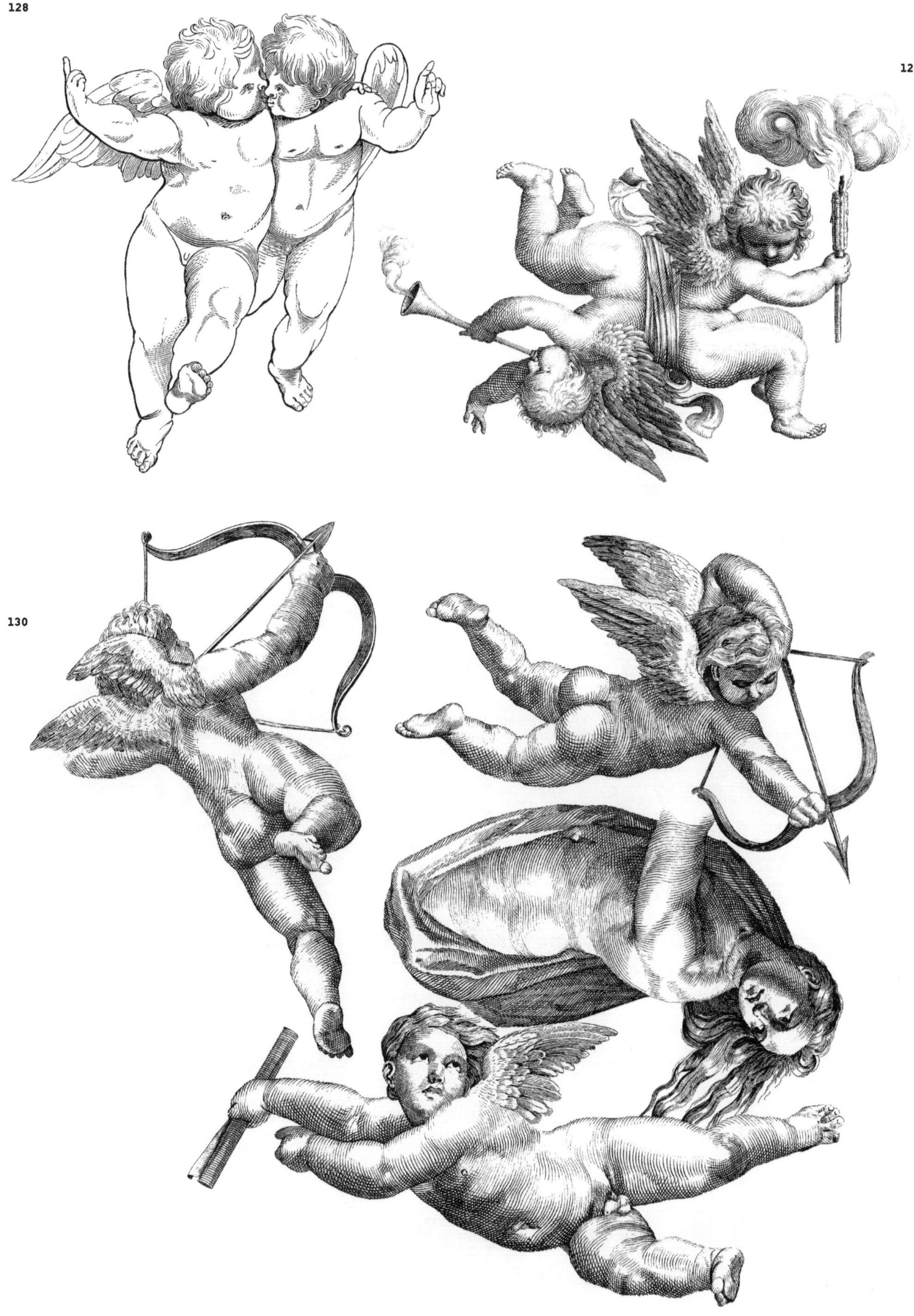

131

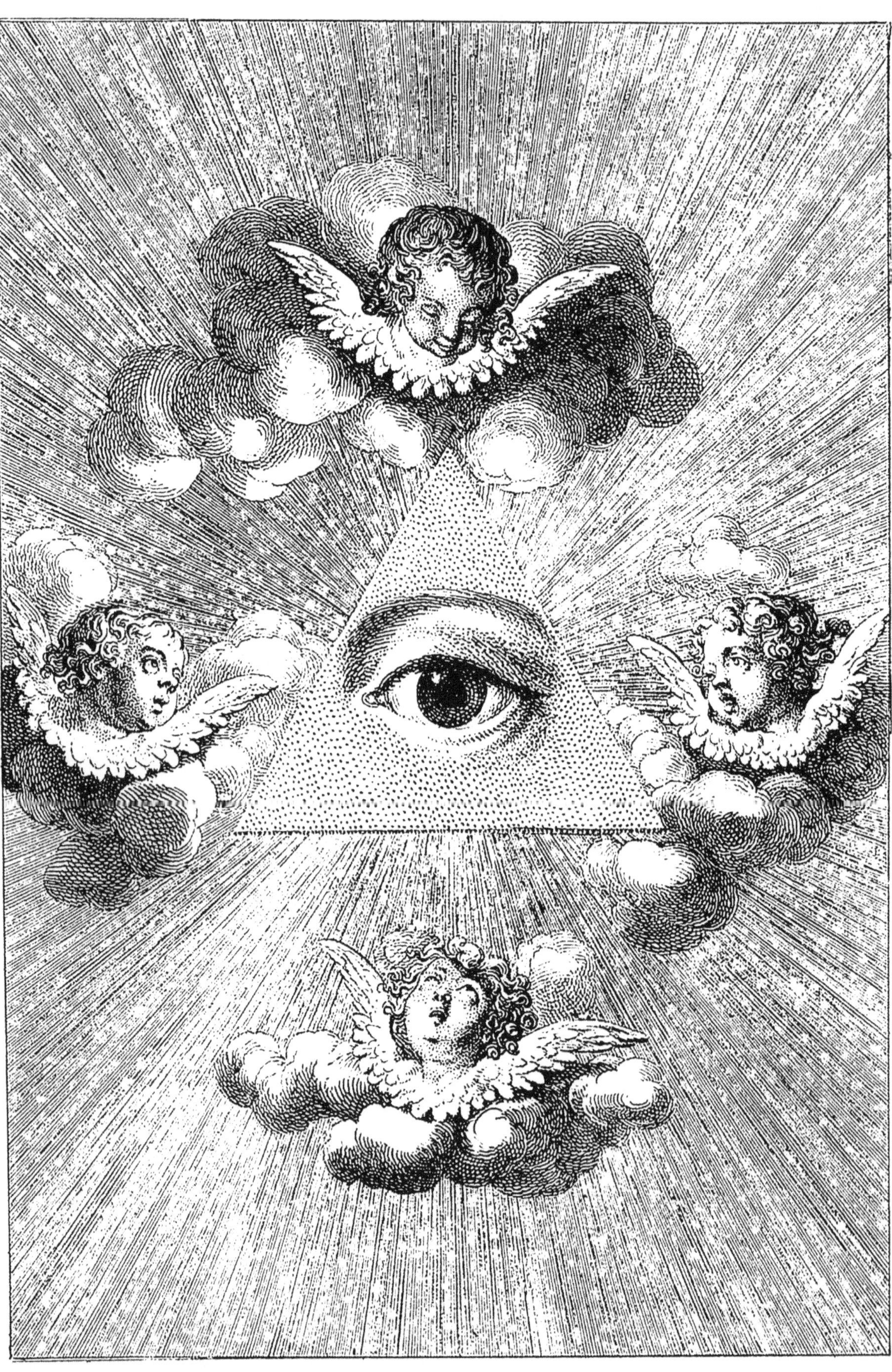

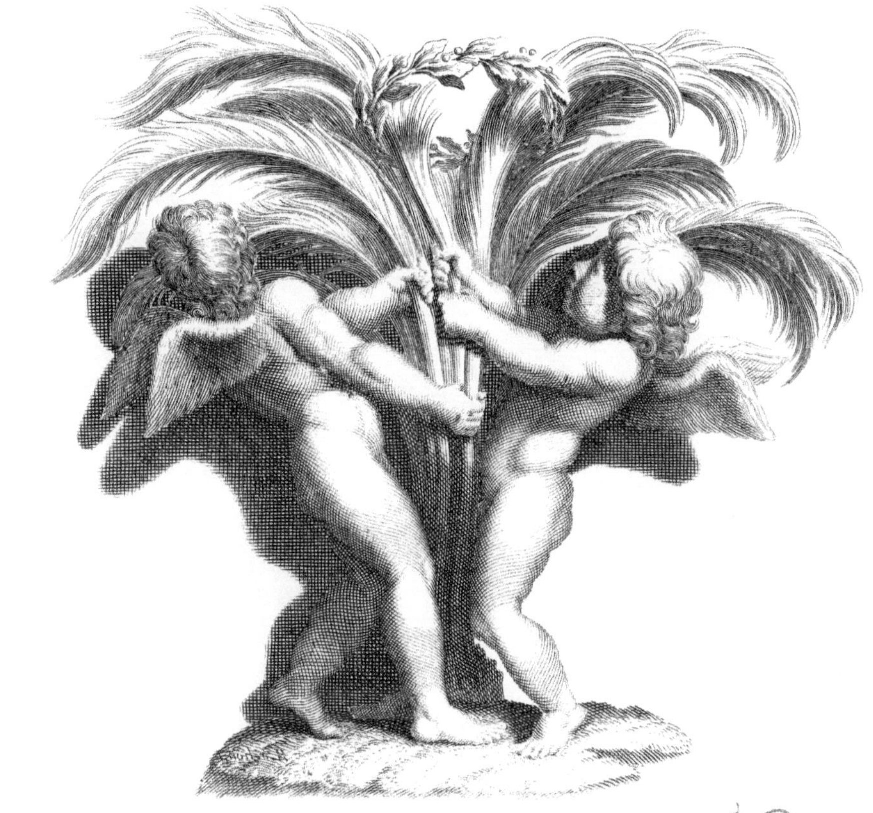

133

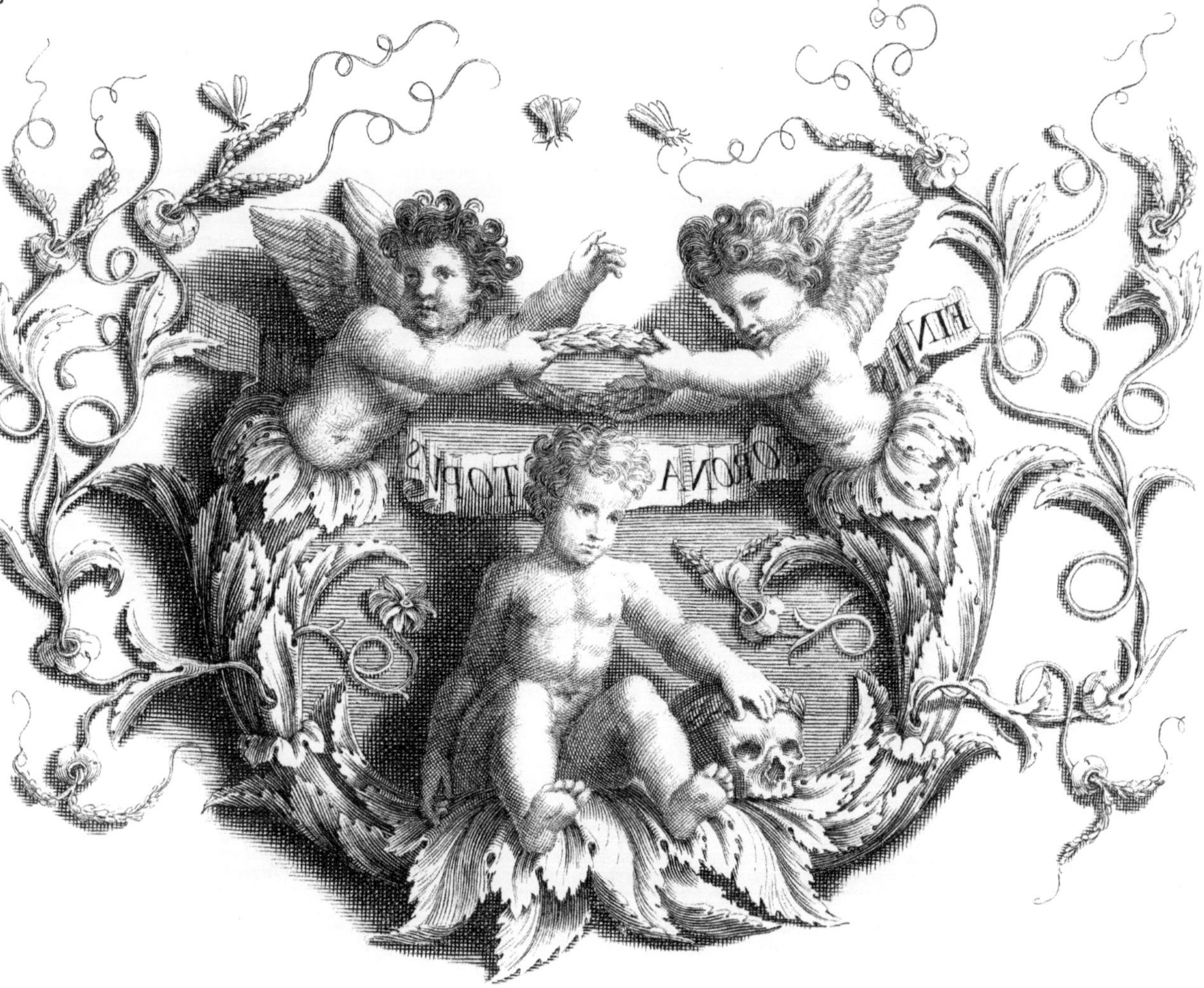

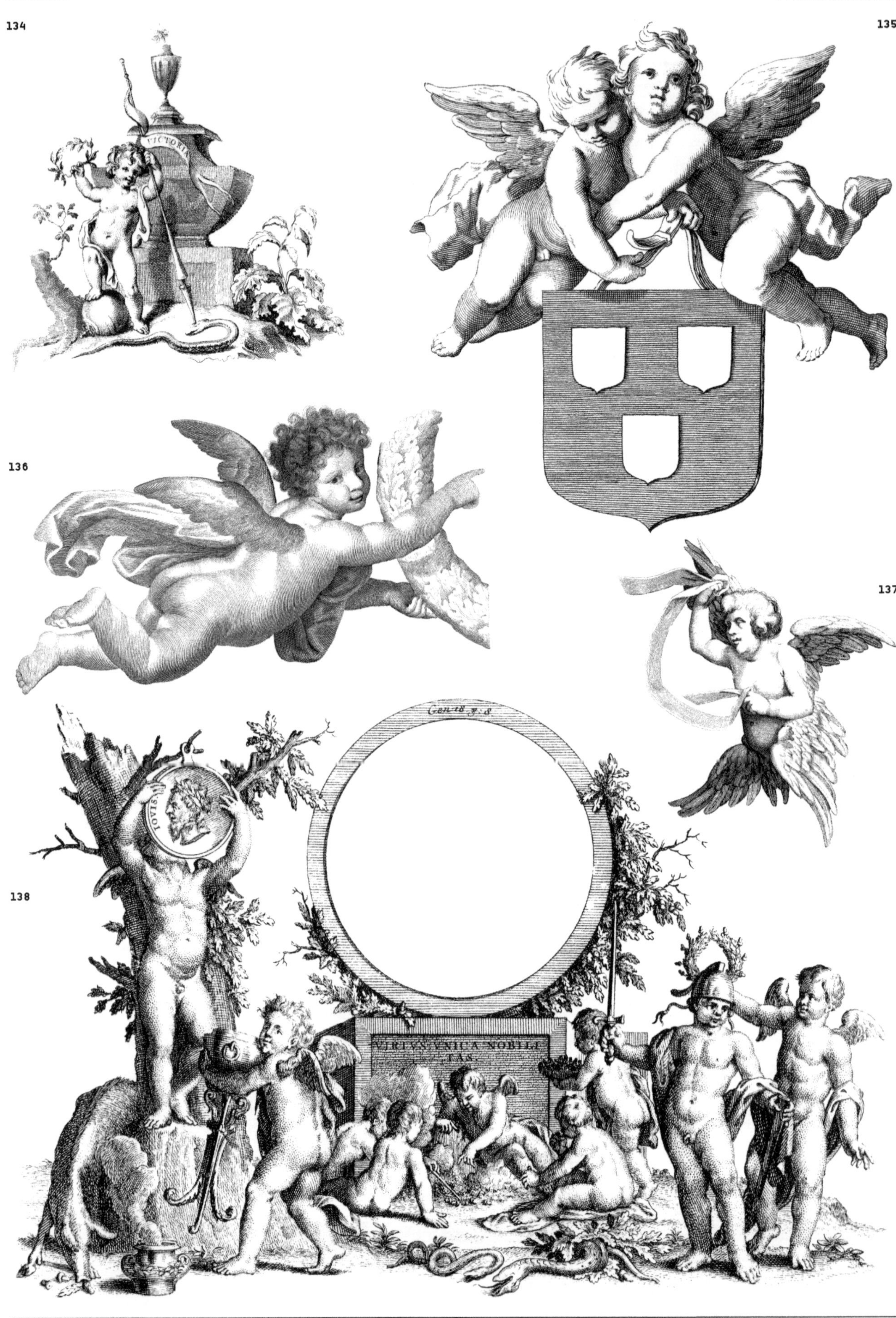

134

135

136

137

138

139

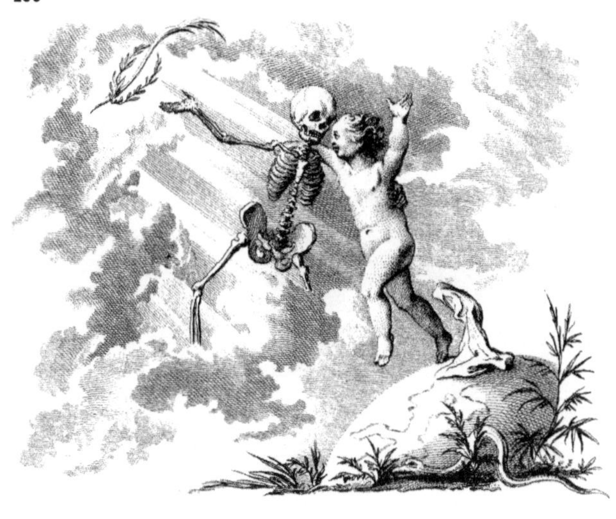

140

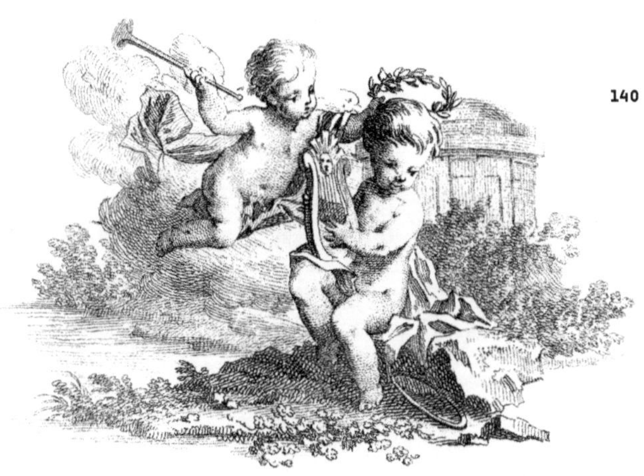

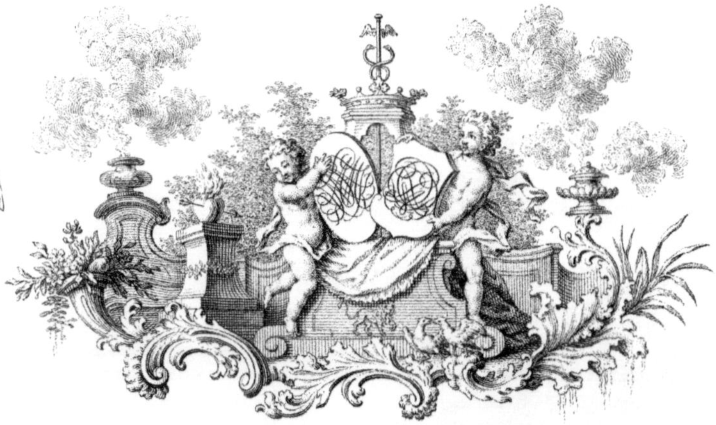

141

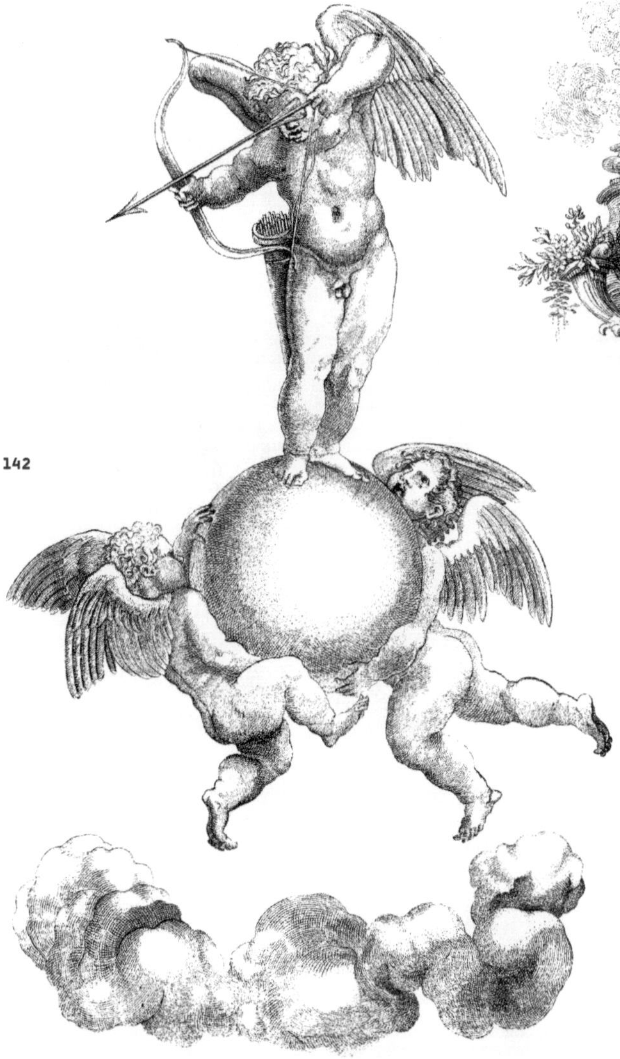

142

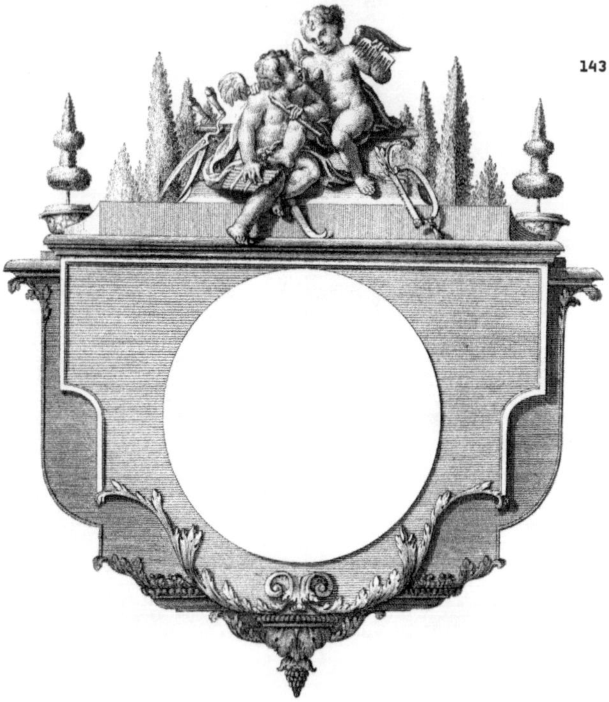

143

144

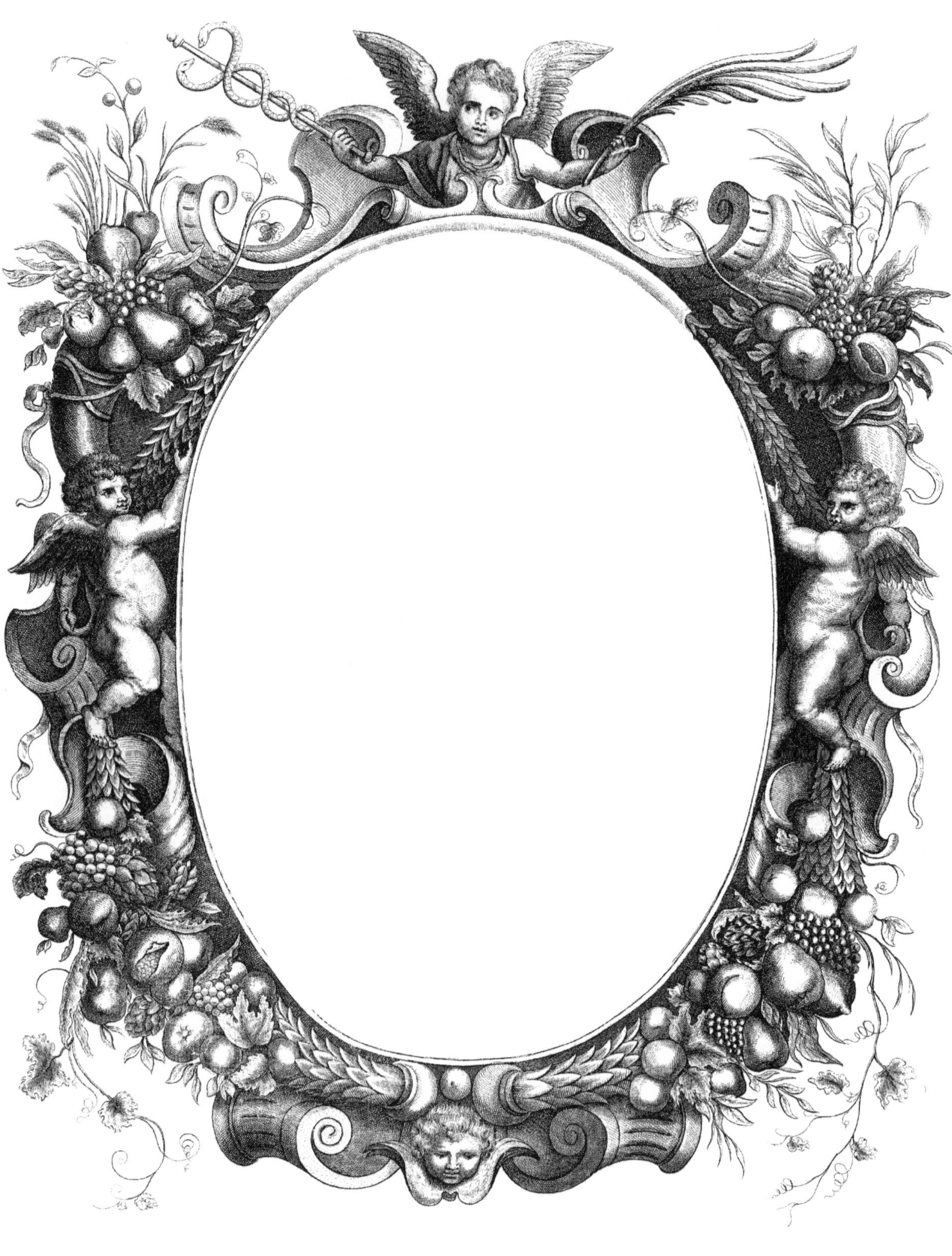

145

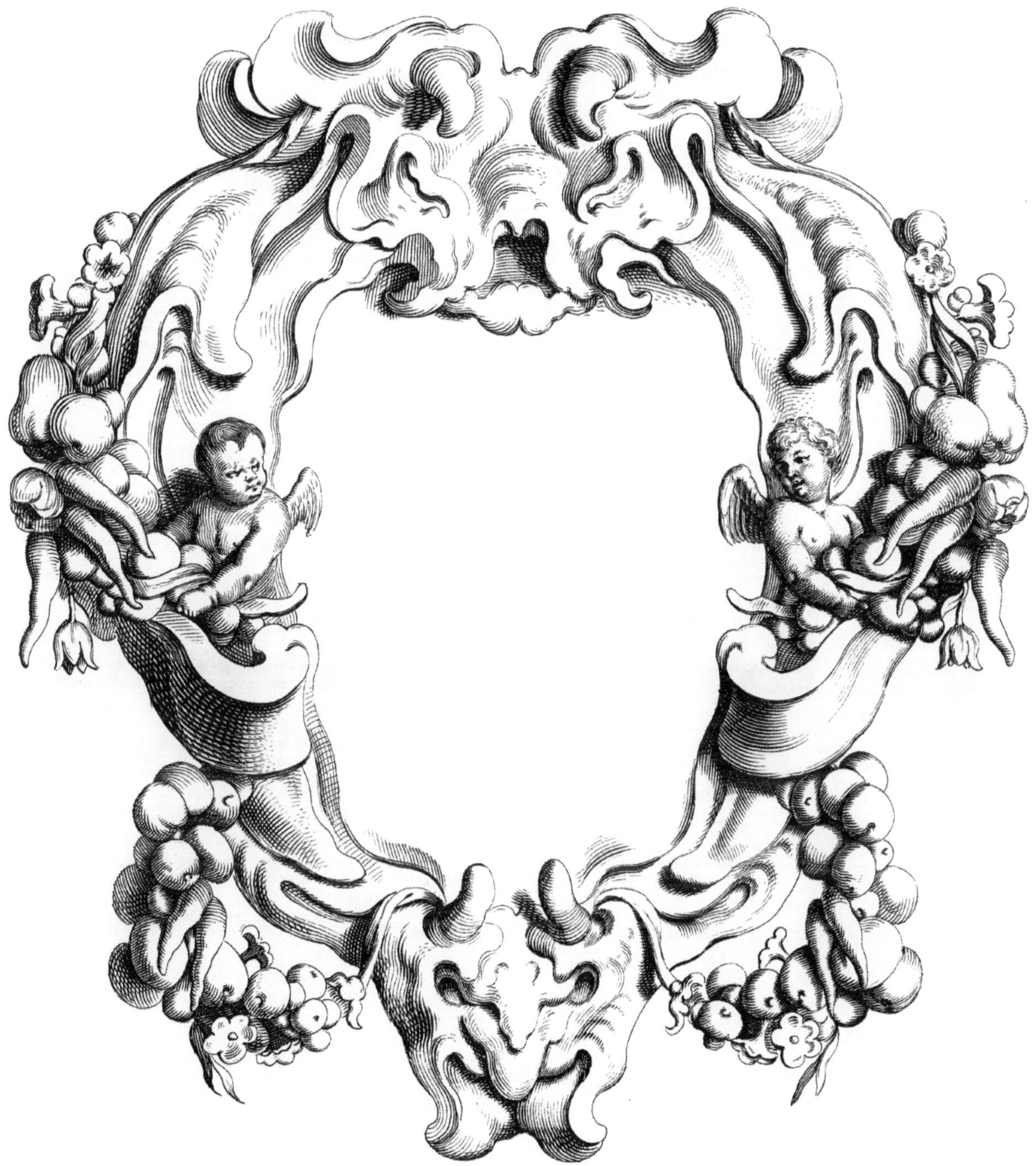

146

147

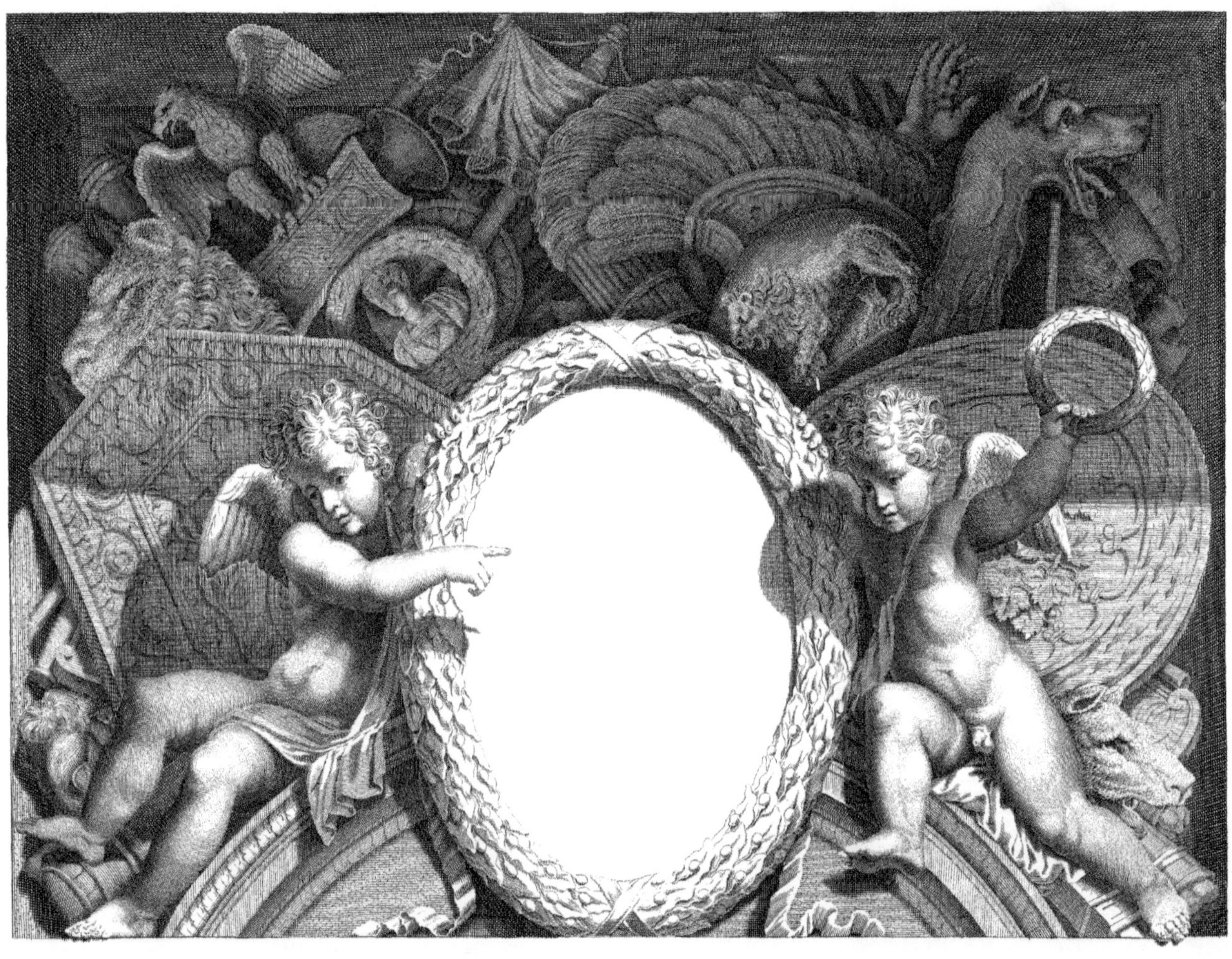

148

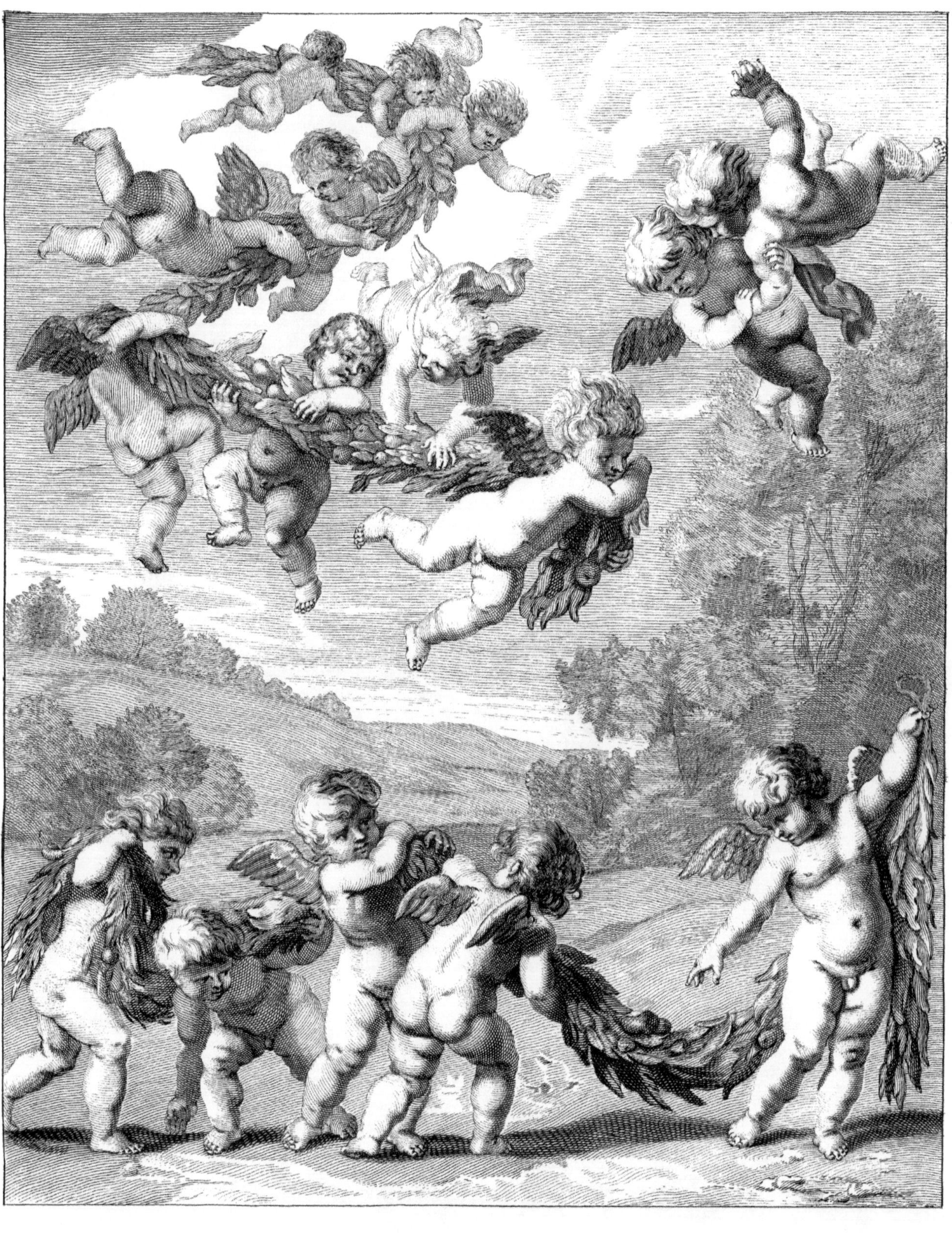

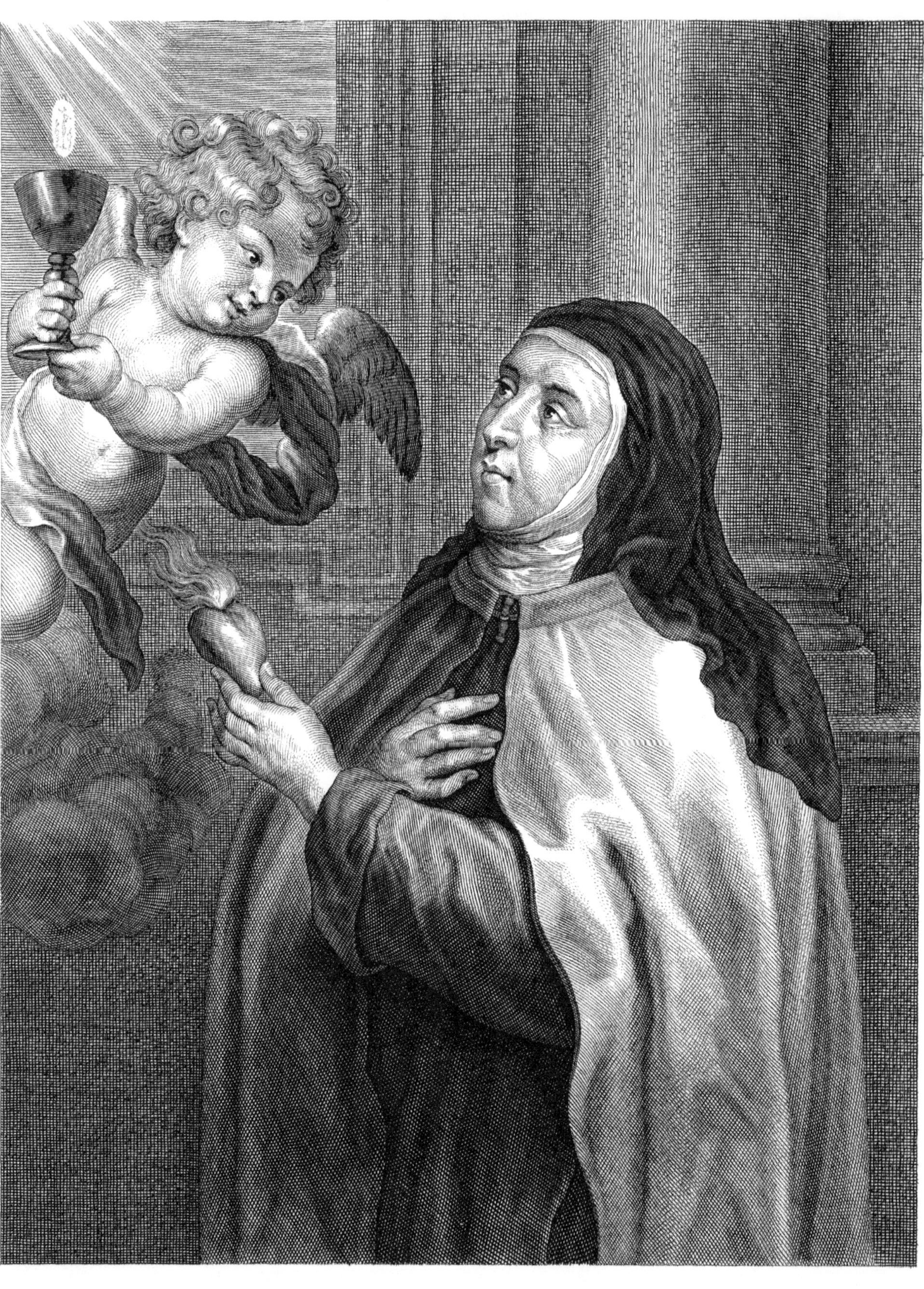

150

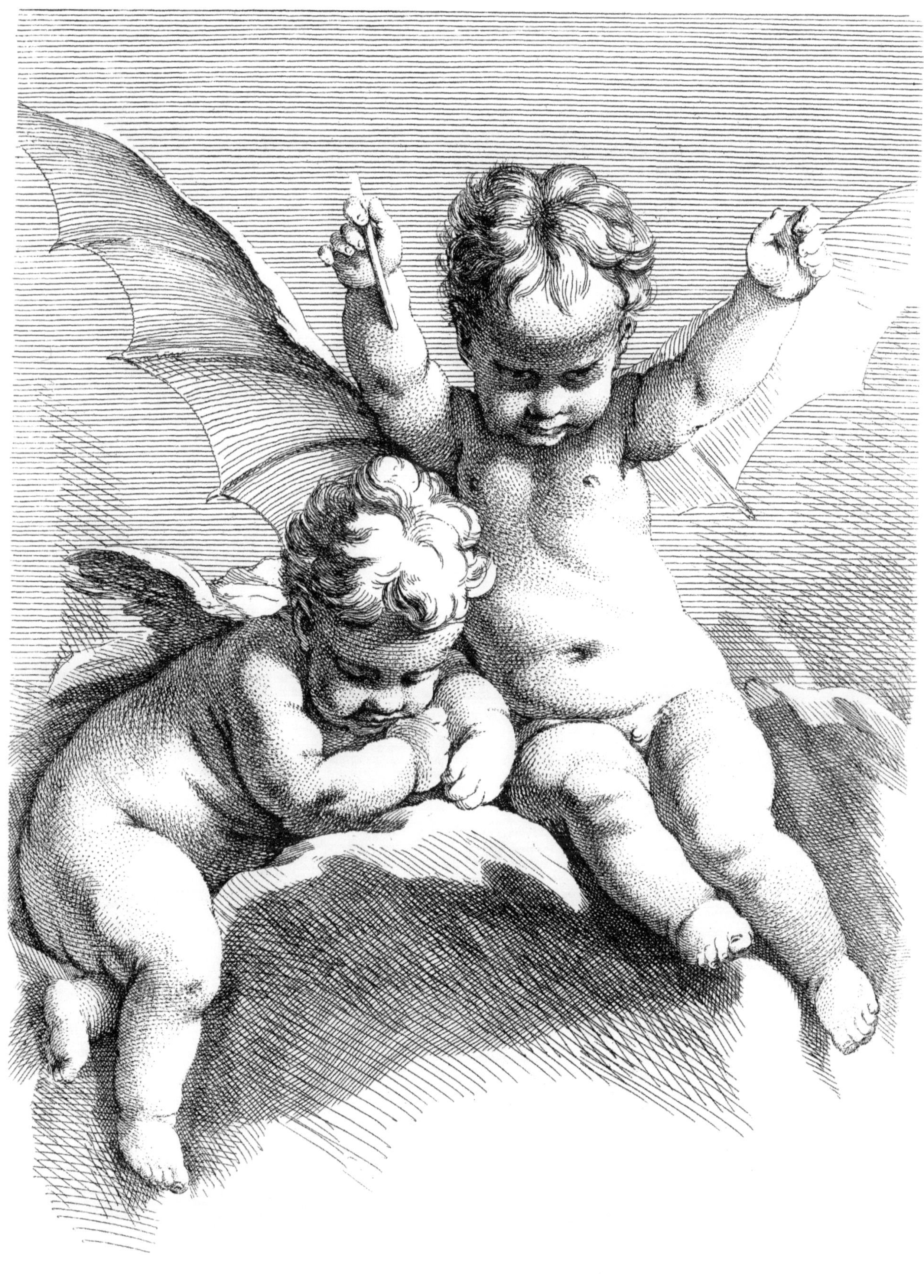

151

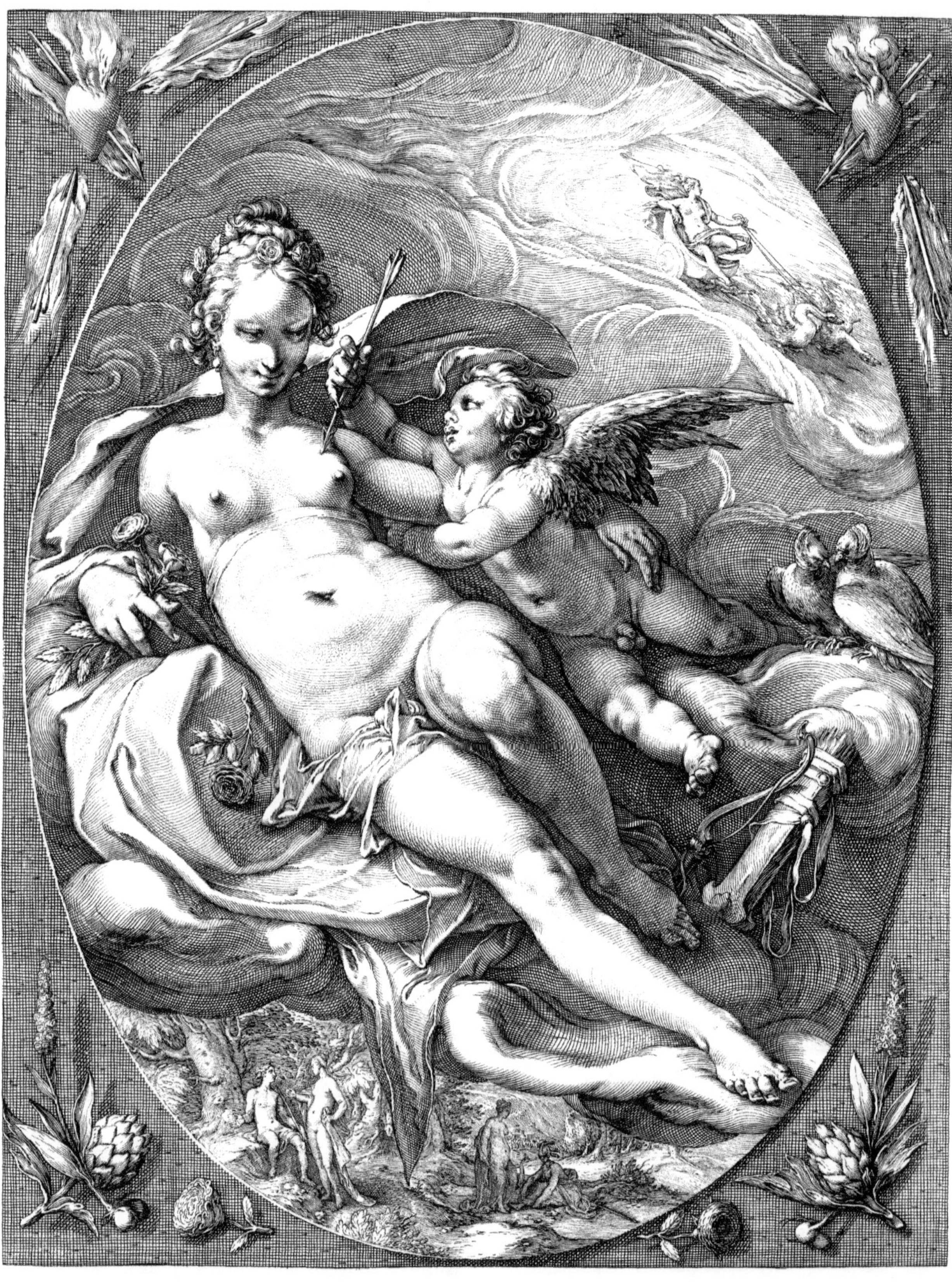

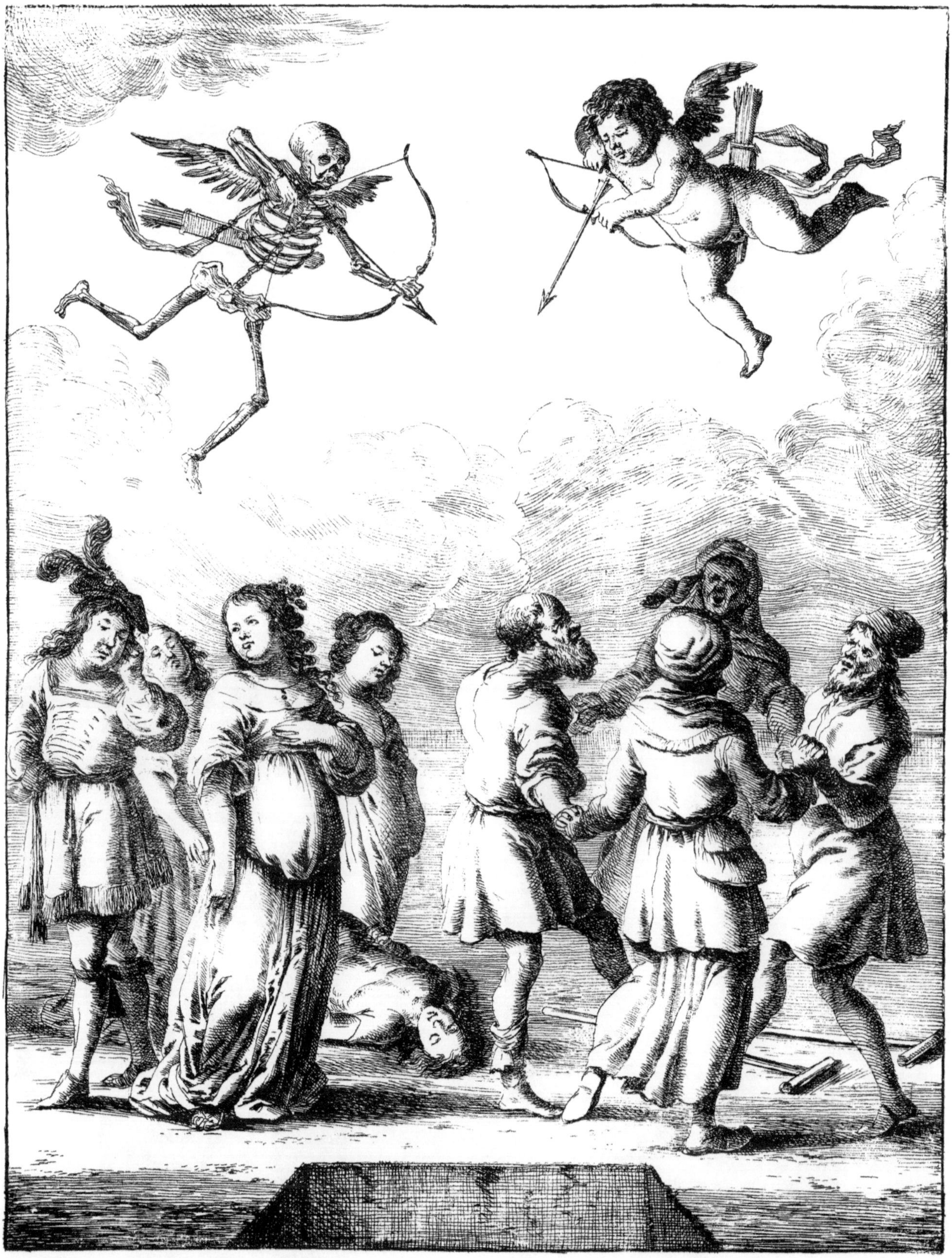

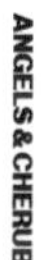
ANGELS & CHERUBS

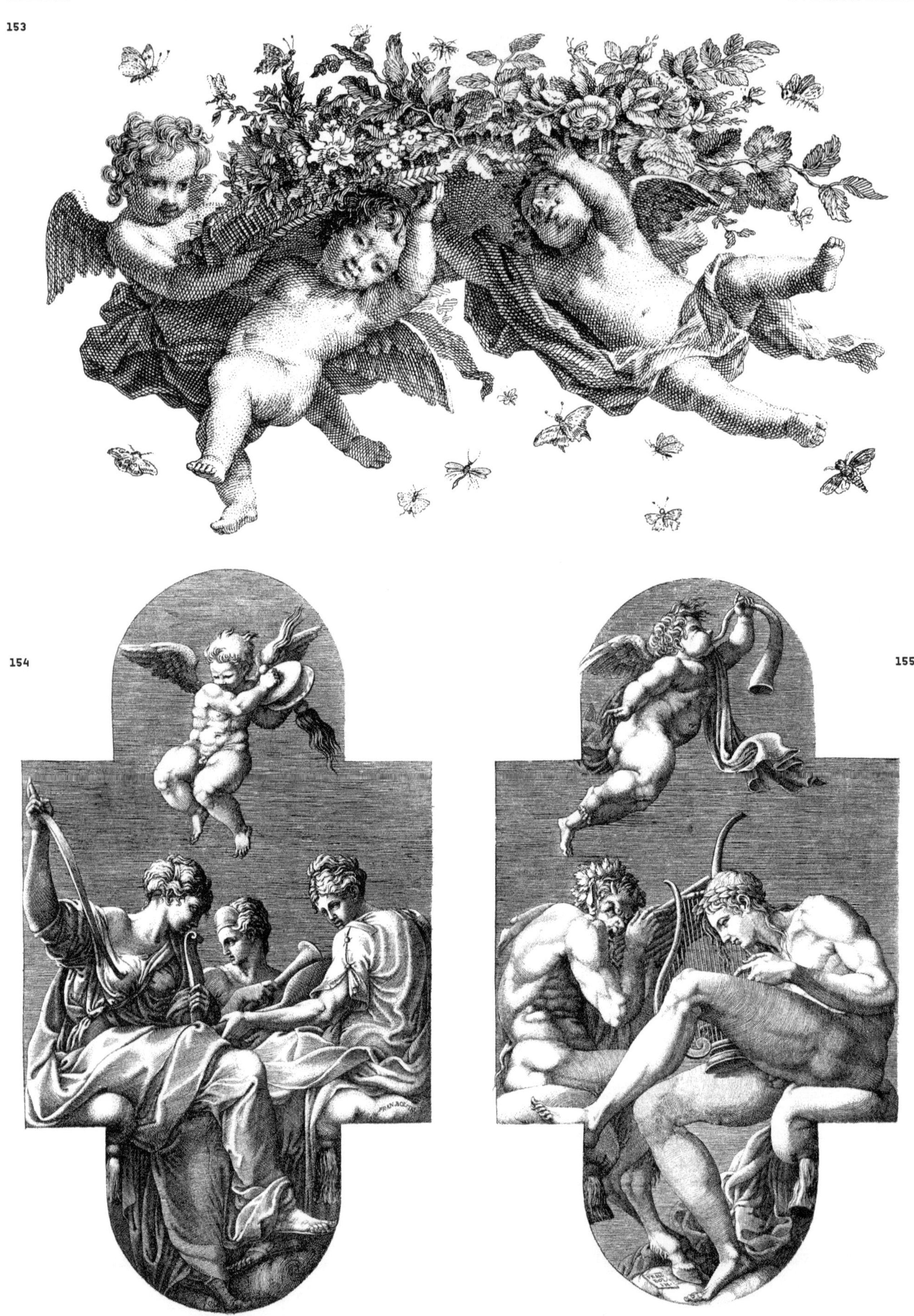

153

154

155

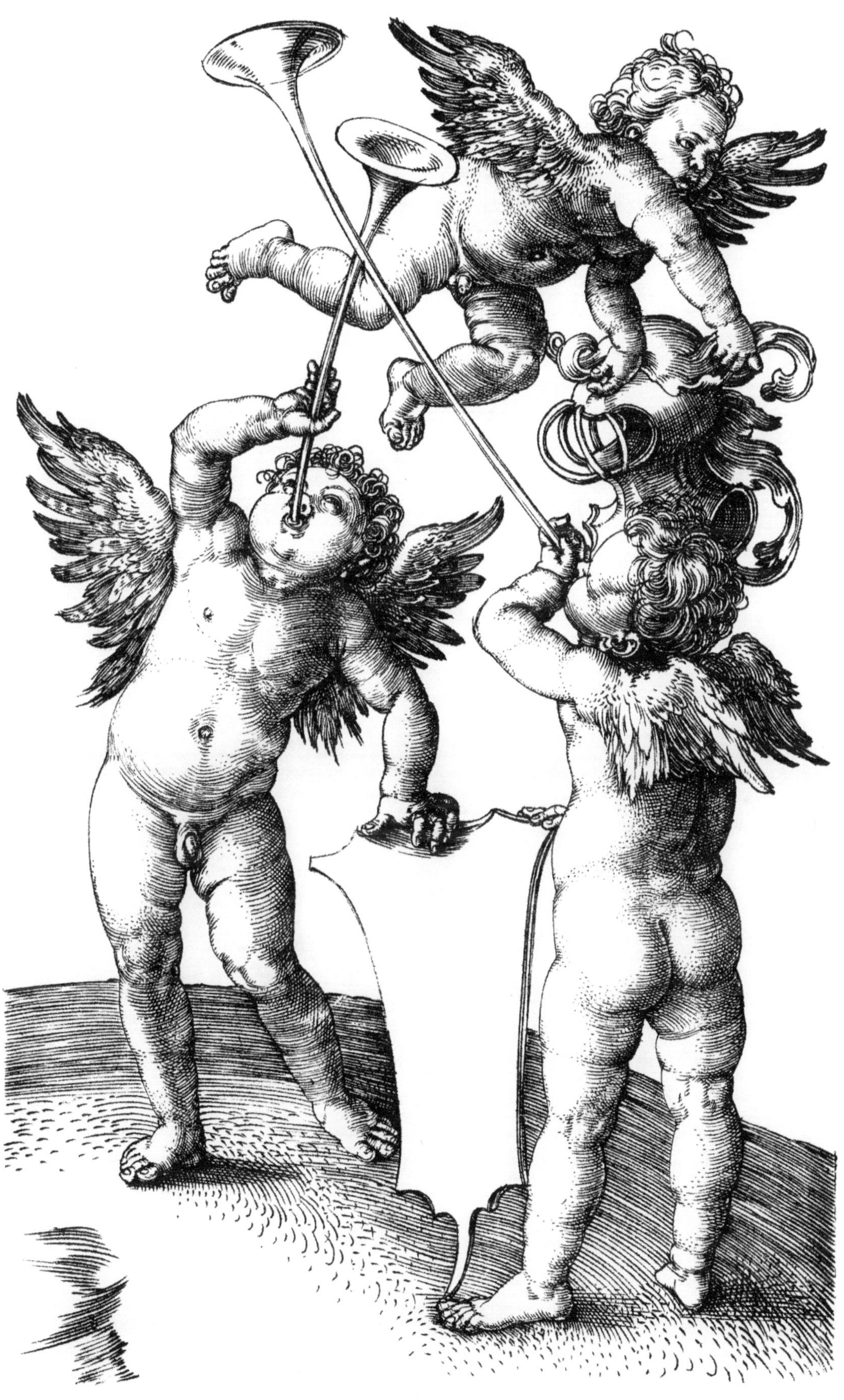

157

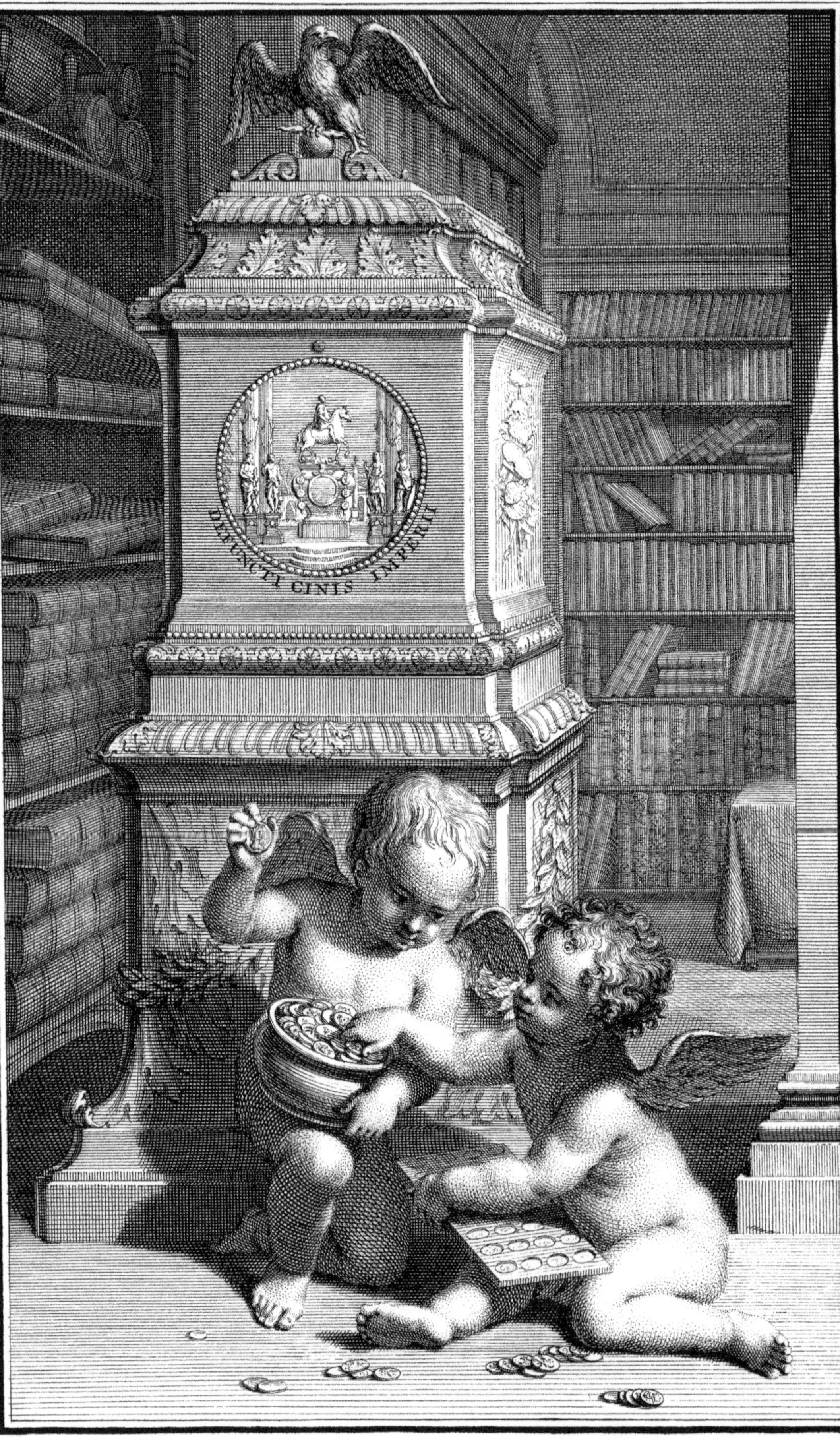

158

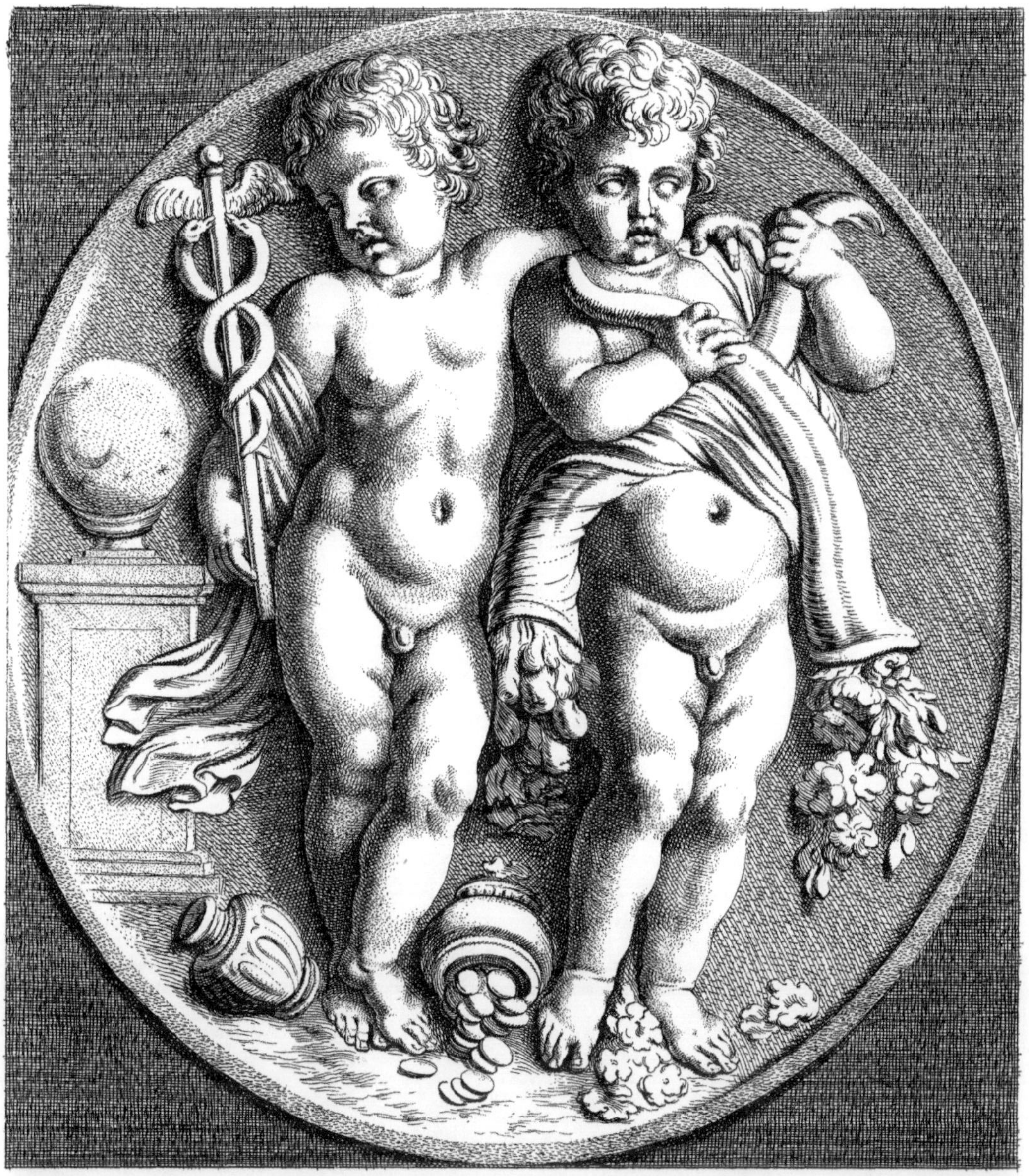

159

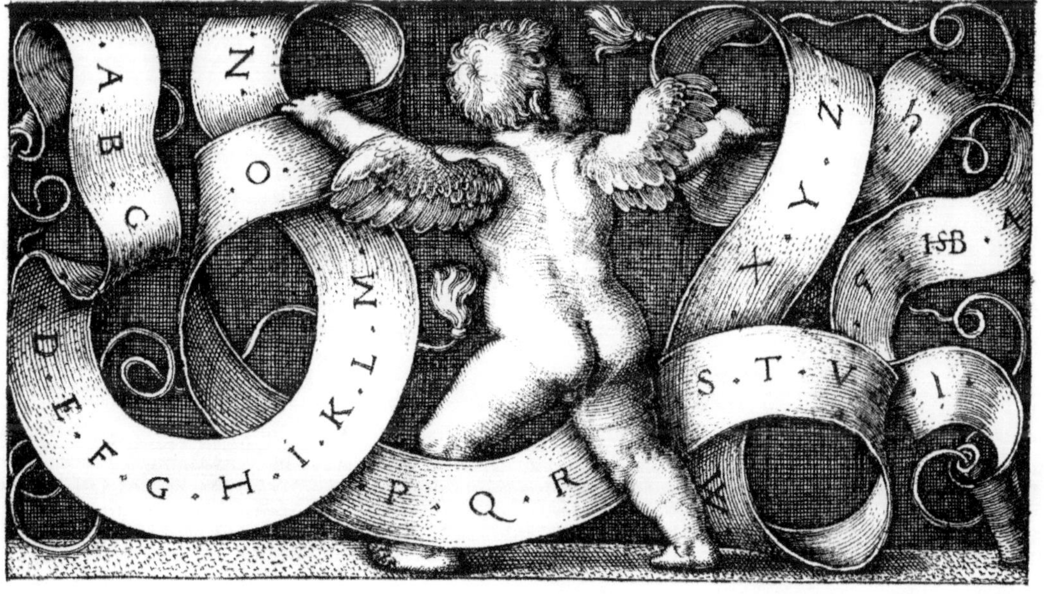

ANGELS

ANGELS & CHERUBS

LIST OF ILLUSTRATIONS

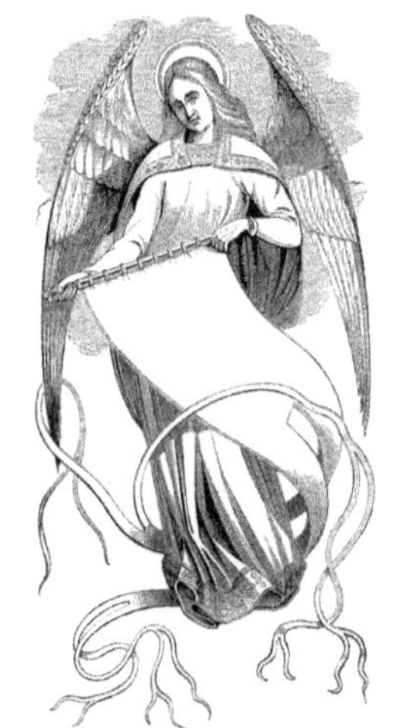

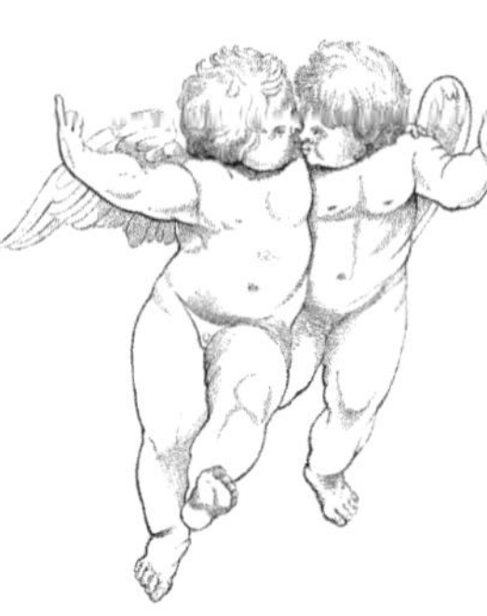

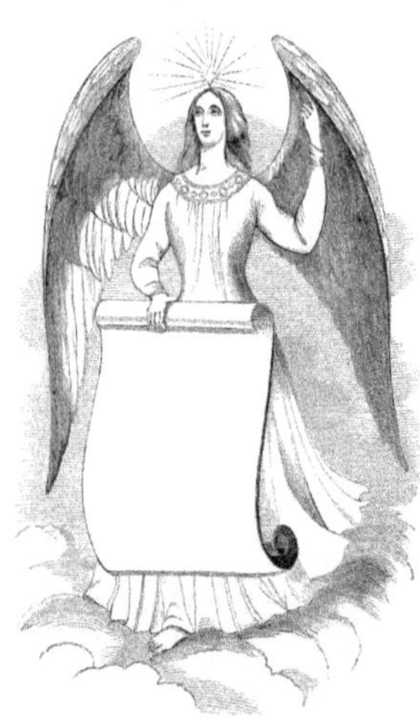

1. The Fall of the Rebellious Angels, 1618, Philippe Thomassin
2. Archangel Michael Trampling the Devil, Raphaël Sadeler (II), after Peter de Witte, 1604
3. Archangel Michael and the Dragon, Jakob Frey (I), after Guido Reni, 1734
4. Archangel Michael tramples Satan, Samuel van Hoogstraten, after Maerten de Vos, 1575
5. Michael Subdues the Devil, Adriaen Millaert, after Peter Paul Rubens, 1645 - 1668
6. Michael and the Fall of the Rebel Angels, Lucas Vorsterman (I), after Peter Paul Rubens, 1621
7. Michael slaying the dragon, Hieronymus Wierix, after Maerten de Vos, 1585
8. Michael and the Fall of the Rebel Angels, Jacob Neefs, after Peter Paul Rubens, 1620 - 1680
9. Archangel Michael protects Christian from Satan, Pieter de Bailliu (I), after Jan Thomas, 1623 - 1660
10. Archangel Michael slaying the devil, anonymous, after Peter de Witte, 1560 - 1678
11. Archangel Michael, Nicolo Billy, after Pietro da Cortona, 1637 - 1691
12. Archangel Michael, Raphaël Sadeler (I) (attributed to), after Peter de Witte, after Hubert Gerhard, 1595 - 1604
13. Archangel Michael, Petrus Clouwet, after Peter Paul Rubens, 1639 - 1670
14. Archangel Michael and the Dragon, Jan Gerritsz. van Bronckhorst, c. 1613 - 1661
15. Archangel Raphael, Crispijn van de Passe (I), 1574 - 1637
16. Archangel Uriel, Crispijn van de Passe (I), 1574 - 1637
17. Michael slaying the dragon, Antonie Wierix (II), 1565 - before 1604
18. Archangel Michael, Hieronymus Wierix, 1563 - before 1619
19. Archangel Michael and the Dragon, Christopher of Shechem (II), after Hieronymus Wierix, 1629
20. Archangel Jophiel, Crispijn van de Passe (I), 1574 - 1637
21. Michael the Archangel slaying a devil, Hans Springinklee, 1500 - 1516
22. Archangel Gabriel with Lily Branch, Joannes Galle, c. 1626 - c. 1676
23. Saint Michael, Jacob Cornelisz van Oostsanen, 1510
24. Saint Michael and the Dragon, Martin Schongauer, c. 1470 - 1491
25. Archangel Michael and the Dragon, Agostino Veneziano, after Raphael, 1500 - c. 1536
26. Angels show the sudarium, anonymous, after Jan van der Straet, 1570 - 1612
27. Angel supporting Christ, who is also resting on clouds, 1570–1615, Cherubino Alberti (Zaccaria Mattia)
28. Lamentation of Christ by Angels, Nicolas Pitau after Guercino, 1668
29. Christ in the Tomb, with Two Angels, Jacob Matham, after Hendrick Goltzius, 1607 - 1611
30. Angels Support the Body of Christ, Conrad Goltz (possibly), after Hendrick Goltzius, after Bartholomeus Spranger, 1594
31. Christ Kneeling Before Passion Tools Held by Four Angels, Pieter de Bailliu (I), after Jan Thomas, 1623 - 1660
32. Christ as Man of Sorrows, Jan Harmensz. Muller, 1608 - 1612
33. Christ supported by an angel standing on a cloud, 1600–1610
34. Christ as Man of Sorrows with Two Angels and Two Cherubim, Cornelis Galle (I), after Gerard Seghers, 1586 - 1633
35. Dead Christ Lamented by an Angel, Jan Harmensz. Muller, after Jacopo Ligozzi, 1593 - 1597
36. Two Angels with the Sweat Cloth, Albrecht Dürer, 1513
37. Entombment of Christ, Aegidius Sadeler (II), after Marco dell'Angolo del Moro, 1588
38. H. Veronica with the sweat cloth, Jacob Matham, after Abraham Bloemaert, 1605
39. Pagan Nations in Adoration of Christ in Heaven, Jan Punt, 1744
40. Christ giving the Sacred Host to the kneeling Saint Catherine of Siena, surrounded by various angels, 1750-1812, Giuliano Traballesi
41. Communion of Saint Bonaventura, anonymous, after Anthony van Dyck, 1636 - 1679

42. Angels Proclaim the Fame of Louis XIV, Simon François Ravenet (le vieux), after Jean Baptiste Massé, after Charles Le Brun, 1752
43. Angel with a Banderole, Claude Mellan
44. Mary Magdalene Carried to Heaven, mid-16th century, Léon Davent
45. Four Trumpet-Blowing Angels, Bernard Picart (studio of), 1683 - 1733
46. Annunciation, Cornelis Galle (II), after Abraham van Diepenbeeck, 1650 - 1653
47. Mary with Child and angels with reliquary in heaven above the church Notre-Dame in Wavre, Boëtius Adamsz. Bolswert, after unknown, 1590 - 1633
48. Guardian Angel Takes a Child by the Hand, Guillaume Chasteau, after Pietro da Cortona, 1645 - 1683
49. Angel and Holy Spirit, Gerard Edelinck, after Philippe de Champaigne, 1666 - 1707
50. Child with Guardian Angel, Pietro Aquila, after Carlo Maratta, 1660 - 1692
51. Child with Guardian Angel, anonymous, Cornelis Galle (II) (possibly), after Anthony van Dyck, after Cornelis Galle (I), 1600 - 1699
52. The Guardian Angel, stepping off a cloud and putting his arm around a young boy at left while a demon walks away at right, 1729–40, Nicolas Gabriel Dupuis
53. Angel Gabriel, C.A. Tuchs, after Willem van de Passe, 1865
54. Sacrifice of Manoah, Antonie Wierix (II), after Maerten de Vos, 1585
55. Farewell to the Archangel Raphael, anonymous, after Maarten van Heemskerck, 1556 - 1633
56. Annunciation of the Nativity to the Shepherds, Adriaen Collaert, after Hendrick Goltzius, 1586
57. The Annunciation (after Pierre Dulin) 1700–56 Jean Audran
58. Liberation of Petrus, Nicolaes Lastman, after Jan Symonsz Pynas, 1601 - 1652
59. John the Baptist and the Christ Child with Lamb and Angel, Cornelis Galle (II), 1638 - 1678
60. John the Baptist is accompanied by angels as he goes into the desert, Cornelis Galle (I), after Jan van der Straet, 1595 - 1636
61. Group of Angels Ready for the Coronation of Mary, Cornelis Galle (I) (attributed to), 1586 - 1650
62. Three seraphim in different guises, François van Bleyswijck, after unknown, 1681 - 1746
63. Vision of Isaiah, Gilliam van der Gouwen, after Bernard Picart, 1728
64. Title page for La Sainte Bible, 1669, Theodor Matham, after Nicolaes Pietersz Berchem, 1669
65. Flora, Pieter Tanjé, after Parmigianino, 1734
66. Lot and the Two Angels, Hans Collaert (I) (attributed to), after Frans Menton, 1579
67. Landscape with Abraham and the Three Angels, Julius Goltzius, after Hans Bol, c. 1560 - 1595
68. Mankind Begs Forgiveness From Its Sins, Gilliam van der Gouwen, 1681 - 1702
69. Hagar and Ishmael in the Wilderness, Robert van Audenaerd, after Carlo Maratta, 1685 - 1723
70. Title page for Justus Lipsius, De crvce libri tres. Amsterdam, 1670, Abraham Bloteling, after anonymous, 1670
71. Annunciation (angel Gabriel), Crispijn van de Passe (I), 1574 - 1637
72. H. Cecilia with Angels, Jacob Matham (attributed to), after Hendrick Goltzius, 1588 - 1592
73. Raguel welcomes Tobias, anonymous, after Maarten van Heemskerck, 1556 - 1633
74. Annunciation, François Stuerhelt (possibly), after Cornelis Galle (I), 1629 - 1729
75. Christ as Man of Sorrows with Two Angels and Two Cherubs, Cornelis Galle (I), after Gerard Seghers, 1586 - 1633
76. The Angel Gabriel, Martin Schongauer, c. 1485 - c. 1490
77. The Assumption of the Virgin, Nicolas de Larmessin (III), 1694 - 1755
78. Saint Louis IX Carried to Heaven by Two Angels, François Tortebat, after Simon Vouet, 1664
79. Coat of arms of Amsterdam between two angels, anonymous, c. 1688

80. Angel with Crown of Thorns, Petrus Clouwet, after Peter Paul Rubens, 1639 - 1670
81. Angel with lance and nails, Petrus Clouwet, after Peter Paul Rubens, 1639 - 1670
82. Design for a group of angels, engraving, c. 1850
83. Allegorical representation with an angel and a fallen horse, Pierre Philippe Chhoffard, 1776
84. An Angel Holding a Scroll, c. 1840
85. Original designs for an inscription tablet, engraving, c. 1850
86. Winged genius holding the Crown of Tuscany in his left hand and a palm in his right, 17th century After Cherubino Alberti (Zaccaria Mattia)
87. Winged genius with the Arms of the Medici in his right hand and foliage in his left, 17th century After Cherubino Alberti (Zaccaria Mattia)
88. Winged angel holding a palm in his right hand and with drapery behind him, 17th century After Cherubino Alberti (Zaccaria Mattia)
89. Winged genius holding a olive branch and a banderole, 17th century After Cherubino Alberti (Zaccaria Mattia)
90. Winged Victory holding a trophy of arms in her right hand and a shield in her left, 17th century After Cherubino Alberti (Zaccaria Mattia)
91. Angel with banderole, Crispijn van de Passe (I), 1601
92. Allegorical representation with angel and shield, Pierre Philippe Chhoffard, 1788
93. Study for a Naked Flying Angel, Jan de Bisschop, after Giuseppe Cesari, 1668 - 1671
94. A winged figure of Fame standing facing left and sounding a trumpet, 1570–1615, Cherubino Alberti (Zaccaria Mattia)
95. Nemesis, Albrecht Dürer, 1499 - 1503
96. Assyrians - Sennacherib's Empire Destroyed, Jeremias Falck, after Claude Vignon, 1645 - 1646
97. Emblem with Father Time as a symbol for the passing of time, Boëtius Adamsz. Bolswert, 1620
98. Fire, Antonie Wierix (II), after Marten van Cleve (I), 1565 - before 1604
99. Three Angels, Pieter Willem van Megen, 1772
100. Winged putto holding a cardinal's hat over a dragon head ,17th century After Cherubino Alberti (Zaccaria Mattia)
101. Alliance between Dutch and French Republic, 1795, Lambertus Antonius Claessens, after Jacques Kuyper, 1795
102. Annunciation to the Shepherds, William Skelton, after Thomas Stothard, 1794
103. Two singing angels, anonymous, after Cherubino Alberti, after Polidoro da Caravaggio, 1583 - c. 1650
104. Two Singing, Embracing Angels, anonymous, after Cherubino Alberti, after Polidoro da Caravaggio, 1583 - c. 1650
105. Five Cherubim on a Cloud, Wenceslaus Hollar, after Pieter van Avont, 1646
106. Frieze with putto and birds, René Lochon, after Charles II Errard, 1651
107. Little Angel with Triangle, Pieter van Avont, 1630 - 1652
108. Title print with putto with announcement, Cherubino Alberti, after Polidoro da Caravaggio, 1590
109. Putto Playing the Flute, Pieter van Avont, 1630 - 1652 (1)
110. Cherubs around a crowned coat of arms, Simon Fokke, 1744
111. A Child Dancing Between Two Angels, Pieter van Avont, 1622 - 1652
112. Harp-playing angel, Pieter van Avont, 1630 - 1652
113. Standing Angel with Orange, Pieter van Avont, 1630 - 1652
114. Standing Angel, Pieter van Avont, 1630 - 1652
115. Standing Angel with Arms to the Right, Pieter van Avont, 1630 - 1652
116. Putto with two dogs on a leash, anonymous, after Charles II Errard, after 1616 - before 1689
117. A group of angels embracing in flight, framed by clouds, ca. 1607, Guido Reni
118. Two Angels Facing Each Other, Pieter van Avont, 1622 - 1652
119. Cherub head, Crispijn de Passe (the Younger), 1642.
120. Leaf ornament with seated putto, Bernard Picart (studio of), 1683 - 1733
121. Putto with a shield with the coat of arms of Witsen, Reinier Vinkeles (I),

after Cornelis Ploos van Amstel, 1765
122. Floating putto and a putto with an extinguished torch, Reinier Vinkeles (I), after Rhijnvis Feith, 1751 - 1816
123. Vignette with three cherubs at a grave framed with symbols of impermanence, Reinier Vinkeles (I), 1751 - 1816
124. Putto, Edouard Taurel, after Raphael, 1834 - 1892
125. Cherub head 3, Crispijn de Passe (the Younger), 1642.
126. Cherub head 2, Crispijn de Passe (the Younger), 1642.
127. Two putti with the tablets of the law and a censer, Bernard Picart (studio of), 1683 - 1733
128. Two Putto, engraving, c. 1850
129. Two gods of love (Amor) connected by a ribbon, Boëtius Adamsz. Bolswert, after M. Reen, 1590 - 1633
130. Three cherubs and a female figure, Leopold Löwenstam, after Raphael, 1852 - 1898
131. Eye of Providence, Daniel Nikolaus Chodowiecki, 1787
132. Two cherubs holding palm leaves, anonymous, after Charles II Errard, after 1616 - before 1689
133. Putto with skull and two putti with lower body of leaf vines, anonymous, after Charles II Errard, after 1616 - before 1689
134. Vignette with a putto with symbols of victory, Reinier Vinkeles (I), 1751 - 1816
135. Two cherubs with a coat of arms, anonymous, 1700 - 1800
136. Floating cherub with wreath, Lubertus Teunis van Deth, 1824 - 1875
137. Cherub, anonymous, after Arent van Bolten, c. 1637 - c. 1638
138. Emblem noble, Jan Goeree, 1722
139. Vignette with Death and a Putto, Reinier Vinkeles (I), 1751 - 1816
140. Vignette with two cherubs, Simon Fokke, 1722 - 1784
141. Cherubs with two coats of arms, Jacob van der Schley, 1746
142. Love, Giulio Sanuto (attributed to), 1540 - 1570
143. Emblem forest wood, Jan Goeree, 1722
144. Frame with putti and fruits, anonymous, 1670 - 1680
145. Cartouche with lobe ornament with two putti, Michiel Mosijn, after Gerbrand van den Eeckhout, 1640 - 1655
146. Allegorical representation with the cross, Pieter Tanjé, after JG a Borckeloo, 1750
147. Divers Trophées, René Lochon, a.Charles II Errard, a. Polidoro da Caravaggio, 1651
148. Earth, Michiel Mosijn, after Cornelis Holsteyn, 1640 - 1655
149. Saint Anne of Saint Bartholomew, Cornelis Galle (II), after Peter Paul Rubens, c. 1641 - c. 1678
150. Two Cupids, One with Bat Wings, mid to late 18th century Jacques Gabriel Huquier
151. Venus and Amor, Hendrick Goltzius, 1596
152. Fable of Cupid and Death, Dirk Stoop, 1665
153. Three cherub with a flower basket and butterflies, Jan Wandelaar, 1750
154. Three Muses and a Putto with Cymbals, Giorgio Ghisi, after Francesco Primaticcio, 1530 - 1582
155. Apollo, Pan and a Putto Blowing a Horn, Giorgio Ghisi, after Francesco Primaticcio, 1530 - 1582
156. Three cherubs with trumpets, shield and helmet, Albrecht Dürer, 1498 - 1502
157. Two cherubs in a library, Jacob Folkema, after Nicolaas Verkolje, c. 1720
158. Heavenly and earthly happiness depicted by two cherubs, Louis Ferdinand I Elle, after Gerard van Opstal, after Tetelin, 1654
159. Surface decoration with cherubs, seen from the back, Hans Sebald Beham, 1510 - 1542

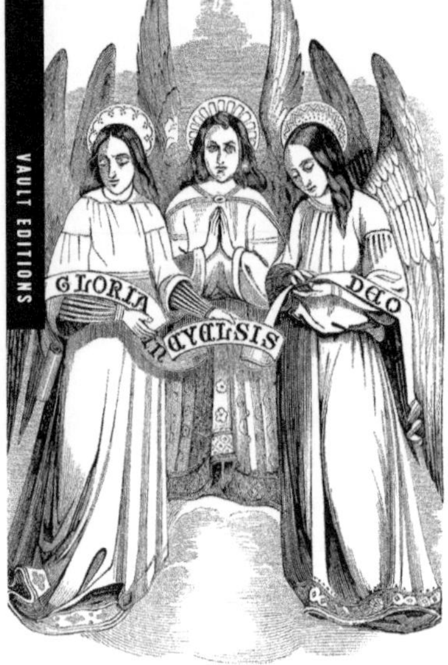

LEARN MORE

At Vault Editions, our mission is to create the world's most diverse and comprehensive collection of image archives available for artists, designers and curious minds. If you have enjoyed this book, you can find more of our titles available at vaulteditions.com.

REVIEW THIS BOOK

As a small, family-owned independent publisher, reviews help spread the word about our work. We would be incredibly grateful if you could leave an honest review of this title wherever you purchased this book.

JOIN OUR COMMUNITY

Are you a creative and curious individual? If so, you will love our community on Instagram. Every day we share bizarre and beautiful artwork ranging from 17th and 18th-century natural history and scientific illustration, to mythical beasts, ornamental designs, anatomical illustration and more. Join our community of 100K+ people today— search @vault_editions on Instagram.

DOWNLOAD YOUR FILES

STEP ONE

Enter the following web address in your web browser on a desktop computer.

www.vaulteditions.com/pages/ang

STEP TWO

Enter the following unique password to access the download page.

ange2346488sxda

STEP THREE

Follow the prompts to access your high-resolution files.

TECHNICAL ASSISTANCE

For all technical assistance, please email: info@vaulteditions.com

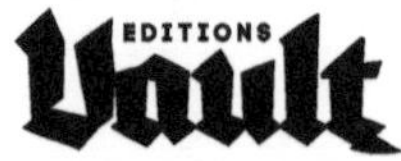

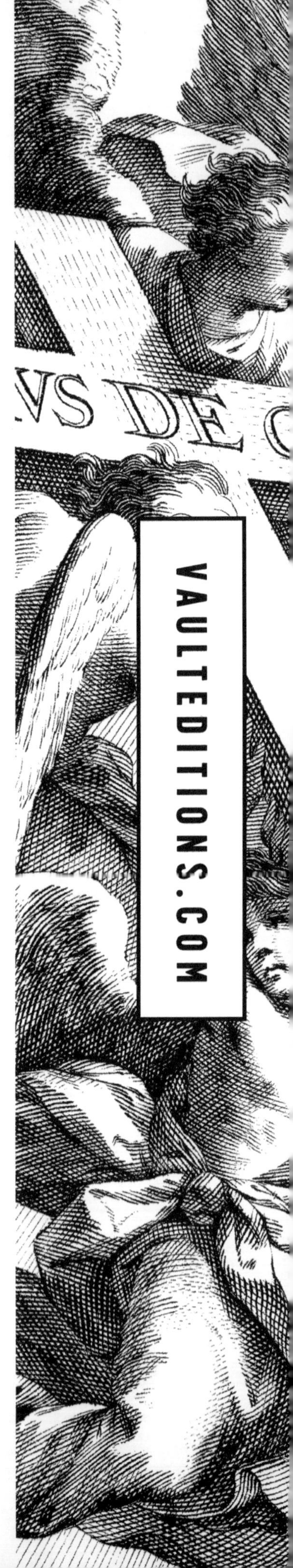